Power to the Parents

Reversing Educational Decline

Antony Flew

The Sherwood Press

First published 1987

© Antony Flew 1987

The Sherwood Press Ltd, 35 Westminster Bridge Road, London SE1 7JB

ISBN 0 907671 32 2

Typeset in Times by BookEns, Saffron Walden
Printed and bound by Biddles, Guildford and Kings Lynn

Flew, Antony
    Power to the parents: reversing
    educational decline.
    1. Parent-teacher relationships—Great
    Britain
    I. Title
    370.19′31   LC225.33.G7

Contents

Abbreviations

BERA	British Educational Research Association
BCC	British Council of Churches
BSA	British Sociological Association
CND	Campaign for Nuclear Disarmament
CORE	Congress for Racial Equality
CPSU	Communist Party of the Soviet Union
CRE	Commission for Racial Equality
CSE	Certificate of Secondary Education
DES	Department of Education and Science
EE	*Education for Equality*
EVA	Educational Value Added
GCE	General Certificate of Education
GCSE	General Certificate of Secondary Education
GLC	Greater London Council
HMI	Her Majesty's Inspector
IEA	Institute of Economic Affairs
ILEA	Inner London Education Authority
LEA	Local Education Authority
LP	Labour Party
NAHT	National Association of Head Teachers
NATO	North Atlantic Treaty Organisation
NCB	National Children's Bureau
NCDS	National Child Development Study
NCES	National Council for Educational Standards
NFER	National Foundation for Educational Research
NHS	National Health Service
NIESR	National Institute of Economic and Social Research
NM	*No, Minister*
NUS	National Union of Students

NUT	National Union of Teachers
PCR	Programme to Combat Racism
SAT	Scholastic Aptitude Test
SHA	Secondary Heads Association
SR	*The Salisbury Review*
TES	*Times Educational Supplement*
TLS	*Times Literary Supplement*
TP	Teachers for Peace
TRJ	Towards Racial Justice
TUC	Trades Union Congress
UCCA	Universities Central Council on Admissions
UN	United Nations

'It is a subject of wonder how people so destitute of education as labouring parents commonly are, can be such just judges as they also commonly are of the effective qualifications of a teacher. Good school buildings and the apparatus of education are found for years to be practically useless and deserted, when, if a master chance to be appointed who understands his work, a few weeks suffice to make the fact known, and his school is soon filled, and perhaps found inadequate to the demand of the neighbourhood, and a separate girls' school or infants' school is soon found to be necessary.' (Assistant Commissioner Goode, in evidence to the Royal Commission on Popular Education, Newcastle, 1861, p. 175.)

Acknowledgements

The three final chapters of the present book are more or less drastically revised and extended versions of works published earlier. These were: *Power to the People!* (London: Centre for Policy Studies, 1983); *Education, Race and Revolution* (London: Centre for Policy Studies, 1984); and 'Peace, "Peace" Movements, and "Peace Studies" ', in L. Grob (Ed.) *Educating for Peace: Testimonies of Spirit* (New York: Orbis, 1987). However, all the other chapters also contain some recycled material. The substantial sources of such salvage were: 'Sincerity, Criticism and Monitoring', 'Competition and Cooperation: Equality and Elites', and 'Education against Racism', all in the *Journal of the Philosophy of Education* for, respectively, 1979, 1983 and 1987; 'Democracy and Education', in R. S. Peters (Ed.), *John Dewey Reconsidered* (London: Routledge and Kegan Paul, 1977); 'Examination not Attempted', in J. Wilson and R. Straughan (Eds), *Philosophers on Education* (London: Macmillan, 1987); Educational Fundamentals: The Four Es', in C. Cox and J. Marks (Eds), *The Right to Learn* (London: Centre for Policy Studies, 1982); 'Spend Less and Learn More', in D. Anderson (Ed.), *Pied Pipers of Education* (London: Social Affairs Unit, 1981); and 'Clarifying the Concepts', in F. Palmer (Ed.), *Anti-Racism: An Assault on Education and Value* (London: Sherwood, 1986). Thanks are due to the various editors, publishers and institutions for permission to re-employ this material; and thanks are gladly given.

Power to the Parents was wholly composed in the Social Philosophy and Policy Center at Bowling Green State University, Ohio. Fred Miller, Ellen and Jeffrey Paul, and John Ahrens have, with a strong support staff, created an ideal environment to encourage such work. Excellently equipped, friendly, alive and in a most salutary way untroubled by any distracting temptations, this Center is all that a think tank ought to be. It was, as the great Duke said of Waterloo, "a damned nice ... nearest run thing", but Tamara Sharp even managed to complete all the typing the day before I was due to fly back home.

Antony Flew

1

The Need for Alternatives

For the $(n + 1)$th time, let me repeat the warning that a public good should not necessarily be run by public rather than private enterprise. (Paul Samuelson, in Margolis, 1969, p. 108.)

In doing this [demanding a total and uniform state monopoly in the supply of educational services] they set themselves against both the UN Declaration of Human Rights, which asserts "The prior right of parents to determine the kind of education that shall be given to their children"; and the European Convention, which speaks of "the right of parents to ensure the education of their children in conformity with their own religious or philosophical convictions." (Marjorie Seldon, in Cox and Marks, 1982, p. 134.)

An overpopulated island with few natural resources, heavily dependent on imported raw materials and food, cannot avoid catastrophic impoverishment if it does not remain in the forefront of progress, which requires making the utmost use of the available brainpower. If Britain fails in this, it will quickly sink to the level of a cold Haiti when the oil runs out. . . . (Stanislav Andreski, in Cox and Marks, 1982, p. 164.)

Power to the Parents may be seen as a sequel to *Sociology, Equality and Education*, self-described by its author as "a one man volume of philosophical *Black Papers*" (Flew, 1976, p. 1). There are, nevertheless, several substantial differences of scope and direction. For a start, whereas two of the eight papers in that earlier collection dealt with topics relevant primarily or exclusively to the management of tertiary institutions, *Power to the Parents* is directly concerned with the tertiary only in so far as doings there have indirect effects upon the lower levels; effects mediated mainly through those people working at these levels who themselves have been or are being instructed in schools, institutes, colleges or departments of education. Again, in the dozen years since *Sociology, Equality and Education*

1

was put together some of the subjects which it treated have become less topical than they were. These also have, therefore, dropped out completely.

1.1 Where we have been, and where we are going

So much for what *Power to the Parents* is not. Two other topics which were treated in the previous collection, and where the current controversial focus has both shifted and widened, are now to be treated again, but this time much more extensively. Here the discussion of ideals of equality in Chapter 3, 'Clarifying Crucial Concepts', is much wider and more systematic. There the treatment of race and racism constituted a commentary on 'The Jensen Uproar', an affair which at that time had a negligible impact on British schools. But here Chaper 5, 'Three Concepts of Racism', refers to documents directing policies which actually are being implemented, in all schools subject to their power, by an ever-increasing number of Local Education Authorities (LEAs); including the very largest, the Inner London Education Authority (ILEA).

(i)   Both that Chapter 5 and Chapter 6, 'Peace, "Peace Studies" and the "Peace Movement" ', take note of a too-little noticed phenomenon of the 1980s. In earlier decades there seems to have been precious little partisan political indoctrination in British state schools, and what there was was never systematically and officially promoted by any of the LEAs. Today, thanks mainly but of course not only to the New Left transformation of the Labour Party, things are often changed, changed utterly. What has been born, however, is not the "terrible beauty" of Yeats's poem about Easter Week 1916 in Dublin but a plethora of programmes for 'Anti-racist Education', 'Peace Studies' 'World Studies' and the like (Lewis, 1986).

Almost without exception, these programmes are found to be not only heavily biased and biased in an always socialist sense but also founded upon assumptions which are at best questionable, if not demonstrably false. For instance, 'Anti-racist Education' often falsely assumes that no whites have ever been enslaved, while significantly overlooking both the part played by other whites in the struggles for emancipation and the apparent absence of indigenous abolition movements in Africa or Asia. Again, the revealed first premise of 'World Studies' would seem to be that any Third World country which is now poor must originally have been made so by First World exploitation, and is indeed still being 'kept underdeveloped' by 'capitalist neo-colonialism'.

Who, one wonders, do they think first enslaved most of the unfortunates whom the white slave-traders bought on the coast of West Africa? Have they never heard either of the long-continuing Arab slave trade in East

Africa or of the British efforts to suppress that trade in the nineteenth century and after? And do they really themselves believe, what they apparently want the pupils to assume, that every Third World country now rated poor and underdeveloped was, until the Europeans arrived, prosperously enjoying the fruits of its unchecked economic growth over a period of many years?

For more information about programmes for 'Anti-racist Education', 'Peace Studies', 'World Studies' and the like, consult the growing literature (Palmer, 1986; Gwynne, 1985; Marks, 1984; Scruton, 1985; Cox and Scruton, 1984; Tingle, 1986; and Scruton *et al.*, 1985). Quite apart from the objections brought against the content of such often intentionally indoctrinatory enterprises, the opportunity cost of their achievement is heavy. For the most obvious foregone alternative to any class period of—say—'Peace Studies' is that same period devoted to some instead neglected, mainstream, traditional subject.

Yet the promoters of these too flatteringly described disciplines are rarely content to control only those class periods specifically allocated to their own favourite missionary enthusiasms. Usually they want these enthusiasms to permeate the whole of the rest of the curriculum as well; and perhaps most especially what, when whether rightly or wrongly it is perceived as controlled by others, they love to identify as 'the hidden curriculum'. Some old men who do not forget cannot, when they see such things going on in our own country, help recalling the pervasive intrusions of National Socialism into every subject taught in the primary and secondary schools of Germany during the late 1930s and early 1940s. Those too who have opened their eyes to the realities of the Second World of 'actually existing socialism', Marxist–Leninist style, will be forewarned of what can and surely will happen here if the electorate at the national level ever gives unchecked and undivided power to the likes of those who have recently been exercising a happily somewhat limited and strictly local control through LEAs such as those of Inner London, Brent, Bradford or Manchester.

(ii) Two of the other topics treated in *Sociology, Equality and Education* are now perhaps making even greater demands than they did then upon the attention of everyone concerned for the maintenance and improvement of the standards presently both demanded and achieved at the primary and secondary levels in the UK. One of these is the neo-Marxist sociology of knowledge—a systematically misleading expression employed to describe the sociology of belief (Ryle, 1931; and compare Flew, 1982a and Stove, 1982). Here "sociology of education is no longer conceived as an area of enquiry distinct from the sociology of knowledge" (Young, 1971, p. 3). In the earlier book I tried to show not only that the supposed findings presented by members of this collective constitute a preposterous farrago of falsehood and fallacy but also that, had V.I. Lenin been confronted with their pretensions to be propagating a theoretical as well as a practical Marxism, his own response would have been a characteristically furious rejection (Flew, 1976, Chs 2 and 3).

Although Lenin himself could scarcely have accepted such a distinction, it can be illuminating nonetheless. For today, especially in academic circles, many of those who cherish an abiding allegiance to Marx profess to have abandoned one or more or even all of those propositional beliefs which earlier generations would have considered to be essential and constitutive elements of Marxism. Their allegiance thus apparently results from, or perhaps consists in, their practical commitments. (See, for instance, Ollman and Vernoff, 1982, and compare this with any work by any classical Marxist.) These commitments are, it seems, both to give sustained day-to-day support to all Leninist regimes and Leninist insurgencies and to promote 'Peace' policies, policies for impotent defencelessness against the ever-expanding Soviet power.

About this neo-Marxist sociology of education, however, I have myself nothing more to say. Nevertheless—since so many practising or aspiring schoolteachers have been or are being exposed to such doctrines, in as much as they continue to be uncritically preached both from the electronic pulpits of the Open University and in the lecture rooms of the University of London Institute of Education—I must not neglect to recommend one compelling demonstration of their lamentable implications for schoolteaching and, presumably, equally lamentable effects upon it. This article concludes: "That subject started out by being harmless but ineffectual, eschewing any attempt to solve teachers' problems. It is no longer ineffectual, but it is no longer harmless either. Its influence on teachers is entirely deplorable" (Dawson, 1981, p. 59).

(iii)   The other topic of continuing importance was in the earlier volume treated beneath the heading 'Teaching and Testing'. There the conceptual contention was that anyone sincerely trying to teach anything must be constantly concerned to monitor their success or failure in ensuring that their pupils master whatever it is that the teacher is trying to teach them. Here, in Chapter 2, 'Examination not Attempted', that particular contention is first generalised to produce a critical weapon as potentially devastating as Hume's distinction between propositions stating or purporting to state only the relations of ideas and those stating or purporting to state matters of fact and real existence (Flew, 1986a, Ch. 3). Later in that chapter this critical weapon is directed at some positions taken in various current disputes about issues of public educational policy. It is also given employment later, wreaking further havoc among the Philistines.

All the essays in the present volume are offered as "essays in the philosophy of independent education", but they are, for better or for worse, philosophical in a perhaps rather broad instead of the narrowest sense of the word 'philosophy'. They are, that is, by no means purely theoretical and apriori. Often they start from, and again and again return to, what are, or at any rate what the author believes to be, matters of fact and real existence. Always they take note of actual or alleged findings of relevant empirical research. Furthermore, the whole lot is unashamedly deployed in support of an objective of practical policy. In all this I am content to associate myself with the authors of *Mixed Ability Grouping: A Philosophical Perspective*, a contribution to a series of Introductory Studies in Philosophy of Education. They conclude their prefatory manifesto: 'We believe that this approach is an appropriate one . . . and, more important, a necessary one if educational practices are to be rationally grounded. If we can do something to advance this last cause we will risk the accusation of 'impure' philosophy" (Bailey and Bridges, 1983, p. xiii).

1.2 An independent education for all?

It remains to explain that and why 'independent' is a key word in these "essays in the philosophy of independent education". During the 1964 General Election campaign Harold Wilson as Leader of the Labour Party promised that "The grammar school will be abolished over my dead body" (quoted Shaw, 1983, pp. 40 and 163). During the 1970 General Election campaign the same Harold Wilson, still visibly alive and flourishing, and now Prime Minister of a Labour administration which had largely succeeded in achieving its longstanding stated aim of replacing all the (state) maintained grammar and secondary modern schools by (neighbourhood) comprehensives, repeated a claim first made by his immediate predecessor as Leader of the Labour Party, Hugh Gaitskell, in a letter to *The Times* (5 July 1958). The claim was that his party's policy of universal compulsory comprehensivisation (a.k.a. 'comprehension') was intended to provide, and was in fact providing, "a grammer school education for all" (quoted Marsden, 1971, p. 11). Since, by definition, whereas grammar schools must be and comprehensives cannot be academically selective, this claim was not just straightforwardly false—as was perhaps to be expected—but strictly self-contradictory.

(i) My own ideal, and the ideal to which all these essays are directed, is one of variety rather than uniformity, of freedom instead of compulsion. Thus it is not of a comprehensive or—incoherently—of a grammar school but of an independent education for all. The crux is for all schools, however they are in future to be owned and managed, to become separate education firms, subject like the presently existing independent schools to the incentives and disciplines of the market. From whatever pocket, public or private, the fees paid by or on behalf of the parents ultimately come, those fees must be paid directly to whichever separate educational firm provides educational services for the children of those parents; and must be available to that particular firm to spend as it thinks fit.

Only when and in so far as this ideal is achieved will families be able themselves to shop around for whatever best suits the individual needs of their own children. If later they are seriously dissatisfied with what is being provided, then they will be in a position to put direct pressure on the particular educational firm: initially perhaps by threatening to withdraw their custom and afterwards, if need be, by actually withdrawing it. Since all fees, whatever their ultimate source, are being paid immediately into the firm earning them, management is always subject to strong incentives to maintain and, if possible, to increase custom. Both success and failure become at all times equally visible.

If and in so far as this ideal is realised, effective teachers will become— what the teachers' unions are always complaining that all teachers are not but ought to be—properly independent and appropriately respected professionals. Since the fees coming into each school would be available for spending there, some of any increase in the total could and surely would be spent on raising the incomes of those teaching in that school; especially perhaps the incomes of the teachers perceived as being most valuable to it. This, after all, is how things once were with all the paradigm professionals— doctors, lawyers, architects and so on—and how they still are for teachers in the remaining independent schools. Presumably the teachers whom the managements of such independent suppliers of educational services perceived as most valuable—and they would certainly be in a better position to judge than any outside officials or committees in shire or city halls—would be those who were most effective in teaching, although managements might also need and want to offer bonuses to those qualified in what were, from time to time, shortage subjects.

So far we have presented what is, and is intended to be, no more than a bare outline of the essentials of the ideal epitomised in the slogan, 'An independent education for all!' It would be misleading and even counterproductive to fill in much more detail. For the sketch does contain all the essentials, and nothing else. A large part of the point of this ideal precisely is to provide for the maximum of variety and choice, while correspondingly rejecting any and every attempt to impose and sustain a state monopoly; a monopoly intended to produce—although, as we shall soon be seeing, certainly not in fact producing—an uniform service for all its conscript customers.

It was, therefore, not merely excusable but necessary to leave open the questions on whether fees should be paid by or on behalf of the parent or parents and from what pocket those fees should ultimately be drawn. One possibility is a tax-financed voucher system, under which the parent or parents of every child within the relevant age set would be allotted a voucher cashable only by a provider of, and in return for, educational services. Within such a framework there are again many alternative possibilities. Thus vouchers could, and presumably always would, be in different amounts for children of different ages; with additions for the blind or for the otherwise grievously handicapped.

Again, vouchers could, and under administrations of a certain political colour no doubt would, be refused to parents belonging to such disfavoured social sets as 'the rich'. (By Cantor's Axiom for Sets the sole essential feature of a set is that its members have at least one common characteristic, any kind of characteristic. Thus 'set' is the term to use whenever we want to avoid the implications of terms such as 'class' or 'community' or 'collective'.)

Any kind of voucher system is, however, only one of several alternative methods of financing which are all equally consistent with the proposed ideal. Alternatively or even additionally you could have education tax allowances or education tax credits, or you could have the funds still following the pupils, as in a voucher system, but somehow going from central government directly into the individual schools. The difference between an education tax allowance and an education tax credit is that the former excuses the parent paying school fees from all tax on some slice of income otherwise taxable, whereas the latter is a sum credited to every parent paying school fees. This sum is offset against tax owed wherever there is a corresponding tax liability. However, where there is not, it is simply paid to the parent— a refund of tax not paid! Various arrangements under which central government funds follow the pupils into the individual schools are already working in other countries. The possibilities are numerous. The two things which are essential to the proposed ideal of an independent education for all are first, that all parents should be free and able to take their children out of one school and into another and, second, that every school should have strong financial incentives to attract and to hold custom, and have sufficient reason to fear disaster if it fails.

Another dimension in which several alternatives are all equally possible and equally consistent with the same ideal is that of the methods of managing the independent and self-reliant educational firms. The management certainly does not have to be a single more or less dictatorial headmaster or headmistress. Perhaps in fact it usually would be. However, it would be no less consistent with our ideal for the management to be by some collective— perhaps a collective consisting of all or some of the teachers, or of the entire staff, or perhaps even of some altogether different set. For it is both theoretically and actually possible for sovereignty over a subordinate organisation, as well as sovereignty over the state, to be held either by a collective or by an individual. Hence, despite his own strong personal pref-

erence for individual despotism, Thomas Hobbes was in his *Leviathan*
careful always to write "one man, or assembly of men".

Yet another dimension in which there are many possible alternatives, all
consistent with an approach towards a full realisation of the proposed ideal,
is that of ownership. Schools could, for instance, continue to be owned by
LEAs or by other state institutions; and some, designed to fulfil special purposes, no doubt always would be. The two cruces are, again, first, the extension of parental choice and, second, the subjection of every individual
school to ordinary market disciplines. So the breaking of *The Public School
Monopoly* (Everhart, 1982), and the effective denationalisation of primary
and secondary education, does not have to, and scarcely could, be brought
about on a single glorious Divesting Day.

An independent education for all, like an independent education for some
but not all, can also consist of a deal of regulation by central or local government. For government can perfectly well insist upon minimum standards
for this and that, or require the teaching of some basic or core curriculum in
all schools, both independent and maintained: just as it ought to and does
insist upon high minimum standards of cleanliness and of quality in the production and marketing of food, and of other things important for sustaining
the health of its citizens.

This said, however, it is necessary at once to insist that we have always to
be alert to the fact that various interest groups, both official and unofficial,
will be forever manoeuvring to extend and to exploit any such regulatory
machinery for the furtherance of their own ends; ends which will almost, if
not quite always, be in flat conflict with the parental consumer's interest in
the preservation of variety among and competition between the suppliers of
educational services. (Compare, for the UK, West, 1970, and, for the
USA, Blumenfeld, 1984, passim.)

The truth that an independent education for all is completely compatible
with a deal of general government regulation may appear less obvious in
Britain than it does in countries where the private sector of the educational
economy is larger. For here today only 6 per cent of children in the relevant
age group attend independent schools. The main reason is, of course, that
only a tiny minority of parents are both able and willing to pay twice: once
by paying taxes to the state and then a second time by paying fees, to a
private school. (By the way, we do have scrupulously to eschew the word
'public' in this context, since by no means all the existing independent
schools are what have traditionally been called public schools, while these
independent schools themselves most emphatically are not state
maintained.)

(ii)   The ideal outlined in Subsection (i) above is about as far as could be
from present actuality. For, as has just been noticed, in Britain today 94 per
cent of all children of primary and secondary school age are attending main-

tained schools. Compared with those for some nearby nations that figure is extremely high. In France, for instance, 17 per cent of all school-age children are educated privately. These private schools, however, produce a quarter of all candidates for the baccalaureat—which, as an university entrance examination, corresponds roughly to our A-levels. In 1959, under President de Gaulle, all private schools became eligible for a direct state subsidy, provided that they meet national standards of curriculum and enrollment. As one result three quarters of the teachers in these private schools are paid by the state. When in the early 1980s the incoming Socialist and Communist administration of President Mitterand proposed in effect total nationalisation and the establishment of a comprehensive state education monopoly, this provoked the largest protest demonstration Paris has ever seen. The proposal was withdrawn. (As the man so famously and so correctly said: "They order . . . this matter better in France.")

In Holland the majority of all schools are in private ownership, thanks mainly to a constitutional amendment of 1917, putting the public and the private on an equal financial footing. However—unlike France and Britain—in Holland it is the public rather than the private sector which contributes disproportionately to university admissions. The most remarkable institutional peculiarity is that any reasonably large collective of Netherlanders can found a private school. Then, provided that it meets certain fairly stringent curricular and other standards, it will qualify for a state subsidy (Wilkinson, 1977, Ch. II).

Coming back home, our maintained schools are not directly managed or wholly financed by central government. The managerial function, and part of the responsibility for financing, is instead delegated to a hundred and four separate LEAs. In the circumstances, and for present purposes, these can most illuminatingly be thought of as Local Education Monopolies (LEMs). There are, of course, many differences between LEMs. A few, for instance, have been both resolved and able to preserve both grammar and secondary modern schools. Again, among the wholly comprehensive majority, some try to provide A-level teaching in the institutions in which lower secondary work is done, whereas others have established 'sixth form colleges'. And so on.

However, whatever the differences between one LEM and another, particular families, necessarily resident within the area of one LEM, have precious little choice of school for their children. Certainly there are some possibilities of getting a child into a school under an adjacent authority; which can be important. At the latest count nearly a fifth of the schoolchildren from the London Borough of Brent had found and taken this escape route (Marks, 1987, p. 28). It is also true that there has been some movement since 1979; and that in what, in more than one sense, is the right direction. But not much; certainly not enough to allow the senses—the directions—of parental choice to become either an effective constraint upon poor instructional performance or an effective incentive for all concerned to do better. How could it be, so long as every reference to parental wishes in every Education Act allows that these may be overriden by the LEM, and even that the monopolists themselves are to be the judges in their own causes, determining whether their own actions were or were not reasonable? Section 76 of the 1944 Act states the principles very clearly. The precedent thus established has been followed ever since:

> In the exercise and performance of all powers and duties conferred and imposed on them by this Act the Minister and local education authorities shall have regard to the general principle that, so far as is compatible with the provision of efficient instruction and training and the avoidance of unreasonable public expenditure, pupils are to be educated in accordance with the wishes of their parents.

The most important of the recent shifts was the inclusion of the 1980 Education Act of a clause requiring that all maintained schools publish whatever results their pupils achieve in independently assessed examinations. There had been cases before in which this information was refused even to school governors (Cox and Marks, 1980a, p. 1). Yet obviously it is essential for any family wanting to make a rationally grounded choice between alternative schools seen as competing for its custom, as well as for anyone wanting to do a decent job as a governor. No doubt it was in part because this is indeed quite obvious that the National Union of Teachers (NUT) and various other similarly interested parties declared—in the words of the NUT—their "total opposition" to this clause in the Bill. The reason stated was that, if such dangerous information were to be published, then 'league tables' would be constructed, which would be very unfair to schools labouring under various special disadvantages.

Certainly information, like everything else, may be misused; and, by some people, it very likely will be. However, given that human nature and the human condition are what they so regrettably are, then the least insecure resort must be to publish not only the examination results but also whatever supplementary information is thought necessary if these results are to be fairly understood. Since it is the schools which are required to make the information available, the sovereign remedy remains in their hands. They are free to insist that their results are supplied only alongside whatever supplementary information they themselves consider necessary to complete a fair picture.

All this being so, it is hard not to infer that the true concern both of the NUT and of all the other educational supply side interest groups then protesting was concern for those institutions which they suspected to be failing without excuse. Adam Smith was no doubt thinking primarily of the producers of dry goods rather than of services, but his reproachful warning applies equally in the present more elevated context: "People of the same trade seldom meet together, even for merriment and diversion, but the conversation ends in a conspiracy against the publick, or in some contrivance to raise prices" (Smith, 1776, I(x)c, p. 145).

(iii)   Subsection (ii) indicated that the British maintained system of primary and secondary education is a network of local education monopolies, offering to its customers precious little choice of, and hence almost none of the usual benefits of competition between, suppliers. One consequence of what unsympathetic centralisers might put down as this form of disorganisation is that most universal statements made about the services actually provided by these LEMs either have to refer to some kind of average or have to be qualified as, at best, true only 'in general' or 'with exceptions'. Those making such statements therefore expose themselves to the indignation of objectors thinking to refute contentions about the average (the arithmetic mean) by insisting that these contentions do not apply to every single member of the set in question; and, most especially, not to that particular member about whom or which the objector happens to be best informed.

Suppose, for instance, that it is said that, in some given human set, the average intake of one particular kind of food is such and such. Then a moment's thought should tell us that, in all probability, some members of that set eat more, some less and some perhaps none at all. After all, if it were known that every member of the set regularly ate exactly the same amount, then that is surely what would have been asserted; and indeed ought to have been.

However, neither we nor she should have been surprised by the uproar provoked by Mrs Edwina Currie when, as a junior minister with some public health responsibilities, she publicised statistics showing that various unbalances of diet are much more common in the North of England than in the South. Editors and talk-show hosts and hostesses were joyously overwhelmed with people raring to refute Mrs Currie with protests that they themselves had never eaten so much as one single, small, solitary black pudding. Those who are seized of the necessary truth that not every denial constitutes a refutation will relish a poet–scholar's acerbic deflation of a critic colleague: "Three minutes' thought would suffice to find this out; but thought is irksome, and three minutes is a long time" (Housman, 1931, p. xi; and compare Flew, 1975, § §1.54-5 and 5.6).

Whatever may be the case with Hume's "rabble without doors" (1739, p. xiv), it would be comfortable to believe that, inside what Tom Lehrer would have us call Edbiz, it is unnecessary to labour such obvious truths about arithmetic means and qualified universal generalisations. However, recent experience shows any such belief to be too optimistic. Thus when in

December 1986 the Hillgate Group published *Whose Schools? A Radical Manifesto* (Cox, 1986), and although their every statement about what they considered to be going wrong was of one or other of these two logical forms, even some directors of education rushed forward to dismiss every anxiety and every positive proposal with an insistence that, at least in their particular bailiwicks, all is well. Perhaps it is, but that was not the point. Nor is it now.

(iv) In a country where only 6 per cent of the children attend independent schools, and where the noisest organised demands are all for the destruction rather than the extension of that tiny private sector, our thinking is apt to be crippled by "mind-forged manacles" of parochial habituation and intellectual inertia. To break these blinkers, to pull ourselves out of the ruts, we need to travel a little both in space and time, even if only mentally.

We have already noticed both that France has an independent sector three times as large as ours and that in Holland nearly two thirds of the schools are privately owned. Nor were things in Britain always as they are now. Yet it is, it seems, still widely believed that popular education began with the Forster Act of 1870, and that educational services for the masses have always been provided by maintained schools. That such false beliefs are still so common even among the latest entrants to the profession is an indication of one of the many major deficiencies in the instruction currently provided in courses under the curriculum rubric 'Education'. My then colleague, the Senior Tutor of the University of Keele, knew what he was talking about when he told our Senate: "You have made your B.Ed.; and now you must lie about it!"

The truth is that Britain had achieved remarkably high levels of basic literacy long before there was any substantial infusion of tax money into the system. In 1834 the Factory Commission reported that 96 per cent of a sample of 28,000 Scottish millworkers could read. For writing, including English and Welsh millworkers with the Scots, the average—to no Scot's surprise—went down; but to a still astonishing 56 per cent (West, 1975, p. 68). The Commission commented: "The returns from factories in the rural districts are quite as favourable as those from the towns, which is attributable to the parochial schools." A modern specialist concludes, referring to the late 1830s, that "In so far as one dare generalise about a national average. . . the figure would seem to run between two thirds and three quarters of the working classes as literate. . . " (Webb, 1963). Compare these figures with some given by UNESCO for 1950, more than a century later: Portugal 55-60 per cent, Egypt 20-25 per cent and Algeria 15-20 per cent (West, 1975, p. 39).

Again, the 1851 Census revealed that, twenty years before the passing of the Forster Act, the percentage of children attending primary schools in England and Wales was already, at 66 per cent, higher than that for the whole world in 1961 (*ibid.*, p.28). The author of *Education and the State*, who has done so much to transform understanding, noticed back in 1965, when this first book was first published, that historians of education were, curiously yet consistently, both inclined to identify their subject with the history of the maintained system only and reluctant to give credit to achievements previous to the development of that system.

Mark Blaug has since constructed a handy measure of the extent of this reluctance: it is a list of ten much recommended books on the history of British education which do not even include the word 'literacy' in their indices (West, 1975, pp. 43-4). Those familiar with the operations of what, with apologies to the retiring President Eisenhower, we could christen 'the bureaucratic–educational complex' will recognise this lack of interest as yet another expression of a characteristic disinclination; the unwillingness to press on, beyond questions about the amounts of teaching to which pupils have or ought to have been exposed, in order to ask what actually has been achieved. (See, for that christening, Andreski, 1982; and, for the characteristic disinclination, Anderson, 1981, p. 35 and passim.)

Another widespread false assumption is that working-class parents—the "working people and their families" of Labour Party election manifestos—could not possibly afford to pay for the education of their children. West shows that in fact, even in the nineteenth century, both before and after 1870, most of them did. For in those days most of the national revenue was raised by indirect taxes on items of common consumption, making the whole system regressive rather than progressive. Even in 1962 the tobacco tax, raising £879 million, was by itself more than sufficient to cover expenditure on education, £797 million (West, 1970, Ch. 4). With the disproportionately rapid decline of smoking in the Registrar General's higher social classes that particular tax becomes progressively more regressive.

Of course, there were in that century many parents too poor to pay any school fees, however modest. Even given the most drastic reductions both in indirect and in direct taxation, there would still today need to be tax-financed support for the education of some children. However, it is salutary, especially for those habitually despising our Victorian forebears, to contrast the arrogant authoritarianism of the 1970 Donnison Commission with Forster's meticulous respect for both the choices and the dignity of poor parents (West, 1970, pp. xvii-xx). In Section 25 of the 1870 Act it is laid down that:

> The school board may. . . pay the whole or any part of the school fees. . . [of]. . . any child. . . whose parent is. . . unable from poverty to pay the same; but no such payment shall be made or refused on condition of the child attending any public elementary school other than such as may be selected by the parent; and such payment shall not be deemed to be parochial relief given to such parent.

West's revisionist essays in the history of education, informed as they are by the new economics of bureaucracy and public choice, also provide an abundance of instances to confirm the truth of the statement that "the professional suppliers of education (administrators, teachers, etc.), who are more politically organised than dispersed consumers. . . , like any other supplier, have a constant wish to operate in the comfort of decreasing market sanctions" (West, 1970, p. 1). That statement itself, defining what was earlier christened 'the bureaucratic–educational complex', constitutes a reproduction in modern and rather more technical dress of Smith's cold-eyed comment, quoted previously with reference to the "total opposition" of a teachers' union to the publication of information reflecting on the quality of the services provided.

The same essays uncover many examples to show how bureaucratic and other interest groups work to control, and sometimes even to corrupt, the supply of relevant information. Thus they will sponsor analysis and statistics of the services they provide, but will ensure that this research and information is never such as to threaten the growth of demand:

> If, as sometimes happens, some study sponsored by bureaus turns out to be objective, thorough, penetrating and lucid, it will usually be classified or otherwise restricted; if the distribution of the few penetrating studies cannot be restricted, the bureau will usually sponsor other studies on the same subject as an excuse for delaying action or to dilute the effects of the former studies (Niskanen, 1971, p. 210).

In later chapters we shall be meeting further, contemporary examples. The use of such history, therefore, is to put us on the alert to what is going on here and now. T. S. Eliot's 'Little Gidding' epitomises this value of travel, concluding with the moral that:

> We shall not cease from exploration
> And the end of all our exploring
> Will be to arrive where we started
> And know the place for the first time

1.3 The present absence of accountability

Section 1.2 expounded the nature and some of the implications of the ideal of an independent education for all. The next task is to offer reasons for adopting and for striving to realise that ideal. For the present author the first and overriding consideration happens to be that it is an ideal which follows as a corollary from a recognition of the most fundamental and universal human rights. He himself also suffers from an almost physical revulsion against an authoritarian enemy eager to impose upon everybody—or, it sometimes seems, only upon everybody else but fellow-members of a socialist power elite—one single, uniform, all-comprehensive Procrustean system.

On some other occasion he would be happy to sketch (indeed on other occasions he has already sketched) a rationale for recognising the three option rights proclaimed in the American Declaration of Independence. He has also offered extensive justification for feeling irreconcilably hostile to all enemies of freedom (Flew, 1982b; and compare Flew, 1978, 1981 and 1983). The too-commonly collapsed distinction between option and welfare rights is, by the way, the distinction: between option rights to be left alone to do your own chosen thing, providing always that you do not violate the corresponding equal rights of others; and welfare rights to be provided with specific goods or services, presumably by the state, and presumably at someone else's expense.

(i) Here and now, however, the appeal is going to be not to what opponents might dismiss as abstract and theoretical rights but to concrete and practical considerations of educational improvement. The main contention is that by far the best prospects for progress lie in moves towards the realisation of that ideal. So those who really want such progress have got to make or accept moves in that direction, whether or not it is a direction in which they would otherwise wish to go. In the proverbial nutshell, the hardheaded reason why is this; that the nearer you get to our ideal, the more the actual producers of educational services become effectively accountable to the families from which the pupils come. These families are those who both have the strongest and most immediate interests in the quality and appropriateness of provision and are in the best position to maintain a continuous watch on what is going on. (By the way, the point of sometimes writing not 'parents' but 'families' is to remind ourselves that, as children grow up, they should play a steadily increasing part in making the decisions about their futures.)

Those who owe their livelihoods to the bureaucratic–educational complex, whether as teachers or as officials, and whose hopes of personal advancement must rest mainly within that complex, have perhaps a stronger interest in the educational economy than any parent. However, that interest, at least directly and necessarily, must be in the welfare and the expansion of the apparatus rather than in the nature and the quality of what that apparatus is actually producing. Because it is their own children who are receiving the provision, it is the families from which the pupils come which have the strongest interest in its nature and quality. In as much as the major interests of the apparatniks and of the parents are thus not merely different but also bound from time to time to be conflicting, it becomes, for anyone who for any reason shares that parental interest, a mandate of the most elementary political prudence to strive to increase the influence of the parents—to shift the whole balance of power in the education economy from the supply side to the demand side.

However, parents are not only the people who have the greatest interest in the nature and quality of educational provision; they are also those best able and most disposed to maintain a continuous watch when—one hopes rarely, but none the less importantly—something dreadful is being said or done within the privacy of classroom walls. For members of the outside inspectorates, and seniors within the hierarchies of individual schools, can observe only when and where they are themselves visibly intruders. In the nature of the case they are thus handicapped in discovering anything which the individual teacher does not want them to discover. That is why, until and unless parents obtain effective rights to escape from offending schools, it must remain impossibly difficult to impose any effective check even upon those indoctrinative and other malpractices which are not—as nowadays so many are—actively promoted by whatever particular LEA is supposedly in charge (Scruton *et al.*, 1985, Tingle, 1986; Lewis, 1986).

(ii)   Recently the authoress of the second of the three mottos of the present chapter was, as is her wont, vigorously advocating a system of education vouchers. The Director of Education in an authority which includes an ancient university town replied that he had no need of any such system to tell him which of the schools in his charge were good and which were not. No doubt any other competent and conscientious Director of Education could with equal truth have said the same. Following this remarkable yet obviously true confession that the system is not in fact producing—what it was never reasonable to expect that such a system would produce (Friedman, 1986, Ch. 6)—universal equality of educational opportunity, my friend then asked (but without either hoping for or needing an answer) whether it was to the good or to the bad schools that the Director directed the children of the dons.

The question which she ought to have asked (but is much too polite to have pressed) is why he had failed to raise the bad schools up to the standards of the good. The answer, presumably, is not that he was unwilling—we have absolutely no reason to suspect that he was doing anything but his level best—but that, subject to all the various constraints under which he was operating, he was unable. Reflect that it took a full-scale official enquiry, lasting for months, and costing a quarter of a million less-devalued early 1970s pounds, before anything effective could be done to clean up the scandal of William Tyndale School. This was so even though the authority (ILEA) was at that time under a more 'right-wing' and certainly a more right-thinking political control than it is now, and was then without doubt sincere in its expressions of concern.

Had those splendid and incontestably working-class mothers who later crowded towards the television cameras, bursting to protest that they wanted their children "to be learnt to read proper", been able to defect, and had every defection impacted immediately upon the funding of that dreadful school, then it becomes extremely doubtful whether there would ever have been any call for an official enquiry. For, had they indeed been under a credible threat of imminent personal disaster were they to persist in their several follies, then the responsible staff even in that school would most likely have been fairly quick to reform themselves. Dr Johnson displayed all his usual shattering good sense when he remarked that the prospect of execution on the morrow "concentrates the mind wonderfully".

(iii) Indeed it does, and would. Compare and contrast such ideally direct and immediate accountability to the individual customers with the near-total lack of any accountability either to them or indeed to anyone or anything else under the present perhaps not strikingly systematic system. Primary and secondary education services are in England and Wales, as was said before, provided by 104 LEAs, subject to various pulls and pushes from the central Department of Education and Science (DES). The political control of both the LEAs and the DES is granted to members of parties elected to office by the grossly unfair and unrepresentative first-past-the-post method. The parties themselves are elected, or not elected, on the basis of programmes embracing policies for almost everything. So the individual voter is offered a choice between three or, at most, four paradigm package deals.

Politicians achieving educational office then have to try to fulfil the promises and threats of their latest party manifesto, enterprises which may or may not in fact accord with the majority wishes of their electorates. However, the lines of communication down from either the Minister's desk or the Council Chamber to the chalkface are very far from constituting a crisply efficient chain of command. That this is so is, of course, often a blessing, but it is a blessing with a price, and the price is that teachers within the state system are very little accountable for what they do or fail to do in their classrooms. As was originally said of teachers in institutions wholly supported by endowments: "Their subsistence, so far as it arises from their salaries, is evidently derived from a fund altogether independent of their success and reputation in their particular profession" (Smith, 1776, V(i)f, p. 760).

1.4 Some causes for national concern

It is a paradoxical yet profound truth that the gravest ground for anxiety about the present condition of the state educational system in the UK is the very lack of comprehensive and criteria-related indices of performance. A system of academic testing is, in the barbarous jargon of educationists, said to be criteria-related in so far as a given class or mark or grade is awarded to all but only those candidates whose performance matches some fixed standard. A system is, by contrast, norm-related in so far as roughly the same proportions of the total numbers of all candidates are awarded all the various classes or grades on every successive occasion of examination, irrespective of the absolute levels of their achievement.

(i)   You do not need to be a pathologically suspicious or hostile critic to insist upon asking and answering the Roman lawyer's question *Cui bono?* when you learn that in 1960—during, so to speak, the first February dawn of the Comprehensive Revolution—the word went out from the former Secondary Schools Examination Council (SSEC) that (roughly) 70 per cent of candidates must pass, and with what proportions in what grades. (See the SSEC's third report *Examination in Secondary Schools: the General Certificate of Education and Sixth Form Studies*, Appendix F.) This ruling necessarily, and presumably of intent, invalidates all direct, year-on-year comparisons of A-level performance. (Much the same apparently applies at O-level, though there 60 per cent have to pass and 40 per cent to fail.)

A-levels, being in effect entrance qualifications for the tertiary sector, are taken by only about a fifth of those attending the state secondary schools. The General Certificate of Education (GCE) at O-level, and the less demanding Certificate of Secondary Education (CSE), were at the time of writing in process of being amalgamated into a new General Certificate of Secondary Education (GCSE). Because they are all normally taken round about the age of 16 these are all known as 16+ examinations. The old CSE allowed for a large element—and, if the NUT is permitted to have its way, the new GCSE will allow for a much larger element—of what was called Mode III. Under this, work was both set and assessed by the teachers teaching the particular pupils to be examined. Everything was supposed to be 'moderated' by externals. However in practice no system introducing a substantial element of Mode III can realistically be rated a system of independent assessment. The significance of all this, and the outrageousness of the NUT's demands, can best be appreciated by reflecting on a possible proposal that driving tests should be conducted by the very same instructors as taught the candidates. It would be a great day for British education if the Minister would tell the next NUT delegation to argue this scandalous case to shut up, clear out and hang their heads in shame (Naylor and Marks, 1982)!

However, these 16+ examinations are taken by only about 60 per cent of all state secondary school pupils. The much-abused Sir Keith Joseph was the first Minister to raise the question of school-leaving examinations for 'the bottom 40 per cent', a constructive initiative which, like several others, appears to have been lost somewhere along the corridors of Elizabeth

House. One consequence of this lack of a fully comprehensive, criteria-related system for assessing the output is that when official committees are set up to investigate the problems presented by illiteracy or innumeracy, these committees have to begin their business by scratching around for evidence indicating what the present situation actually is (Bullock, 1975; Cockcroft, 1982).

This absence of precise and comprehensive statistics, even of skills which can easily be tested with absolute objectivity, ought to be alarming. For, as will be argued more fully in Chapter 2, every rational being sincerely seeking to attain some objective—any objective—is bound to be constantly monitoring its success or failure in that pursuit. So, in so far as our system really was enthusiastically and unreservedly devoted to achieving high minimum levels of literacy and numeracy it would inevitably be producing, as it were, as a by-product, an abundance of information about progress, or the lack of it; and this even were there still no independently assessed national tests. In Japan, afflicted with what must surely be the most difficult of all surviving systems of writing, with much larger classes, taught by teachers who can therefore be correspondingly better paid, the results achieved in such tests are phenomenal. (I can here reasonably claim some special expertise, since I spent the years 1942-5 working on that written language; at the end of which three-year period of intensive effort and involvement I could scarcely have competed with today's average Japanese twelve-year-old.)

The *Public School Monopoly* in the USA is, of all contemporary systems, perhaps the least dissimilar to our own (Everhart, 1982; and compare Blumenfeld, 1985), but there they do have criteria-related Scholastic Aptitude Tests (SATs). These in fact test achievement rather than aptitude (Jencks and Crouse, 1982), and are taken by those aspiring to proceed to the tertiary stage. Scores of these SATs have been sharply and almost continuously declining since 1965, a year which, perhaps by coincidence, marked the beginning of a massive increase in federal funding (Blumenfeld, 1984, Ch. 10). So it is no wonder that in 1983, under the title *A Nation at Risk*, a National Commission on Excellence in Education had to conclude:

> The educational foundations of our society are presently being eroded by a rising tide of mediocrity that threatens our very future as a nation and as a people. . . . If an unfriendly foreign power had attempted to impose on America the mediocre educational performance that exists today, we might well have viewed it as an act of war. As it stands, we have allowed this to happen to ourselves.

None of this is intended to show, or possibly could show, that the situation in the UK is equally lamentable, but it should serve, and is intended, as a warning. Not notwithstanding, but rather because of, the lack of any UK equivalent to these criteria-related SATs, we have nevertheless as best we can to try to find out where things are going in our own country. As we proceed we shall discover that findings giving grounds for alarm are regularly received both by the bureaucratic–educational complex and by its allies in the media and elsewhere with, at best, complacency and, at worst, a pontificating and sometimes unscrupulously active hostility. Suffice it for the moment to point out that such is not the behaviour of people unreservedly committed to ensuring that all our children shall achieve the best of which they are capable and zealous to locate and correct every systematic fault which can be corrected.

(ii)   Since, in the words of Tobias Danzig, number is the language of science, and since science provides the foundations for all modern technological developments, it is appropriate to begin with mathematics. In 1983 the National Institute of Economic and Social Research (NIESR) issued its Discussion Paper No. 60, *Schooling Standards in Britain and Germany*, containing "Some Summary Comparisons Bearing on Economic Efficiency" (Prais and Wagner, 1983). Of course, as the NIESR realises, such international comparisons are difficult to execute, but, after all qualifications and allowances have been made, the general conclusions were as decisive as they are disturbing.

Except for the tiny elite continuing with mathematics to A-level, an elite whose achievement outstrips that of their West German counterparts, every other comparison is in our disfavour. Since there is no reason to suspect greater innate ability in the Federal Republic, the defects must lie in our school organisation, curriculum, teaching and/or, perhaps, in motivation. However, wherever they lie, their seriousness can be appreciated by savouring a few such NIESR statements as that "about half of all German pupils compared with a quarter of all pupils in Britain achieve a standard equivalent to a broadly-based O-level"; that "the German system has raised the level of attainment of its weakest 50 per cent of pupils to about that of the average pupil in England"; and that "those in the lower half of the ability-range in England appear to lag by the equivalent of about two years' schooling behind the corresponding section of pupils in Germany".

None of this should have been surprising to anyone who had noticed the findings of an Institute of Mathematics survey taken in 1977. (Their report is handily reprinted in Cox and Marks, 1982, pp. 59-66.) In this survey the same studiously elementary test was given to 8,000 pupils in maintained secondary schools in England and Wales. All the pupils tested were eligible to leave school during the following summer, although the sample included its due quota of those who would in fact be continuing their education. There were, of course, large variations as between different LEAs; with, as usual, the most deplorable levels of performance those achieved under the

ILEA—the authority which contrives to spend more per pupil than any other. However, the Institute concluded, with restraint, that "None of the results. . . for any authority is satisfactory. They all give strong support to the concern that has been expressed for some years and in many quarters about the level of numeracy of school leavers."

Almost needless to say, little or nothing seems to have been no more nor less than actually done either about this cause for concern or about the Institute's incidental finding that actual absenteeism was everywhere higher than the officially recorded truancy rates—rising under ILEA above 25 per cent. It is worth pausing briefly to ponder that incidental finding, for it reminds us of something which everybody really knows but which, in many of the contexts in which it matters, many choose to overlook. This familiar but often conveniently forgotten fact is that the desire for eduction is something less than universal, and that it is presumably both less strong and less common in some social sets than in others.

The neglect of this fact vitiates virtually all the available research on equality of educational opportunity, most of which is in any case already vitiated both by its insistence on collapsing the distinction between opportunity and outcome and by failing to distinguish chance (probability) of achievement from chance (opportunity) of achievement (Flew, 1981, Ch. II 4-5; and compare Murphy, 1978, 1981 a, b. He is the first social scientist, to my knowledge, to gain a firm, if awkward, grasp upon all these points.)

A similar neglect afflicts a lot of the discussion within Edbiz both about larger matters of policy and about teaching small individuals. Entering that enchanted garden, even normally sharp philosophers unthinkingly identify "children who are very difficult to teach" with "children with severe learning difficulties" (Bailey and Bridges, 1983, p. 36). Nor have any LEAs been over-keen to enquire how many of the children under their charge have, after answering the daily roll call, been refusing any longer to expose themselves to the educational services provided. (Why the teachers do not do so will be sympathetically understood by everyone knowing the difficulties of disciplining an unruly class!)

Returning to the NIESR, their findings too do not appear to have made any deep impression. Apart from reports of the knee-jerk response of the NUT, construing this, like everything else, as one more reason for increasing the public education budget, there was in *The Times* one feature article on 'A German Lesson for Our Schools' (1 November 1983) by Anne Sofer, at that time a member of the Greater London Council (GLC) and still prominent in the educational affairs of the Social Democratic Party (SDP). This article is significant both in what it did and in what it did not contain.

It did not say anything about the qualifications of teachers or about the consequences of comprehension. It would, for instance, surely have been relevant to notice that most other countries in Western Europe make some sort of qualifications, pay and status division between schoolteachers at the upper secondary level and the rest; or that in Britain, until very recently, virtually all applicants have been admitted to teacher training (Wilkinson, 1977, pp. 97ff.)? It was, presumably, in order 'to improve teacher/pupil ratios'—to what educational effect?—that as many as 41 per cent of those accepted had, as late as 1975/6, no O-level in mathematics, while 25 per cent had never got beyond O-level in anything (Cox and Marks, 1982a, p. 58). Since Sofer has been, and apparently remains, a militant of the Comprehensive Revolution, she very understandably, if less excusably, forbears to mention that, even in 'Red Hesse', West Germany has been extremely cautious about comprehension. The norm remains a choice of three types of specialist school. (It is this sort of thing, incidentally, for which the radical right in education has been begging for years, and which would very soon emerge if once the existing individual state schools had to compete for custom.)

Sofer, however, draws a very different moral: "The bottom half of the pupil population is failing so abysmally because they are subject to an examination system which is designed to pick out the brightest and fail the rest." She sees this as an expression of the attitudes of "the conservative (with both a large and a small 'C') academic establishment", which is alleged to exclaim: "Exams that everyone can pass. What nonsense!"

The true nonsense is all on the other side. GCE O-level was not designed to be taken by all but then inescapably failed by most. It was designed to be taken by all but only those higher-ability pupils who could reasonably be expected to pass. What is wrong is not that we make everyone take examinations which most—however hard they study and however well they are taught—are bound to plough but that we fail to demand that everyone takes some examinations, but different examinations for different interests and different levels of ability.

What the West Germans have is a more varied and more comprehensive battery of examinations, not one single uniform examination with a minimum grade set so low that every candidate is bound to pass. As the NIESR report makes clear, candidates can and do fail all these different West German examinations. Sofer's protests notwithstanding, it would be—indeed, since it does happen, it is—a nonsense to conduct examinations which candidates cannot by any means contrive to fail (Flew, 1976, Ch. 6). For how can a pass constitute achievement, or serve as an indication of the attainment of any standard in anything, if such a 'pass' is awarded to all candidates quite irrespective of the work done or not done?

(iii)   In 1981 the newly appointed Minister was a man who had declared himself to be "philosophically sympathetic" to the idea of the voucher. The first move in the campaign to kill it was the production of the DES document later to be mischievously nicknamed *No, Minister* (Seldon, 1985). This was later published, in December 1982, as an Appendix to *Bulletin No. 6* of the (unofficial) National Council for Educational Standards (NCES). Of most immediate interest to us are two sentences which the DES officials had the effrontery to present as an objection. They stated that:

> the quality and scope of the school curriculum is a matter of great national import-
> ance and its improvement is very much the concern of all those affected by it.
> How far would parental preference for what schools offered coincide with the
> needs of employers, and indeed of the pupils themselves?

This bold bit of intellectual judo, confounding the opponent with his own strength, might well have led the innocent to believe that there already is a core curriculum mandated for all state schools, and that the apparatniks of the bureaucratic–educational complex are demonstrably more likely than parents to take thought for the future employability of the children taught. The truth on both counts is quite contrary. No standard curriculum ever has been centrally prescribed: under a clause of the 1944 Act, honoured nowadays at least as often in the breach as in the observance, the sole com- pulsory subject is Religious Knowledge. The flagrant failure actually to meet "the needs of employers", and hence "of the pupils themselves", is most vividly and convincingly illustrated by the establishment of the Manpower Services Commission. For here we have a fresh engine of the state, with an annual budget now of over 2 billion pounds, one of its main functions being to run another fresh institution, the Youth Training Service. The function of that—in a nice and delicate choice of word—is to 'supple- ment' the work of the state primary and secondary schools.

Anyone urging that anything more than a very basic and sketchy outline should be prescribed from the centre needs carefully to ponder warning words from John Stuart Mill:

> A general State education is a mere contrivance for moulding people to be exactly
> like one another: and as the mould in which it casts them is that which pleases the
> predominant power in the government, whether this be a monarch, a priesthood,
> an aristocracy, or the majority of the existing generation; in proportion as it is
> efficient and successful, it establishes a despotism over the mind, leading by
> natural tendency to one over the body (1859, p. 240).

However, the fact is that just such a basic, outline, ideologically inoffensive, core curriculum did originally emerge as the result of the interactions of various separate and autonomous initiatives. Shortly after World War II its hold was, to put it no stronger, drastically weakened, not through the choices of wayward and irresponsible parents but by central government decree.

For at that time, following recommendations from an official committee chaired by Sir Cyril Norwood, it was laid down that the various once wholly independent Examination Boards, originally established by individual universities or groups of universities, should no longer award School Certificates and Higher School Certificates. Instead there were to be GCE O-levels and GCE A-levels. So far, if not so good, or at least no great matter. However, the new GCE could be awarded for the achievement of no more than the barest pass in a single subject. Under the old regimen you had to get passes in at least five subjects, as well as good passes, called Credits, in—was it?—at least three of those five. Certainly, in order also to be granted exemption from the Matriculation Examination of the University of London, you needed at least five Credits. Without that exemption no one was admitted into what is now called 'the old Sixth Form'.

To us the relevance of this long-forgotten School Certificate system was that, in order to be awarded any certificate at all, you had to have performed satisfactorily in Mathematics, English and one foreign language. So, for any school containing any pupils aspiring either to obtain a qualification which was in fact universally respected by employers and/or to enter a real Sixth Form, these three crucial subjects constituted the inescapable core curriculum. There could be no question of dropping any one of these, just because it was too hard or otherwise unappealing. When applicants for itions showed their School Certificates, whether with or without 'exemption from London Matric', they provided proof of some modest level of competence in all three areas. There was therefore, in those more demanding days, no question of finding that "41 per cent of those admitted" to teacher training courses "had . . . no O-level in mathematics".

The third element in that long-since abandoned core curriculum was "one foreign language". The failure of our state monopoly system to satisfy this important cultural and economic need is, if possible, still more spectacular. Thus, of all the boys entered for A-level French in 1977, some 34 per cent came from the private sector. For German, the proportion was 36 per cent. Greek and Latin shares were, respectively, 66 and 46 per cent. The schools from which these candidates were drawn took, in that year, only 5.5 per cent of the total secondary school population.

A more recent analysis, covering all but only the schools run by ILEA, shows that entries for French and German O-levels *fell* by 42 per cent between 1977 and 1983 (Marks *et al.*, 1986; and compare O'Keeffe, 1986, p. 196). In 1984 the number entering for German fell yet again, by a further 29 per cent, with only 242 achieving the 'pass' grades of A-C, and in all ILEA schools only 69 pupils passed A-level German. What an indictment of state education in our capital city: from schools catering for more than

25,000 pupils each year, only 69 emerge with either a decent facility in speaking or writing the language of our largest European trading partner, or an ability to appreciate the literature of one of the great civilisations!

Later we shall try to show why we can reasonably hope that an increase in the possibilities for parental choice between schools would do a lot to solve this particular problem, but the immediate task is to point out a curious fact. It is that the confidence of the heaven-born, the Administrative Class elite within the DES, is generously shared by revolutionary diehards of Marxism–Leninism outside. Both sets profess to be sure that the present system abundantly satisfies the needs both of employers and of those who aspire to be employed. Entrenched in so many positions in colleges and departments of education both in the UK and in other countries of the First World overseas, made deaf by their cherished eschatological revelation to the hubbub of complaints from earthly employers, such revolutionary diehards somehow sustain uncritical and uncriticised convictions: both that the needs of that hypostasised abstraction Capital are always, without means or mechanism, magically met, and that a "differentiated labour force" is not required to run an economy which has once been fully socialised. (See, for instance, Levitas, 1974; and compare Sarup, 1982, 1986, or any of the works of those listed in Partington, 1987. Again, to distinguish some individual voices in that hubbub of complaint, listen, for instance, to Anderson, 1982, 1984.)

It will perhaps be of some passing interest to note (whether or not these indoctrinators truly believe their own extravagant preachings) that these teachings have long since been abandoned by those in fact most unequally powerful people, the nomenklatura under 'actually existing socialism'. In August 1960 *Kommunist*, the theoretical organ of the CPSU(B), tacitly parodied an oft-quoted passage from Marx, adding only the realistic but crushing comment: "It will not be so." Some may be happy to hear terms of abuse so often employed by Marx rebounding on him in this parody:

An unintelligent person and philistine might form his own picture of communism approximately as follows: you rise in the morning and ask yourself, where shall I go to work today—shall I be chief engineer at the factory or go and head the fishing brigade? Or shall I run down to Moscow and hold an urgent meeting of the Presidium of the Academy of Science?

It remains to conclude this Subsection by noting a further curiosity. To the extent that these misteachers of teachers succeed in their propagandist endeavours, they must thereby themselves, however indirectly, make it even less the case than it might otherwise have been that the system into which such indoctrinated pupil teachers enter will help all its pupils to become employable. Thus Professor Roy Edgley under the title 'Education for Industry?' in *Radical Philosophy* for Spring 1978, reflects, with evident approval, that "many teachers and students, certainly the socialists among them. . . will insist on raising the question 'Education for Industry, or—in its present form— against it'?"

1.5 Black Paper prejudices?

Any contemporary consideration of 'The Need for Alternatives' has to relate to the Comprehensive Revolution. This truly radical reorganisation has sometimes been described as a great experiment; just as, in the 1920s and the 1930s, the operations of the regime established by the Bolshevik coup of October 1917 were regularly characterised as 'that great social experiment in Russia'. Certainly the continuing effects of the Comprehensive Revolution are both very extensive and extremely important. However, the word 'experiment', in as much as it suggests an open-minded and flexible willingness to monitor progress and to change course if the actual results are found not to be as expected or promised, is not in either case anything but totally inappropriate.

(i)   At least in that of the Comprehensive Revolution part of the reason lies in the fact that the chief promoters of the policy have had a variety of objectives, not all of which are in practice or even conceptually compatible. In so far as the project of universal comprehension ever has been sold to the wider public, the stated aim was both generous and strictly educational. The contention of those addressing the electorate in general or parents in particular was always, very simply and appealingly, that here we had the only practical way to ensure that all our children would have the best chance of achieving the most of which they are capable.

The truth, though this has sometimes been denied, is that the wider public never has been completely sold on the idea of universal comprehension. If or in so far as that project is to be taken to include either the destruction of all independent and all grammar schools or 'mixed ability teaching' and the ending of all 'streaming' and 'setting' within the comprehensives themselves, then it most certainly has not. About the first of these possible further implications, it is doubtful whether the rank and file even of the most militant teachers' union agrees with the ferociously totalitarian demands of its national executive. Not even the NUT executive has declared unreservedly for the second. The whole situation was nicely summed up in a traditionally honest though carelessly written Fabian Society pamphlet: "Claims of a mandate for comprehensives was [sic] so much eyewash" (Marsden, 1971, p. 14). The militants had also had grievous difficulties in persuading even some traditionally Labour LEAs to abolish grammar schools which they had themselves established and of which they were rightly proud (Shaw, 1983).

Since the Comprehensive Revolution, like the Glorious Revolution of 1688, was effected through Parliament we do well to quote the operative resolution of the House of Commons:

> That this House, conscious of the need to raise educational standards at all levels, and regretting that the realisation of this objective is impeded by the separation of children into different types of secondary schools, notes with approval the efforts of local authorities to reorganise secondary education along comprehensive lines, which will preserve all that is valuable in grammar school education for those children who now receive it and make it available to more children;... and believes that the time is now ripe for a declaration of national policy.

The then Minister, Anthony Crosland, forthwith implemented this resolution by issuing DES Circular 10/65, instructing all LEAs to prepare their plans to go comprehensive. In private, as we now know from the memoir written by his widow, he expressed himself in a very different and less generous way: "If it's the last thing I do, I'm going to destroy every fucking grammar school in England and Wales. And Northern Ireland" (Crosland, 1982, p. 149).

Presumably her husband saw this destruction as what moral philosophers of an earlier generation would have called an intrinsic good; something to be pursued for its own sake rather than to be judged by its actual consequences. Certainly there are many others who have by deed or word or both made it clear that, for them, universal compulsory comprehension is just such an intrinsic good. Often this is a somewhat sordid business: the policy is by all means to be defended, either because it is the policy of the party or the bureau with which proponents identify or because they have in some other way become personally committed to it. Sometimes, however misguided, it is at least not sordid. A Lecturer in Philosophy at the London Institute of Education expresses himself with none of Crosland's gutter vulgarity: "Comprehensive schooling is an integral part of the socialist vision" (White, 1977, p. 60).

The immediate relevance of all this is that it can help to explain why so many defenders of the Comprehensive Revolution are not merely indifferent but hostile to serious discussion of evidence or argument suggesting that it is in truth not yielding the excellent results promised in that parliamentary resolution. The point is that, although perhaps themselves indifferent, they know that others, and in particular the parents of children whose education may be suffering, do care, and their caring might well lead them to challenge a policy to which some of its defenders are devoted for quite other reasons. After all, as one of those defenders and would-be extenders so ingenuously has it: "Parents would believe, perhaps, that reorganisation was intended to improve schooling" (Steedman, 1980, p. 201; and compare Cox and Marks, 1981).

(ii)   One of the objections which proponents have been especially keen to see never seriously discussed was put by R.R. Pedley in the first volume of *Black Papers*, and reiterated or developed by others in every successor: "It is one of the more grotesque ironies of our times that a Labour Government, claiming a particular interest in the needs of the poor and the lowly. . . should have determined a policy for secondary education which will beyond doubt lead to. . . a reduction in the opportunities open to able children, from whatever social background they come" (Cox and Dyson, 1969, p. 45).

This would be so for two reasons; first, because selective grammar schools drew the brighter children of all classes into what had to be intellectually more stimulating environments and away from environments which were often hostile to education. Both the Editors and many of the other contributors come from homes which were very definitely not 'middle class' and they well knew both what and how much they owed to their (maintained) grammar schools.

Second, unless most of the new comprehensive schools were going to be inhumanly and unmanageably large, comprehension was bound to employ a scarce resource wastefully and thus wantonly to deprive a lot of children of a good which they might, ought to and, under the previous dispensation, would have been able to enjoy. Later *Black Papers* deployed evidence which showed that this was already happening. The scarce resource is, of course, people able and willing to teach hard subjects well and up to higher levels: the schools which do contrive to hire, for instance, properly qualified physics teachers will be able to give them only uneconomically small A-level classes. Able working-class children are likely to be still further disadvantaged because such teachers, having a choice, will mostly choose to work in generally middle-class areas.

It might reasonably have been expected that an objection so serious and so plausible would have met an equally serious and considered response, and that the same would have applied to many other points raised in the first and subsequent volumes of *Black Papers*; even though, at least in the present case, that argued response could scarcely hope to constitute a refutation. Any such optimistic expectations were in fact disappointed: those thinking of themselves as educational progressives preferred to howl down rather than to heed the voices of dissent. (See, for instance, for some of the lowlights of the reception of the first volume, Amis and Conquest in Cox and Dyson, 1970.) Typically, at an Easter conference in 1969, the then Minister of Education claimed that the publication of the first volume marked "the blackest day in English education for a hundred years".

The Prime Minister of a later Labour administration, in a famous speech at Ruskin College in Oxford (18 October 1976), dismissed all such dissent as mere "*Black Paper* prejudices", adding "We all know those who claim to defend standards but are simply seeking to defend old privileges and in-equalities". Realising that Prime Ministers are impossibly busy men, we may charitably conclude that Mr Callaghan was misled by advisers. It is, however, impossible to be equally charitable about some of those advisers. To the personal knowledge of the present writer, more than one of the most prominent militants of the Comprehensive Revolution, when confronted with this particular *Black Paper* objection and in the company only of per-sons he could not reasonably attempt to deceive, has first admitted that it is correct and then revealed that he himself did not care. That many young people should be thus deprived of the opportunity to better themselves through education seems to such socialist loyalists to be, at worst, only a mildly unfortunate cost of enforcing the Procrustean ideal. Sometimes they call this ideal 'social' justice—the adjective presumably being inserted to indicate that what is to be imposed is precisely not old-fashioned, without prefix or suffix, justice (Flew, 1984).

(iii)   We have already made something, and shall in Chapter 2 be mak-ing much more, of the fact that we have no fully comprehensive battery of criteria-related tests by which to measure the achievements of British primary and secondary schools. It is equally significant that there has been almost no official effort to monitor the results of the Comprehensive Revolution or to discuss how far, if at all, these have in fact fulfilled that promise made in 1965 by the House of Commons. Bodies such as the National Foundation for Educational Research (NFER) have been handsomely funded to study several comparatively narrow aspects of public educational provision, but they have kept away from investigating the biggest question. Perhaps we might even be justified in suggesting that they have been kept away.

Fourteen years after the House of Commons passed that crucial opera-tive resolution one very honest and sensitive research worker confessed that he was, both as a social scientist and as a moral being, scandalised by this negligence:

> The advent of the comprehensive education system. . . stands as one of the most significant developments in secondary education since 1902, that is, from the time when the State first supported secondary education. Yet. . . this event has remained virtually unaccompanied by any sustained research of an empirical variety. To be sure, we have had £100,000 worth of bromide from the NFER. But that ceased in 1972, after the appearance of three reports remarkable only for the virtuosity with which they avoided the major issues.

He goes on to say that this is unjustifiable scientifically:

because, without adequate up-to-date information we can only discuss the issue in terms of prejudice. Morally unjustifiable also because, without such enquiries and information, we are, in effect, asking parents to endorse our convictions, beliefs and prejudices either for or against comprehensive education, without the opportunity of making their own judgment on the development of a national education system (Neave, 1979).

(a) During that period of official negligence—and before the 1980 Act, enabling privately funded researchers to review *Standards in English Schools* more thoroughly and systematically than before (Marks *et al.*, 1983)—it was nevertheless possible for diligent and persistent enquirers to dig out some bits and pieces of relevant and disturbing information. For instance, in the second volume of *Black Papers* Tibor Szamuely published an article under a provokingly paradoxical title, 'Comprehensive Inequality'. It is interesting to note, by the way, that Szamuely had himself both taught and been educated in Soviet-occupied Hungary and in the Soviet Union itself before escaping—through Nkrumah's Ghana—to lecture in Politics at Reading University. Arguing on the same lines as, in Subsection (ii), we saw that R. R. Pedley and others had argued in the first volume, Szamuely concluded "that comprehensive education in this country *will inevitably lead to far greater social inequality than exists at present*" (Cox and Dyson, 1970, p. 53: emphasis original).

This article contains a rich store of information both about the achievements and failures of comprehension within the Soviet Empire, and about then recent moves there to repair these failures by establishing academically selective and specialist schools; information which ought to be, but so far as I know never has been, taken into account by those directing all their energies to exposing the perceived outrage of structured inequalities in 'late capitalist societies'. However, for us the immediate interest begins with Szamuely's reminder that a year or two earlier Mrs Shirley Williams, as a junior minister at the DES, had announced to a conference of European Ministers of Education that over 26 per cent of our university population (and 35 per cent of students in all institutions of higher learning) are of working-class origin. The parallel (university) scores for some of our Continental neighbours were: Sweden—14 per cent; Denmark—10 per cent; France—8.3 per cent; West Germany—5.3 per cent; and Switzerland—4 per cent (*ibid.*, p. 49). No figures from Eastern Europe were available.

Apparently it did not then occur to Mrs Williams, nor has it ever since occurred to her, to wonder whether this outstanding performance, in a country which all left-thinking people know to be quite extraordinarily class-ridden, might not just possibly have had at least something to do with what she would surely have been too much of a lady to follow Crosland in describing as "those fucking grammar schools". The British figures are now compiled by the Universities Central Council on Admissions (UCCA), and published annually in their *Statistical Supplement*. Throughout the 1920s and 1930s—when the statistics must have been compiled by some predecessor organisation—and right up till 1961, the annual figures hovered very closely around 26 per cent. They reached a peak at 31 per cent in 1968, the year of Mrs Williams' speech. By 1973 we were down to 28 per cent, while by 1978 it looked as if we were bottoming out onto a new and lower plateau. The latest percentage figures available at the time of writing were 1978—23; 1979—22; 1980—19.4; 1981—17.5; 1982—18; 1983—19.5; 1984—19.7; and 1985—20.5.

Now, of course and notoriously, no argument goes through from post hoc to propter hoc. Certainly too a fully adequate analysis of such data would have to ask and answer several further questions: whether, for instance, there have been changes in the proportions of all children rated as coming from the Registrar General's three lowest social classes. However, the suggestion that the decline is a consequence of comprehension does, surely, become the hypothesis to beat? This is so: first, because it began just when any effects of comprehension might have been expected to start to show themselves; second, because there seems to have been nothing else happening during the relevant period which might constitute a plausible alternative explanation; and third, because the *Black Paper* writers provided us with very good reasons to predict that a major cost of comprehension would be to deprive able children from working-class homes of educational opportunities which they might otherwise have enjoyed.

(b) Persisting with this same shameless apologetic for antique "privileges and inequalities", we notice next some astonishing discoveries made at a time when LEAs were still permitted to conceal the results achieved by individual schools in independently assessed external examinations. The secret 1978 A-level results from 90 of the then rather more than 180 always comprehensive schools run by ILEA fell into the hands of two extremely energetic members of NCES. (Perhaps, as the phrase goes, these secret results 'fell off the back of a lorry'?) They were unable to obtain the results from the rest. Peter Newsam, at that time ILEA's Chief Education Officer, put the two researchers down as having suffered "a complete intellectual collapse" (Marks *et al.*, 1986, p. 57) because they had not included results from all ILEA schools which, he suggested, he could supply. However, when the researchers were planning a later study, Newsam declined to send them this information. Since no addition of material referring to the others could have discredited revelations referring only to the available 90, Newsam's own response was not so much an "intellectual collapse" as an offensive manoeuvre.

Against much protest from ILEA and elsewhere, the NCES researchers proceeded to make and to publish an analysis of all they had (Cox and

Marks, 1980). It was, surely, bad enough? Indeed for anyone genuinely concerned, as they are, for the education of all our children it was appalling. Of those 90 ILEA comprehensive schools, 36 had no A-level French or Geography, 28 no Physics, 25 no Chemistry, 22 no Mathematics and 20 no Biology. Just how wastefully the available teachers were employed is seen from the further fact that 46.5 per cent of the subject groups in eight major subjects produced no more than two A-level entries; and, hence, even fewer passes.

These and other figures given in that NCES report point to two important conclusions. First, and certainly, that some very precious teachers were being very wastefully employed to teach tiny classes. Second, that presumably a lot of able and willing children were confined in schools unable to provide A-level teaching from which they could have benefited, and which was available elsewhere under the same LEA.

When they have at last been forced to recognise this problem the stock response of LEAs is to withdraw post-O-level responsibilities from their schools and to establish Sixth Form Colleges. It is only one of many objections to this policy that it must tend to deprive the schools of teaching by all those academically superior teachers qualified up to A-level. Yet it is a problem which could scarcely arise at all where information about every school's results was freely available, and where parents were free to rescue their children from those schools which could not, and take them to those which could, teach what they wanted to learn, or, at any rate, and in some cases more realistically, what their parents wanted them to learn. It is therefore salutary both in this and in many similar contexts to recognise that for many members of the bureaucratic–educational complex their own power rather than pupil learning is the true name of the game. Rarely has this truth been expressed so frankly as by the author of *The Family, Education and Society*: "It is the business of education to eliminate the influence of parents on the life-chances of the young. . . ." (Musgrove, 1966, p. 135).

2

Examination Not Attempted

The unexamined life is not to be endured. ((Plato's) Socrates, *Apology* 38 A.)

[During the administration in which I served a spell as Minister, tax] expenditure on education rose from 4.8% of GNP in 1964 to 6.1%. As a result, all classes of the community enjoyed significantly more education than before. (C.A.R. Crosland, *Socialism Now*, p. 20.)

It will be needful that all *efficient* schools be registered and publicly recognised as such. . . . [Any parental protests are, therefore, to be overriden. Yet it] certainly will be very difficult at first to convince parents. . ., especially in cases where the instruction of a School is efficient, but the premises are unsatisfactory. It will be very difficult to convince a Yorkshire farmer that the School is not "efficient" when his child is getting on very well in it. (Report of one of Her Majesty's Inspectors of Schools (1871).)

At the beginning of Part I of Section IV of his first *Enquiry*, David Hume makes much of a distinction between two quite fundamentally different sorts of what we should now call propositions. It was, of course, a distinction which had been made before. So what is new in Hume is not the drawing of the distinction but the use which he makes of it. It is in this aggressive employment that it has been aptly nicknamed 'Hume's Fork'. By wielding that weapon he is able to conclude that whole *Enquiry* with a peroratory purple paragraph, which has since adorned many a lesser, drabber essay:

When we run over libraries, persuaded of these principles, what havoc must we make? If we take in our hand any volume, of divinity or school metaphysics, for instance, let us ask, *Does it contain any abstract reasoning concerning quantity or number?* No. *Does it contain any experimental reasoning concerning matter of fact and existence?* No. Commit it then to the flames: for it can contain nothing but sophistry and illusion.

The starting point of the present chapter is just as simple, just as fundamental and just as apriori. The difference is that here we shall have not the drawing of a fundamental distinction but the vindication of a necessary truth. That truth established, the next task will be to realise some of the possibilities for wreaking havoc. The havoc to be wrought, however, will all be havoc among various hypocrisies, misdirections, false assumptions and other similar obstacles obstructing efforts to get the best and the most possible educational output out of whatever resource input may be from time to time available. The hope is that the appreciation of one simple and, once understood, scarcely deniable point will raise and maintain what has been well characterised, in another context, as a gale of creative destruction (Schumpeter, 1963).

2.1 Rationality, sincerity and monitoring

It is many years since I first applied to the particular case of 'Teaching and Testing' what is now to be an entirely general contention (Flew, 1976, Ch. 6). The crux then was that you cannot truly be said to be sincerely trying to teach—or, for that matter, to learn—unless you are constantly alert to discover how far the material proposed for teaching, or learning, actually is being mastered. It is, therefore, one thing to reject some particular method of testing and assessment, or some particular practice in the employment of the findings thereof. It is quite another to repudiate all testing and assessment in general and as such. When, as does still from time to time happen, professing teachers commit themselves to such wholesale repudiations, then these manifestos ought to be construed, and forthwith accepted, as acts of resignation. For to continue their previous employment in these circumstances is to behave like Silas Wegg in the Dickens novel; who "resigned from the duties but not the emoluments of a teacher".

Again it will not do, notwithstanding that it is all too frequently done, to proceed with ranting polemic confidence from the truistic premise that there are forms of educational attainment which it is not sensible to try to measure through the mechanism of two- or three-hour written examinations to the illicit and necessarily false conclusion that there are forms which cannot be in any way measured or identified at all. Certainly it would be silly to assess the success or failure of a programme of moral education by discovering how well or ill the class was able to regurgitate approved moral maxims (Straughan, 1982, pp. 90–92). It would, nevertheless, be even more absurd not to ask whether there had been any resultant improvement in the conduct of pupils exposed to that programme; whether, for instance, there had been any consequent declines in the incidence of theft or of bullying or of vandalism.

So, if professing teachers are so imprudent as to claim that what they are themselves striving to put across is too elusive and too ethereal to be captured by tests or measures of any kind whatever, then they should be told—kindly but very, very firmly—to find something else to teach, something teachable. For thus to pretend to be teaching something the learning or not learning of which is indiscernible is as grotesque as *The Hunting of the Snark*. What sense does it make to pretend to pursue a quarry which, as the supposed hunters themselves maintain, could not be identified even if it were to be caught?

(i) Wholesale and unqualified denunciations of all examinations have perhaps become less common than they were when the first *Black Paper* was published (Cox and Dyson, 1969). At that time even—or, rather, especially—Edward Short as Minister "condemned examinations as a great disincentive to true education, hanging like a millstone around the necks of the schools" (quoted Cox and Dyson, 1971, p. 7). However, a decade later, from a successor volume to *Education for Democracy* (Rubinstein and Stoneman, 1972), we learn that "Clear guidelines should be laid down by the government that there must be a move towards a situation where all pupils, and not just 20 or even 60 or 80%, have a right to proper assessment and evaluation" (Rubinstein, 1979, p. 223). What was, at the time of writing, the most recent Labour Party (LP) statement on education declared commitments both to an "assessment system for the whole age and ability range" and to regular monitoring of "the progress of pupils, so that weaknesses are remedied and strengths reinforced" (pp. 14 and 9).

Such glimpses of a fundamental truth, even when combined with failures to appreciate its consequences, cannot but be welcome. Yet the fullest mastery of the logical geography of one particular area is still no sufficient substitute for a similar understanding of the general principles of which their application there is only one particular instance, however important. These three general principles all concern what Hume distinguished as the "relations of ideas", rather than "matters of fact and [real] existence". However, though in this sense theoretical, they have the most extensive and indeed often the most explosive practical applications.

(a) The *first* and most manifest is this. Everyone sincerely and rationally pursuing objectives of any kind whatsoever—objectives good or bad, interested or disinterested, particular or general—every such person must be constantly concerned to monitor their success or failure in approaching or attaining those objectives. Suppose—to begin at what may be an embarrassingly stratospheric level—that someone proclaims a Quest for the Holy Grail, and suppose that, almost as soon as the fanfares have died, he settles for the first antique-seeming mug offered by the first fluent rogue in the local bazaar. Then we surely have to say that his neglect of any serious and systematic enquiry, his total lack of interest either in the history of the purchase put in the place of honour on his mantelpiece or in the evidence that the real thing does after all survive somewhere; we have to say that everything conspires together to show that, whatever else he may have been after, he most certainly could not have been sincerely trying to unearth and to acquire the vessel actually used in the original Last Supper. Sincerity of purpose thus absolutely presupposes a strong concern to know whether and how far the purpose that is entertained has been or is being achieved.

Again, take two further, somewhat more pedestrian, examples. First, if an illustration from the workaday world of wealth creation is not insupportable, consider the case of a businesswoman who has dared to declare her resolve to make an overall profit. Now suppose that she takes no steps to ensure that accounts are kept, revealing which parts of her operation are or are not running at a loss. Then, as before, we have no option but to conclude that, whatever her true aim may be, making a profit is no part of it. Perhaps she really is—as the stock phrase has it—in business for the sake of her health? Certainly, if she had been sincerely devoted to the pursuit of profit, then she could not but have insisted upon the keeping of at least one set of books. (Had she been not merely sincerely but ruthlessly and unscrupulously devoted, then she might well have had a second set also—for the attention solely of the Inland Revenue!)

As a final illustration, consider what we would think of a cricket captain who never so much as glanced at the scoreboard, and never even noticed whether runs made by members of his team were or were not being recorded. We should all agree—should we not?—that he must be either stupid beyond belief or simply not playing to win. Perhaps he was conscientiously obeying one of the most persistently proclaimed precepts for self-styled educational progressives: "... to replace the ethic of competition and acquisition by one of cooperation and community" (Rowe, 1970, p. 38). Yet, however commendable his behaviour on other grounds, we certainly cannot allow that such a captain is sincerely trying to win.

(b) The *second* principle is a corollary of the first, for a large part of the point of monitoring progress, or the lack of it, is in order to determine whether and when some alteration of approach is required. So, in so far as those who assert that they are sincerely seeking to attain some particular objective have any claim to the status of even minimally rational beings, they categorically must be ready to change course by adopting fresh tactics if ever and whenever those previously employed prove not to be yielding the desired results.

Here as elsewhere, of course, readiness to act by no means entails action: rational beings, precisely in as much and in so far as they are rational, will change tactics only when some available alternative is perceived to be more promising. Both such readiness to change when a more promising alternative is perceived to be available and such conservative unwillingness to alter when it is not constitute a large part, surely, of what we have in mind when we speak of intelligence and of rationality in practical affairs?

(c) The *third* and last of the three principles is somewhat more complex than either of the first two and, both for that reason and for others, perhaps more controversial. Even the first two, whether or not they are legitimately controversial, are in fact sometimes controverted just so soon as it begins to emerge how large, how numerous, and often how uncomfortable are the further conclusions to be derived. (That is why the statements of these principles above had to be supported by several pedestrian and scarcely disputatious illustrations rather than by a solitary single.)

This third principle is that, in so far as any of the resources employed to secure the desired results are scarce—a condition which always is satisfied, even if the resources drawn on consist in nothing but the time and energy of those desiring those results—the purposers must, as rational beings, be concerned to achieve the maximum output of desired results in exchange for the minimum input of scarce resources. They must be so concerned. For, on the same assumptions of single-mindedness and sincerity of purpose, they cannot but want, by means of such greater economic efficiency, either to get more of those particular desired results from an unincreased investment of scarce resources or else to obtain through an alternative investment of the surplus thereby saved some or more of some other goods which are desired.

(ii) It is by reference to that third principle that we justify the introduction of economic terms into a book about education. In Edbiz such terms are often felt to be repugnant: every naturally Platonic spirit is inclined to assume that economic analyses can be relevant only to the banausic. However, the truth—and this is a logically necessary truth—is that economic science deals solely with scarce means rather than with the multifarious ends towards which those means may be directed. (One classic essay on the nature of economic science is Robbins, 1935, Ch. II.)

Economic analyses, therefore, both can be and need to be made whenever and wherever scarce means are deployed in pursuit of ends of any kind, regardless of how banausic or how elevated those ends may be. So it will not do—as has nevertheless so often been done not only in universities but also lower down the academic scale—haughtily to dismiss all enquiries about the costs and cost-effectiveness either of current educational policies or of existing institutions with some supercilliously donnish apophthegm about 'certain prominent persons knowing the cost of everything and the value of nothing'. Nor will it do—as has nevertheless recently been done by one Platonising philosopher of education—to dismiss the teaching of all possible saleable skills or subjects as educationally irrelevant while undertaking "to proclaim and explain the obvious truth that the value of education and the criterion of success in educating is quality of mind—something that cannot easily be measured and something that, though it may be fair to call it priceless, cannot be costed" (Barrow, 1982, p. 189).

In short, there is scope for economic analysis wherever and whenever any kind of scarce resource is deployed to advance any sort of ends, however banausic or however elevated those ends may be. Such analyses are not apt only to what is conventionally considered the wealth-creating element in a national economy or even to the economy only (Radnitzky and Bernholz, 1987). The various scarce resources employed within the welfare state apparatus as a whole do all have alternative possible uses, both within and outside that apparatus. Also, just as the vast resources available to the NHS might be deployed in all manner of alternative ways in order to produce all manner of different quantities and qualities of the very various goods which that organisation exists to produce, so might the resources available in such other parts of that welfare state apparatus as the state system for providing primary and secondary education be deployed in many ways in order to produce different baskets of those different but perhaps almost equally various goods which those other parts have been established and are maintained to produce. Economic analysis can be, should be, and sometimes is being employed to make such allocative decisions more rational in terms of the ends chosen by the deciders, just as in World War II British economists in Operational Research helped to guide our military commanders to allocative decisions making for a speedier and less costly victory.

(iii) The remaining task in this Section is to relate our first two principles to the main methodological recommendations of Sir Karl Popper. He has proposals, which are, of course, closely connected with one another, for the spheres of both theoretical science and practical policy. In each case Popperian methodology can be seen as the direct outcome of sincerity in the appropriate purposes. It is the more worthwhile to present these fundamental Popperian recommendations in this way in as much as he himself seems never to have spelt out any such implications. His apparent reluctance to do so, and the consequent failure to deploy what is perhaps the most powerful argument for his own methodologies, are probably to be explained by reference to his wholly honourable unwillingness to attribute, or even to recognise, either academic bad faith or any other discreditable distractions in any of his intellectual opponents. It is an unwillingness shared, like so much else, with his lifelong friend Friedrich Hayek.

(a) The theoretical aim of science is truth. Given this aim then, the critical approach must follow. The person who truly wants the truth, like the knight who with pure heart and single mind seeks the Holy Grail, cannot embrace unexamined candidates. He must be ever ready to test, and test and test again, if ever and whenever he either himself finds, or is by others confronted with, reasons for suspecting that he has got it wrong.

By the way, whenever there is talk of criticism we need to be aware of a crucial distinction, more frequently collapsed than observed. In one common sense criticism is always hostile. In another, the sense in which Popper employs the word, criticism is rational and enquiring appraisal, which prejudices no verdict, whether favourable or unfavourable. To qualify as, in this second sense, a Shakespearean critic you do not have to be antecedently committed to the judgement that even the best of his plays are no good. Yet almost everyone, not only outside but also within Edbiz, seems sometimes to need to be reminded that it is only in this second sense that to encourage an ever-critical approach is a creditable and constructive educational aim.

In developing his theoretical methodology Popper himself adds various highly contestable claims. These certainly must not be accepted as corollaries of the principles previously commended. Thus he proceeds to assert: "Our science is not knowledge (*episteme*): it can never claim to have attained truth. . ." (Popper, 1959, p. 278). Whatever we may think of any of these additions, and especially of such a confession of incurable scepticism, we have to allow that insistence upon a restlessly critical approach is a mark—indeed *the* mark—of the sincerity of our desire for truth herself and of our refusal to be content with any substitute—however plausible, seductive, comfortable, congenial or otherwise appealing that substitute might be.

(b) Parallel considerations apply to the practical problems of social and political policy. If you propose to maintain that it is in order to secure some relief of man's estate that you are pushing this policy, then you must be on guard to monitor its success or failure by that stated standard. You would indeed be best advised to build provisions for such monitoring into every programme you propose. For it is—is it not?—precisely and only in order to secure that relief that you are introducing that programme? Also, although, of course, you yourself are absolutely certain that it will deliver the goods promised, you do also recognise, as we all must, that none of us humans is either infallible or omniscient and hence that—as, notoriously, Robert Burns observed—"the best laid schemes of mice and men gang aft agley"?

Surely, then, just in case this should turn out to be true of your own particular scheme, you yourself want to be the first to know? For how else will you be able to make, with all possible promptitude, the changes needed to ensure the actual delivery of those promised and longed-for goods? On the other hand, if all things are in fact going to turn out as well as you are insisting that they will, then you have everything to gain and nothing to lose by establishing an honest, thorough system of monitoring. For how can you fail to anticipate and to relish the future demonstration that your policy turned out to be a triumphant success?

Popper's own advocacy of piecemeal and reformist social engineering—

as against its wholesale, revolutionary and Utopian opposite—should be recognised as the consequence and expression of his sincere and rational commitment to the welfare of the beneficiaries or victims. For Popper's crucial objection to what he calls Utopian social engineering precisely is that it must make the monitoring of success, and the cybernetic correction of failure, impossible. Thus, he says:

> the reconstruction of society is a big undertaking which must cause considerable inconvenience to many and for a considerable span of time. Accordingly, the Utopian engineer will have to be deaf to many complaints: in fact it will be part of his business to suppress unreasonable objections. (He will say, like Lenin, 'You can't make an omelette without breaking eggs.') But with it, he must invariably suppress reasonable criticism also (Popper, 1966, I, p. 160).

It is obvious that what Popper here had most vividly in mind was 'that great social experiment in Russia'. However, his contrast between piecemeal, reformist social engineering and its wholesale, Utopian, revolutionary opposite is equally applicable to our lesser and more local Comprehensive Revolution. A paradigm specimen of Popper's second sort, it too was implemented with all possible speed, and enthusiastically enforced from the centre. It too was carried through both with no provision for the systematic monitoring of its effects and with an inflexible resolve to override all objections. The best way to discover or to be reminded of these claims about the Comprehensive Revolution is still to read or reread the relevant contributions to five successive sets of *Black Papers* (Cox and Dyson, 1969, 1970, 1971; and Cox and Boyson, 1975, 1977; but compare also Shaw, 1983). Unfortunately, because the last two sets were each issued in different formats and from different publishers, the complete series bound up together seems never to be found in libraries.

The most relevant and constructive way in which to end this Section is with a manifesto of Popperian politics: the adoption of his piecemeal, reformist, critical method

> might lead to the happy situation where politicians begin to look out for their own mistakes instead of trying. . . to prove that they have always been right. This— and not Utopian planning or historical prophecy—would mean the introduction of scientific method into politics, since the whole secret of scientific method is a readiness to learn from mistakes (*Ibid.*, p. 163).

2.2 Resource inputs or education outputs?

Suppose that, "persuaded of these principles", we proceed to survey our public educational system and to attend to debates about the future development of that system. Then we cannot but be both astonished and appalled not only by the incompleteness and the other inadequacies of the monitoring, but also by the failure in those debates to take account of the findings of what little monitoring there has been. For, typically and customarily, even the more public political debates—in which participants do at least pretend to be approaching issues from the standpoint of the common good rather than of their particular preferred interest group—persistently fail to make one most obvious and fundamental distinction: namely, that between resource input and education output. Just as typically and just as customarily, all the labour unions recruiting mainly or exclusively from within Edbiz, as well as some of the politicians discussing or regulating it, justify Dennis O'Keeffe's comment: "Like so much else in the British economy, our education system is treated by its workforce as fundamentally a source not of *production* but of *employment*" (Anderson, 1981, p. 35: emphasis original).

(i) The passage already quoted as the second motto of this chapter provides an egregious illustration of this failure to distinguish. It read: ". . . expenditure in education rose from 4.8% of GNP in 1964 to 6.1% in 1970. As a result, all classes of the community enjoyed significantly more education than before" (Crosland, 1974, p. 20). The second of these propositions is thus presumably asserted as an immediate inference from the first. For the only further reason offered for believing that conclusion was that "The huge expansion in the supply of teachers produced a steady reduction in the pupil/teacher ratio." What is so extraordinary is that this manifestly unsound immediate inference from input to output was presented as a compulsive argument by an extremely able man; a man who had, before entering professional politics, earned his living as the Economics Fellow of an Oxford college.

(a) Crosland's argument here could go through only given two assumptions: one known to be false and the other, at best, not known to be true. The assumption which he above all should have recognised to be false is that output is always and everywhere precisely proportionate to resource input; that all expenditures are always rewarded with equally good value for money. No doubt in a perfectly competitive market, with many and various suppliers, this must 'with the effluxion of time' tend to become at least approximately true. However, as was emphasised in Chapter 1, our present situation is almost the exact opposite. In Britain nearly all primary and secondary educational services are supplied, free at the point of 'purchase', to captive customers and by local monopolies; while those captive customers, whether we think of them as being the parents or as being the children, are—it should never be forgotten—not always and everywhere the most eager of consumers.

In these circumstances anyone endowed with the merest modicum of common sense and common experience, to say nothing of trained economists, should expect to find what everyone who has looked has found. Certainly, the lack of established criteria-related measures of educational output makes it hard to produce ideally satisfactory quantifications. Nevertheless, there is already quite enough evidence to justify the conclusion that the average differences between LEMs, and still more the differences between the individual 'firms', are far and away greater than any to be observed between ordinary commercial firms which have, if they are to stay in business, to compete hard for custom.

The findings of the researchers who produced *Equality of Educational Opportunity* (Coleman, 1966) have often pulled attention away from all differences of this kind. James Coleman and his colleagues executed, under the auspices of the US Office of Education, the most extensive survey ever undertaken of the public schools in that country. When they started they expected, and indeed were expected, to find two things: first, a strong correlation between resource input and education output and, second, a failure to provide the same resource input into the education of blacks as was being provided for whites. To their own astonishment, and to that of almost everyone else, they discovered both expectations to have been incorrect. (In the light of some much less happy recent experience in our own country we should perhaps commend them for their refusal even to contemplate distorting those findings.)

Many reading this Coleman Report were inclined to infer that schools make no difference; although scarcely anyone seems to have proceeded to the obvious corollary conclusion that, if this were indeed so, then we could afford to make deep cuts in the public education budget or even simply to abolish it. One example of the drawing of the first inference is found in another extremely influential research report: 'We cannot blame economic inequality on differences between schools, since diferences between schools seem to have very little effect on any measurable attribute of those who attend them"; and again, "the conventional wisdom is wrong. The next sections will show that there is no correlation between what a high school spends and its impact on students' attainment. . ." (Jencks, 1972, pp. 8 and 148).

The truth, however, was that Coleman and his team, hoping that their findings would encourage the remedying of any unfairness exposed, were chiefly concerned to discover whether blacks were getting their fair share of that budget. So they collected and compared always averages; never individual schools. In this they made the same mistake, and for similarly creditable reasons, as that made by the judges in *Brown v. Board of Education*. For, notwithstanding that there was, a short walk away from the Supreme Court building, an all-black high school unequal only in its eminent superiority, they ruled, with their eyes solely upon averages, that segregated schools could not be 'separate but equal' (Sowell, 1986, pp. 29-32 and 39-75).

The next most influential book was *15,000 Hours* (Rutter, 1979), a report of work done this time in England. Whereas Jencks and his colleagues were mainly, not to say obsessively, devoted to equalisation, and hence concerned with education only in so far as it might be made to serve their own peculiar Procrustean ideal, the Rutter team concentrated upon the essential business of learning and teaching. Borrowing a useful concept from Coleman—"the *increment* in achievement that the school provides" (quoted p. 7), a concept which for our purposes shall be rechristened Educational Value Added (EVA)— their conclusions confirmed not only the convictions of most widely experienced if perhaps unacceptably oldfashioned teachers but also the more systematic and disciplined findings of much earlier and since forgotten research. (As they themselves remind us, quite spectacular differences had long ago been found in truancy and general delinquency rates between physically similar schools drawing similar pupil intakes from the same neighbourhoods: compare, for example, pp. 8 and 27.)

So what answers does Rutter(1979) give us? They are very clear. Yes; by any properly relevant, EVA test the ethos of the individual school *is* enormously important(p. 182). No; spacious buildings did *not* "seem to be any kind of prerequisite for successful outcomes." However, how the staff reacted to perceived deficiencies of either decor or of structure clearly *did* matter(p. 101). And so on. The most immediately relevant overall conclusion was "that secondary schools varied markedly with respect to their pupils' behaviour, attendance, exam success and delinquency. . . *even after taking into account differences in their intake. . .*" (p. 205: emphasis original).

Just how markedly has emerged only since the 1980 Act gave researchers access to the O- and A-level results achieved in individual schools. Thus the *Second Report* on *Standards in English Schools* finds: that "the differences. . . between comprehensive schools within wholly comprehensive LEAs are even greater than the very substantial differences between LEAs. . ."; and that "pupils at some comprehensive schools obtained. . .*four* times as many O-level and CSE Grade 1 passes as those at other comprehensive schools *within the same LEA*" (Marks and Pomian-Srzednicki, 1985, p. 80: emphasis original).

A more particular study within a single still happily atypical LEA revealed both "enormous differences in resources between schools, the schools with the poorest results obtaining twice as many teachers and twice as much money per pupil as the schools with the best results" and that "the most popular schools were those with better results, fewer resources, more graduate teachers and less mixed-ability teaching" (Marks, 1987, p. 28). The chief present relevance of such material is first, that it shows how grotesque it is to assume that EVA must be constantly proportionate to resource input and, second, that it reinforces the case for granting all parents the right to withdraw their children from schools perceived as unsatisfactory.

(b) Crosland's second assumption was that any "reduction in the pupil/ teacher ratio" necessarily and always guarantees some improvement in the educational outcome. Now the fact—what should strike any outsider as the well-nigh unbelievable fact—is that there appears to be no hard evidence showing that, within the relevant range—say, from 45 to 15—reductions in class size make teaching more effective, as opposed to more agreeable. Even if we knew that this was indeed true, and equally true across all subjects and at all levels, still anyone sincerely and rationally dedicated to obtaining the best possible results from whatever resources may from time to time become available would nevertheless want to press the question with which the poet Yeats is said to have responded to the news of his Nobel Prize for literature: "How much? How much?"

For, unless the consequent improvements in learning were very large indeed, rational policy makers would have to consider alternative possibilities of achieving that greater output at the same cost. Teachers' salaries are, after all, by far the biggest item in every education budget. Even if there are no worthwhile improvements in learning to be obtained by reducing the ratio, but reductions do make the educational process more agreeable to all concerned, still we should demand an answer to the Yeats question.

In so far as it is a matter (not of learning improvement but) of teacher rather than pupil satisfaction, then certainly any reductions in the ratio must be taken into account in salary negotiations, as being equivalent to some increase in teachers' pay. If and in so far as it is the children whose lives are to be made more agreeable, then it is the opportunity cost of alternative expenditures foregone which we must consider. Perhaps the children themselves—defying the objections both interested and ideological of the NUT—would prefer better facilities for competitive sports rather than more classroom teachers? (Jencks, who, as we have seen, falsely concludes that schools make precious little educational difference, is sufficiently the benevolent classical Utilitarian to insist—quite rightly—that the *15,000 Hours* spent in them should nevertheless be made to pass as pleasantly as possible!)

Although the primary concerns of the present book are with philosophical and methodological issues, here the neglect of the substantial questions of policy-relevant fact is so scandalous and so universal that it becomes urgently necessary to present a brief review of the state of the evidence. Until quite recently most of the (mainly North American research seems to have weighed as heavily against the second as against the first of Crosland's assumptions; although these findings have—surprise, surprise!—been constantly ignored or dismissed both by the teachers' unions and by the several other supply-side pressure groups, both in the United States and in the United Kingdom.

Thus the 1950 edition of the *Encyclopedia of Education Research*, after reviewing the work done in the previous fifty years, found: "On the whole, the statistical findings definitely favor large classes at every level of instruction except the kindergarden . . . The general trend of evidence places the burden of proof squarely upon the proponents of small classes" (p. 212). Again, since we are dealing with averages rather than with individual performances, we have to take note how Jencks in the *New York Times Magazine* (10 August 1969) summed up the whole post-Coleman debate: "Variations in schools' fiscal and human resources have very little effect on student achievement—probably even less than the Coleman report implied." After that we should perhaps compare Glass (1982), which leans, not perhaps very weightily, in the opposite direction.

It is also as fair as it should be wryly disturbing to add that, in the UK, and perhaps also in the USA, the possible effects of reductions in class size may have been masked or offset by declines in teacher quality consequent upon the drive to achieve that "huge expansion in the supply" on which Crosland so complacently congratulated himself. It is, however, not our business here to try to track down the true and final answer to any such first-order factual questions. What we have to do is to underline both the fact and the significance of the fact that the DES under several successive Ministers, as well as the whole national and local Edbiz establishment, have been pressing on with a policy of indiscriminately reducing and hence supposedly improving pupil/teacher ratios without having any decisive evidence that this is the best method, or even one method, of getting better learning results, and without even calling for or commissioning the research which might definitively settle all outstanding questions. How can we interpret this fact save as an index, either of a scandalous indifference to the proper objectives of any genuinely educational policy or of an equally scandalous political irrationality? (Since any future Minister who does call for such research will presumably also have some responsibility for the tertiary sector, it would be salutary if they were also to ask why, when departments, schools and institutes of education are all staffed on the assumption that the faculty will spend roughly half its time in teaching and half in research, so very little policy-relevant research ever emerges.)

(iii) When such an intellectual tiger as Crosland is capable of committing himself to those common complacencies in premeditated print there is no call to be surprised by the impromptu bleatings of the sheep. Consider, for instance, a typical House of Commons debate under the rubric 'Education'. In 1981 the Opposition motion, introduced by Mr Neil Kinnock, simply took it for granted that the relations between input and output are here direct, constant and uniform: "That this House", it began, "recognising the direct relationship between the maintenance and enhancement of educational standards and an appropriate investment of resources. . ."; and so it went on, and on and on.

The Ministerial amendment moved by Mr Mark Carlisle did at least mention value for money. It expressed "confidence in the ability of the education service. . . to secure maximum educational value from the extensive resources which continue to be available to it". Yet in the rest of his speech the Minister made no attempt to justify such confidence. Like so many of his predecessors in similar debates he could think only of offering formidable figures of increasing expenditure: "Some 5.5 per cent of the gross national product [GNP] of this country, or twice what it was in 1950, today goes on education. . . . In 1979-80 more was spent on the schools in real terms than ever before, twice as much in total and half as much again per pupil as 20 years ago. Much has gone on additional teachers and the reduction of the pupil/teacher ratio." From this and from this alone the Minister felt entitled to conclude: "There has been a gradual improvement in standards."

At which point, if not long before, someone may object: 'But this is all perfectly obvious; we really did not need a philosopher to rabbit on about things of which every person of sense is already fully master.' To that the reply must be either that obviousness in fact is, as indeed it is, what so much else is nowadays falsely said to be, essentially relative or else—or should it be, perhaps, and furthermore?—that, if the objector is right, then the shortage of persons of sense must be even more severe than we had ever previously realised.

The truth, however, is that these things have not always been, and indeed still are not, obvious to everyone: not even, or perhaps we should say especially not, to many of those most heavily involved with or in Edbiz. Opposition politicians, and their numerous allies in the media, have dinned it into the public's head that tax-funded expenditure on education has, since the General Election of 1979, been drastically reduced. However, although there have indeed been heavy cuts in Treasury support for the universities, with heavier still threatened for future years, state spending per pupil head has at the primary and secondary levels actually continued to increase, even in real terms. Anyone believing the contrary of this truth, as it would seem that most people do, will be too easily persuaded that any and every perceived deficiency in the state-provided education services can properly be put down to 'the cuts'.

It is important to appreciate three main reasons why so many people, not only outside but also inside Edbiz, have been and remain thus deceived about 'the cuts'. First, all the figures are of national, arithmetic mean averages, which embrace indiscriminately a multitude of differences both between LEAs and between individual schools subject to individual LEAs. Second, this has been a period of drastically declining enrollments, in which a great deal of surplus capacity ought ideally to have been phased out. However, Parliament's Comptroller and Auditor-General calculated that, by the end of 1986, the LEAs in England and Wales—for many reasons, by no means all bad—had succeeded in ridding themselves of only one out of nearly three million redundant places. (He further estimated that the mere maintenance costs of the buildings for a million pupils would be over £150 million *a year*—more than enough lavishly to restock every school library.) Third, education budgets are not spent wholly and solely in and upon schools, while the main allocations as between items are decided by politicians, advised by officials, all of whom may have their own not always strictly educational reasons for preferring one kind of expenditure to another.

These three reasons taken together all go to show that and how it is possible for particular schools, even for all the schools subject to one particular LEA, to suffer cruel cuts notwithstanding that both national and local expenditures under the wide general budget heading 'Education' continue relentlessly to increase; and that in real terms. Here the latest national figures, for the year 1986-7, show LEAs budgeted to spend 8.5 per cent more, against 2 per cent fewer pupils, and inflation (estimated) around 4 per cent.

Desperately repeating these in the *Daily Telegraph* (13 June 1986), a Conservative MP went on to retail complaints from two of his headteacher constituents. One, after "belabouring me on the intolerable parsimony of the Government" went on to list instances of bureaucratic extravagance, none of which, he contended, would have occurred had he himself been allowed to control more of the moneys spent on his school. The other complained that his classes averaged 34; half as much again as the national and considerably above the local average. Deaf to all appeals from the chalkface, his LEA were at that time enthusiastically "recruiting 25 specialist teacher-advisers for 'multi-cultural' education". (Presumably one reason why the average costs per pupil in independent day schools seem to be so closely comparable with those in the state system must be that, precisely because the independents are what they are, they are not subject to either town or shire hall bureaucracies. They therefore do not have to carry on their budgets any expenditures either for these or for other troops of external interferers.)

(b) We may be mildly encouraged to notice that since 1981 there does seem to have been rather more questioning about value for money. Especially since the appointment of Dr Rhodes Boyson, who had before entering Parliament enjoyed well-publicised success as Head of the ILEA comprehensive at Highbury Grove (Boyson, 1974), the speeches of junior ministers have from time to time emphasised the evidence both that similar resource inputs applied to similar pupil intakes do in fact yield very different educational outcomes and that there quite certainly is not here a strong positive correlation between inputs and outputs. Although there is dispute about just how badly ILEA's examination results compare with national norms, no one can deny either that it has been spending roughly half as much again as or that its results are no better than the national average (Marks *et al.*, 1986). Senior ministers, however, still appear reluctant to stress such truths, doubtless preferring to believe that, thanks to their own wise and alert administration, all everywhere is well.

Again, in 1983 a special adviser to the Chief Secretary to the Treasury began his own report by quoting the 1976 Layfield Committee:

> It is difficult to make valid comparisons of unit costs or other comparative measurements of the performance of different authorities. Nevertheless, the need to develop and apply the best measures which can be devised is of outstanding importance.

This adviser agreed about the difficulties, which no one should either deny or minimise, but he then had to comment: "Since the report was published there has been disappointingly little progress in this direction, despite the importance which Layfield attached to it" (Lord, 1983, p. 15). In the same year Her Majesty's Inspectors (HMIs) issued two reports in which—very much in the tradition of their Victorian predecessor, quoted at the start of this chapter—they proceeded, without reference to any of the educational results achieved, to reproach certain LEAs for no other or better reason than that their expenditures under various heads had been below the national norms.

They did this also in their *Annual Report 1982*, and none of the education correspondents of the national dailies at that time seemed to find anything remarkable about this concentration upon inputs and this lack of interest in outputs. However, the following year at least one of them—John Izbicki in the *Daily Telegraph* (19 and 24 October 1983)—did begin to suspect either ideological or institutional bias or partisan political motivation when, in a special report, the Inspectors excoriated schools in the thrifty London Borough of Sutton. They themselves conceded that in this Conservative-controlled LEA, which had successfully held out against the Comprehensive Revolution, "examination results were good, pupils were well turned out, polite, punctual and well spoken. The 'Three Rs' emerged as generally excellent."

It is, though scarcely sufficient, fair to put into the balance against such suspicions—which were at that time further fuelled by the surreptitious transmission of a confidential DES document supposedly 'rubbishing' *Standards in English Schools* (Marks *et al.*, 1983) to various militants of the Comprehensive Revolution—that, in their 1980 report on *Educational Provision by ILEA*, an all-comprehensive authority now controlled by the ultra-left, the Inspectorate did bring themselves to record that, although by every input criterion provision was generally generous, the output was often disproportionately poor. In the present context the most remarkable conclusions were that, under ILEA:

> ... many secondary schools currently seem reluctant to analyse critically pupils' examination performances and other possible measures of the schools' effectiveness. Overall, the secondary sector needs considerable improvement... This improvement certainly does not call for extra resources; it can largely come from increasing teachers' awareness of pupils' abilities and from developing a greater capacity and willingness to assess their performance (21.8 and 21.17).

We should also notice, before proceeding to attend to the true nature of the NUT's concern for educational standards, some of the things said by the HMIs in their general report on *The Effects of Local Authority Expenditure Policies on Educational Provision in England—1985*, published in May 1986:

> In over a quarter of the schools visited poor leadership and management at one or more levels was considered to be adversely affecting the quality of work, the levels and deployment of resources, the organisation and planning of the curriculum,... and the morale of teachers. In only half the schools visited was the planning and organisation of the pupils' work, including relating tasks carefully to the age, ability and aptitude of the pupils, judged satisfactory (9.6).

> Few involved in providing or providing for education can take much, if any, pride in a national service within which three tenths of all the lessons seen were unsatisfactory;... in three fifths of the schools where an assessment was possible, the teachers' perceptions of pupils' potential and needs were inadequate; and half the schools visited needed to widen their range of teaching styles to bring about a better match with what was being taught... (18.12).

In reading any of the HMI's reports on their observations in the classroom we have to remember that schools usually have some warning that Inspectors are likely to call, and will presumably react accordingly.

(c) The NUT is by far the most numerous and powerful Edbiz pressure group. So let us take a short, distasteful look at the series of leaflets which its Executive issued for their 1979 and 1980 'Campaign against the Cuts'. Attention here, as later and always, was wholly concentrated upon resource input with neither reference to, nor question asked about, the education output. In fury the NUT told the world: that "government policy means... less education for your child" and that "Scrooge lived to regret his meanness".

It called for "protest about the threat to education standards". Yet the only standards over which the leaders themselves appeared in fact to be aroused, and to which what evidence they did produce actually was directed, were not educational at all. They were not, that is, standards achieved in and by teaching and learning. Instead it was all a matter of how many people were being or were to be employed as teachers; of how much tax money was to be spent on school meals; and, generally, of the total public expenditure falling under the rubric 'Education'. The kindest, although not by that token the fairest, thing to be said about the entire campaign is that, while never actually attending to any questions about achieved educational output, it was always assumed, for no good reason given or available, that educational goods are bound to be generated in exact and constant proportion to educational expenditures.

Really it was worse than this. For they were telling us that "there is no leeway in the service", and that "after the years of cutback in education, there is no room for 'economies' ". Yet never anywhere did the NUT make space for certain crucially relevant and in some cases directly falsifying facts: for instance, that over the previous 30 years, public expenditure on education had *in real terms* multiplied fourfold; or that, in the same period, pupil/teacher ratios had fallen from 30.4 to 22.3 in primary schools—and from 21.1 to about 16.3 in secondary schools; or that spending on books and equipment could have been roughly doubled at the price of returning to pupil/teacher ratios of only four or five years before (Marks and Naylor, 1981).

Were we to accept the criteria favoured by the NUT we should, on the basis of such too-often forgotten facts, be able to say that educational standards had been rising at an unprecedented rate, had reached unprecedented heights and both were then and still are set for further record-breaking rises. When, in Anderson (1981), I first published materials since recycled in this Section, that publication provoked the customary chorus of protest and denunciation. The General Secretary of the NUT, its house organ *The Teacher* and several district officials, all joined in. Yet, at least as far as the reach of the Social Affairs Unit's cuttings agency extends, not one of them gave any indication of even having understood the crucial distinction between standards of resource input and standards of achieved output. It is, as the most formidable of British political thinkers once remarked, "easy to see the benefit of such darkness, and to whom it accrueth" (Hobbes, 1651, Ch. XLVII).

2.3 Consequences of comprehension

In one of the many paperbacks on education policy published in the 1960s and 1970s a comparison is made between the Great Debate inaugurated by

Prime Minister Callaghan's speech at Ruskin College and another occurring within what was by Chairman Mao miscalled the Cultural Revolution (Rubinstein, 1979, pp. 266-7). One important similarity not mentioned in that comparison is that in both cases the most important conclusions were pre-empted. For, after all, the opinions of dissidents could not but be discreditably motivated. They were, as the Prime Minister had already ruled, nothing but "*Black Paper* prejudices".

(i)   Considered as a piece of partisan politicking there is nothing either unusual or hard to understand about this. Yet to anyone cherishing only a naive and ingenuous interest in the standards demanded and achieved in education it must seem on two counts rather odd. First, because it is literally preposterous to misdescribe as prejudices argued contentions which you yourself propose to reject without examination. If the word 'prejudice' is to be more than a redundant term of abuse, then it has to be scrupulously employed to pick out just those beliefs—whether right or wrong—which are either formed prior to proper consideration of the evidence or else maintained in defiance of it. It is obscurantist and demoralising to apply the word merely to abuse other people's opinions, or even all strong convictions, simply as such. The judge who instructs the jury to consider carefully, and without prejudice, all and only the materials actually presented in court is not asking them to refuse to bring in a decisive verdict (Flew, 1975, 1.55-6 and 5.6). Second, because it would be perverse, if the object really were to remove the grounds for public anxiety—rather than solely to still it—to silence precisely those who first both drew attention to those grounds and articulated that anxiety.

From the beginning militants of the Comprehensive Revolution have manifested what in Ernest Bramah's Kai Lung stories is delicately described as "well-sustained no-enthusiasm" for the discovery and examination of any evidence suggesting that it might be prudent at least to pause a while and reflect, and then perhaps, on reflection, to change course in some way. Some have clearly thought of their revolution in historicist terms (Popper, 1957; and compare Flew, 1985, pp. 97-102). They have thought of it, that is, as a transformation being brought about by some inexorable natural law of historical development, a progress which could at most be merely temporarily checked, and which it must therefore be in the long run useless to try to resist. Thus, in a book entitled *The Comprehensive School: Guidelines for the Reorganisation of Secondary Education*, we read: "Opposition to such deep and powerful forces is futile" (Halsall, 1973, p. 1).

Whether for this or for other reasons, opposition or even hesitation has regularly been put down to bigoted and interested refusal to accept the light of the New Dawn. Opponents have in consequence been shamefully and shamelessly vilified. Contributions to both the second and the third volumes of *Black Papers* contain long lists of what must have been calculated misrepresentations of their predecessors, calculated misrepresentations often coming from respected, if not by the same token respectworthy, sources. This secular crusade, like some of its religious precursors, seems to have followed and still to be following the principle that against the infidels any and every weapon is legitimate.

It is, therefore, scarcely surprising that some of the leaders have professed not to be aware of— and it is obvious that they are sincere in wishing never to become aware of— any possibly discomfiting evidence or argument. The professed ignorances of Edward Short, who preceded Margaret Thatcher at the DES, were especially notorious. When asked by Mr Biggs-Davison in the House of Commons: "What consideration has he given to the misgivings of American educationists— for all their experience— about an almost universal comprehensive system?" Mr Short replied "I do not know about misgivings on the part of the Americans" (quoted Cox and Dyson, 1971, p. 5).

We have already noticed some such discomfiting evidence and argument. We shall be deploying more in the remainder of this Section. However, all this material, even taken together, does not add up to— and is certainly not offered as— a compulsive case for any categorical, universal, negative conclusion about comprehensive schooling. In fact there never has been any complementarity of contraries in this particular debate. Whereas most of the most militant proponents certainly are resolved to impose universal, compulsory, comprehension— even maintaining that nothing is truly comprehensive if anyone is allowed to escape— none of the active opponents has ever wanted either to prevent the establishment of any comprehensive schools at all or to abolish the lot if once established. For us it always has been, and remains, a matter of what particular arrangements best meet the strictly educational needs of the children in a particular area. This whole book is in any case primarily devoted to theoretical rather than substantive practical issues, and hence more concerned with what has to be taken into account if these are to be rationally decided than with what the senses of the correct decisions would be.

Nevertheless, although the available argument and evidence is not sufficient to determine and sustain history's final verdict upon the Comprehensive Revolution, it is, surely, more than sufficient to warrant "total opposition" to all LP and Trades Union Congress (TUC) proposals both to discipline the handful of LEAs still holding out against the Comprehensive Revolution and to destroy all independent schools. Those of us who knew National Socialist Germany in the 1930s will recall that the name for similarly totalitarian policies there was 'Gleichschaltung', which, being translated, is 'making uniform of homogeneous', 'forcing into line' or— most succinctly— 'equalising'. We cannot but remember, and shudder.

Even some of our British socialists, who as such share no ('bourgeois') liberal scruples, might—if only they would bring themselves to study those spectacularly superior A-level results achieved in the independent schools—become just a little anxious about the long-term economic effects of such a deliberate deskilling of our future labour force. So far, however, they remain stubbornly deaf to every non-doctrinal and unsplenetic consideration. Thus, in a *Statement on Private Schools* issued in July 1981, the TUC–LP Liaison Committee formulated a formidable threat (later alterations have been only in the means proposed in order to secure the same dear destructive end):

> A Labour Government would introduce a second and more substantial Education Bill within the first year of taking office. This bill would. . . enable the Secretary of State for Education to forbid private schools to charge fees for new admissions or to receive payment for places for new admissions. . . (pp. 5 and 6).

(ii) In the beginning the most generous and educationally concerned promoters of the Comprehensive Revolution hoped and believed that the consequent abolition of selection at age eleven (the 11+) would stimulate the discovering and flowering of talents hitherto rejected. The same *Statement on Private Schools* angrily assumes that the accomplishment of that revolution has in fact fulfilled those hopes, and thereby proved that there was indeed that rich reservoir of wasted talents:

> The myth that selective schools enable working class pupils to have the same educational opportunities as middle and upper class pupils has been finally buried. All the 11 and 13 plus did was to dip the ladle a little deeper in the barrel and scoop out more middle class children to be educated in grammar schools rather than private schools . . . . For every one former working class child who today claims that his education at a grammar school was the key to his later success, there are a score of equally bright children whose opportunities were stunted by the very same system (p. 21).

(a) These claims are quite certainly false. It is little short of crazy to propose to base a national policy for education upon foundations so insupportable. For a start there is, to put it no stronger, a measure of reasonable doubt among the tolerably well-informed concerning the educationally beneficial consequences of comprehension. However, what is rationally disputed is whether the admittedly and scandalously inadequate evidence suggests that the educational results are either not vastly, but still significantly and substantially, better or not vastly, but still significantly and substantially, worse or, all in all, pretty much the same. There is not a scintilla of evidence to show that the Comprehensive Revolution has made possible the release and development of such a torrent of previously wasted working-class talent.

On the contrary, what evidence there is suggests that—just as those awful *Black Paper* bogeypersons had warned—it has had a diametrically opposite effect. Earlier we quoted the DES figures, showing an actual decline in the percentage of university entrants coming from families in the Registrar General's three lowest classes. We also cited *Sixth-Forms in ILEA Comprehensives: A Cruel Confidence Trick?* (Cox and Marks, 1980). It is from this study that we have to infer how many talented working-class boys and girls, who under the old regimen could have been able to attend maintained grammar schools—most of them established by the old London Labour Party, under the leadership of Herbert Morrison— were at that time forced to attend comprehensives which could not provide A-level teaching in major, mainstream subjects: "Out of these 90 schools, there were 36 schools with no A-level French or Geography, 28 without any Physics, 25 without Chemistry, 22 without Maths, and 20 without Biology" (p. 4).

(b) As we have also seen, Anthony Crosland in the unbuttoned intimacy of the home expressed his hopes for the educational system, if not his strictly educational ideals, in revealingly violent and destructive terms (S. Crosland, 1971, p. 149). In the event neither he nor any of his successors has so far succeeded in dismantling the old secondary modern and grammar school system in Northern Ireland. They thus failed to dispose of what has turned out to be embarrassing evidence.

In 1968 the DES published a paper estimating that the next ten or fifteen years would encompass a Great Leap Forward. By 1976 there were going to be 124,600 secondary school age children getting two or three A-level passes. By 1981 it was to be 171,900. Somehow, something went wrong. For 1976 saw a shortfall of 34,300—over a quarter. By 1981 this had become 68,000—more than a third. It seemed that a percentage plateau in A-level achievement had been reached in 1971.

Further analysis, significantly neither made for nor commissioned by the (official) DES but the (unofficial) NCES, revealed that between 1969 and 1978 the percentage of boys in state schools getting one or two A-level passes actually fell, with that of those getting three not rising but staying steady (Baldwin, 1981). The girls did better than the boys, managing a marginal improvement over the same period. However, neither sex—or, as those with no knowledge of grammar might prefer to say, neither gender— came anywhere near fulfilling the happy hopes of 1968. The picture would have looked still more disappointing but for the noteworthy but not strenuously publicised DES practice of mixing up the performance figures of the maintained with those of the independent schools. For there the minority had in fact achieved the kind of improvement which had been expected for all. Meanwhile, falling back to an earlier stage, the percentage of 16 year olds obtaining five GCE O-levels or CSE grade 1s stayed the same between 1968 and 1978: and this despite increased expenditure, lower pupil/teacher ratios and the raising of the school-leaving age in 1973/4. (In 1978 all our children had to remain in school till age 16, whereas in 1968 about half had left by that age.)

We therefore have to ask, what neither the DES nor any other members of the comprehensive lobby have ever been heard to ask: What went wrong? Had the predicted rise met and been checked by some sort of ceiling? Had the shift towards less discipline and more informal methods of teaching had some educationally depressing effect? Had there been a decline in teacher calibre? None of these three suggestions would be at all popular in that quarter, although elsewhere many are convinced that both the second and the third do point to causally significant factors. There seems, however, no escape from the conclusion that the Comprehensive Revolution must start as the suggestion to beat. The very reluctance of supporters of universal comprehension to put this hypothesis to a fair test is, surely, symptomatic of some anxiety about the likely outcome? (For revised estimates made by the DES in 1970 see their *Student Numbers in Higher Education in England and Wales*; as usual, published by HMSO. Their expectation then was that the number of leavers with five or more O-levels would rise to 284,000 by 1981, and the number with one or more A-levels to 212,000. This has not happened. Their own later statistics show that the actual numbers of leavers achieving these qualifications in 1981 were, respectively, 191,000 and 120,000. These figures, as usual, embrace both the maintained and the independent schools.)

This is where Northern Ireland comes in. For there the figures—which, being for maintained schools only, are not bumped up by the strikingly superior performance of any independents—are now, for leavers with one or more A-levels, 50 per cent higher and, for those with five or more O-levels, 40 per cent higher than for England. In assessing this information we need to keep at least three things in mind: first, that O- and A-levels are norm- rather than criteria-related examinations; second, that far more of the schools in Northern Ireland are of the so-called voluntary or religious sort; and, third, that Northern Ireland is both much poorer and afflicted with much higher rates of unemployment than most of the rest of the UK.

If, as is sometimes asserted, these examinations have over the years become progressively less demanding, then this will have no bearing on comparisons between the performances of different subsets. However, if this assertion is true, then the overall picture becomes even bleaker than at first it appeared. The second consideration may well be significant, even if unlikely to account for the entire difference. For there is indeed evidence that, both under ILEA and under other wholly comprehensive LEMs, these 'voluntary' schools not only are much more popular with parents but also perform better. It would, however, probably be unfair to suggest that it is any such educationally superior performance which has provoked socialist hostility rather than the defining socialist commitment to total state ownership and control of everything (Cox and Marks, 1982b). For even the notoriously (by present LP standards) 'right-wing' Prime Minister Callaghan had in his Ruskin speech quoted Tawney (1922): "What wise parents would wish for their children, so the State must wish for its children." This saying, perhaps uncharacteristic of Tawney, is certainly reminiscent of Mussolini in his later Fascist period: "All for the State; nothing against the State; nothing outside the State."

What is called deprivation by animistically minded social scientists and by others similarly wishing to suggest that everything unfortunate is always someone's fault—and presumably someone else's fault—is usually recruited to explain inferior rather than superior performance. However, in fact, within the UK there seems to be a strong positive correlation between one fundamental form of educational achievement and domestic overcrowding—something which features among everyone's indices of 'deprivation'.

David Donnison, whom we met earlier as the eponymous Chairman of the Donnison Commission, later, as Director of the Centre for Environmental Studies, wrote the Foreword to a report on the National Child Development Study (NCDS). This particular report, *From Birth to Seven*, was much concerned with reading (Davie *et al.*, 1972). Though formerly Fabian, Donnison here takes on the Radical colour of his mainly Marxist subordinates: "The patterns glimpsed. . . are so deeply embedded in this country's economic and social structure that they cannot be greatly changed by anything short of equally far-reaching changes in that structure." The authors themselves remark: "Poor housing is often mentioned as one of the contributory causes of school failure" (p. xvi); and go on to quote the here also rather Radical R.M. Titmuss, maintaining that it is impossible to do much good in the schools "while millions of children live in slums without baths, decent lavatories, leisure facilities, room to explore and space to dream" (p. 54).

So committed are these authors to these Radical and, for any non-Radical, pessimistic preconceptions that, without for one moment allowing themselves to reflect on educational achievement in any of the places or periods in which all but the most tiny minorities have suffered housing worse than the most deplorable in contemporary Britain, they proceed to calculate how much retardation in reading age is to be put down to over-crowding and how much to the lack of other basic amenities. They thus contrive not to grasp the refutatory significance of certain items in their own tables of data.

If their Titmussian assumptions were correct, then, presumably, areas with a lot of overcrowding would also have to have a deal of poor reading. So what do we find, when we take our own critical look at their data? Far and away the worst region of overcrowding (in the UK) is Scotland, where 39 per cent of children live in conditions rated overcrowded. In none of the other regions distinguished did the figure go above 20 per cent and four were below 10 per cent. Now what about the percentages of those accounted 'good readers' and 'poor readers'? Still without apparently noticing its relevance, they give the decisive answer:

> In reading attainment the most striking feature to emerge from the results (Fig. 34) is that the proportion of good readers (Southgate reading test score 29–30) in Scotland is markedly higher than in any other region of Britain. The difference is even more marked for poor readers (score 0–20). For example, for every eighteen poor readers in Scotland there were, proportionately, twenty nine poor readers in England and thirty in Wales (pp. 107–8).

One reason for attending here to *From Birth to Seven* is that, as we shall soon be seeing, it is by no means the only report on the NCDS in which well-publicised conclusions have not in fact been sustained by the data deployed in their support (Cox and Marks, 1980b). However, after noting both the invalid derivation of a false preconception and the political direction of that preconception, anyone with a sincere commitment to either justice or educational improvement has at once to deplore the consequent failure of these researchers: either to congratulate the Scottish teachers or to urge their English and Welsh colleagues to learn from them how now to do better.

2.4 Publicity and suppression

Among the policy statements presented to and duly approved by the Blackpool conference of the Labour Party in October in 1978 was one supporting a proposal for a Freedom of Information Bill. Arguing, rightly, that the sharing of information is "an essential bulwark against tyranny" it went on, equally correctly, to assert:

> Public authorities must be made to disclose to the citizens, not only what their policies are and how they can be analysed, assessed and interpreted, but what are the intentions, motives, and values behind them. . .

Unfortunately, while it is one thing to assert such sound principles, it is quite another actually to apply them, especially if you are in office and there is something—as there so often is—which you need to hide. Mrs Williams as the responsible Minister at that time was resolute in her support for

LEAs refusing to reveal the examination results of their maintained schools. Her then party later went on to join with the NUT in its "total opposition" to the clause in the 1980 Act requiring these revelations. Readers of Williams (1981), which is alleged to contain the fruits of her post-SDP rethinking, will be at a loss to discover why she ever left the LP: certainly her book gives us no reason to believe that she has since departed, either in this or any other way, from her former collectivist attitudes towards the wishes and opinions of individual parents.

Something of what she and her political associates needed to hide can be seen from Boyson (1978). For the author had, by means which he chooses not to reveal, got his hands on the separate examination results for that year of every school under the since 1967 all-comprehensive City of Manchester LEA. These data clearly showed the enormous differences which everyone, even without the evidence drawn from US experience, ought to have expected from a system of neighbourhood schools recruiting from socially disparate districts. Both in *Politics is for People* and at the 1981 conference of the Secondary Heads Association (SHA) Mrs Williams advocated universal compulsory comprehension and the destruction of the independent schools, on the grounds that these measures were necessary to promote social mixing and equality of opportunity: "The maintained system of education and the economy itself are crippled by this socially segregated system" (Williams, 1981, p. 158). Boyson had already in 1978 given his crushing reply to this contention by asking a still-unanswered question: "What equality is there in opportunity between children going to Parrs Wood with 1562 pupils and 210 A-level passes this year, and those attending Spurley Hey with 1119 pupils and only 8. . .?" (For an analysis of much more, similar material about the performance of different schools under ILEA, see Cox and Marks, 1980a.)

(i)   While still Minister at the DES Mrs Williams set up an official inquiry which, while continuing to conceal the examination results achieved in individual schools, was—in both descriptive and prescriptive senses of the word 'expect' (Flew, 1975, 5.9 and 6.1)—expected to demonstrate that the comprehensive reorganisation of the maintained system had been, in strictly educational terms, a success. Here and elsewhere in the present book the phrase 'strictly educational' is being so employed that a programme will be shown to be, in strictly educational terms, a success if and in so far as, and only if and in so far as, it results in the educational achievements of all our children approaching more closely to the limits of their abilities. It should never be forgotten that precisely this was the single justifying reason for total comprehension given to and accepted as sufficient by the House of Commons in 1965 (p. 27).

It is necessary to put heavy emphasis upon this phrase in the argument: both because so many of what are nowadays advocated as 'policies for education' in fact aim at ends not essentially connected with learning and because supporters of the Comprehensive Revolution are in fact increasingly inclined to resort to justifications which are not, in this understanding, strictly educational. Take, for instance, Professor A.H. Halsey. He has been a leading figure both in campaigning for universal compulsory comprehension and in researching into social inequality. The very first sentence of his article on *Education and Equality*, published in *New Society* in the year of that Parliamentary resolution (17 June 1965) is altogether frank and explicit: 'Some people, and I am one, want to use education as an instrument in pursuit of an egalitarian society."

Again, had the ending of all social segregation been from the beginning publicly presented as one of the main objectives, then even those most resolute in rejecting all overseas (and particularly US) evidence and experience could scarcely have escaped excoriating cross-examination. For, given that so many schools are in areas as socially segregated as those of Parrs Wood and Spurley Hey, how could we achieve an appropriate national social cross-section in every neighbourhood comprehensive without a wildly unpopular, and wildly wasteful, exercise in compulsory bussing? Lacking the support of an imperial judiciary arbitrarily misinterpreting a justiciable Constitution, any such proposition will in Britain surely have to wait on the prior abolition of contestable General Elections? (No doubt this and many similar points have long since been taken by the 'hard left'. For a commitment to an electorally irremovable one-party socialist despotism is, after all, what most sharply distinguishes those people from their softer siblings.)

The report of the inquiry which Mrs Williams had initiated appeared after she had left office, and while she was contemplating a break with the Labour Party. This inquiry had been conducted under the auspices of the National Children's Bureau (NCB), using NCDS materials. Both the entire conduct of this inquiry and the way in which its findings were published and received provide further confirmation of the claim that, for most of its most committed supporters, comprehensive reorganisation neither is nor ever has been any sort of experiment; not an experiment the results of which have to be monitored, with a readiness to make changes of course if it turns out that earlier hopes are later disappointed. Rather it has been, and is, a revolution to be defended against any counter-revolution and/or a revelation to be cherished against all assaults by infidels.

What was actually received, and accepted with uncritical delight by almost all the journalists, was an article announcing the publication of a book, *Progress in Secondary Schools* (Steedman, 1980). This comparatively short paper summarising that massive, and notably expensive, report appeared in the NCB's quarterly *Concern*, in the July 1980 issue (Steedman and Fogelman, 1980). Long before anyone had had much chance to examine the primary document, it was being widely hailed in the press as having completely vindicated the whole comprehensive re-organisation: "Report explodes comprehensive myth," *The Guardian* shouted; "Clever children do as well in comprehensive as in grammar schools—study shows," said *The Times*; and so on. Nor is there evidence that any of the education correspondents who joined in this explosion of applause either then or ever actually got around to studying any of the data presented. Only in the *Financial Times* were there signs of such study, and this resulted in a carefully damning editorial.

Caroline Cox and John Marks, however, devoted the best part of their subsequent long vacations to *Progress in Secondary Schools*. The result was *Real Concern* (Cox and Marks, 1980b). They concluded that the object of their critique is an "extraordinarily shoddy and partisan report", adding that "It is sobering to reflect that the DES not only sponsored but was represented on the Advisory Group which supervised" the whole operation (p. 31). Again we have to note in passing that the critical examination of this "shoddy and partisan" piece of work was not made by anyone employed in any department, institute or school of education but instead by two people who were not and never had been so employed.

Real Concern argues at length and in detail that the much-trumpeted con-clusions of Steedman and her colleagues are not sustained even by their own doctored data. It is, in the circumstances, not unfair to speak of "doc-tored data". For, as Cox and Marks protest, "No raw data are given; all the results are adjusted by unknown amounts and then scaled so that the reader has no idea what the original figures were" (p. 8). Furthermore, ". . . the report is so biased in its interpretations that it is hard to avoid the suspicion that those concerned, including the Advisory Group on which the DES were represented, were culpable of gross partiality and/or influenced by vested interests" (p. 21).

The nature and degree of that partiality is most vividly, indeed comically displayed in Steedman's consideration of the fact that, on the NCB researchers' own showing, comprehensive parents are far more inclined to express dissatisfaction over the schooling of their children than the parents of children at either grammar or secondary modern schools: "Of course it may be that indications of dissatisfaction reflect a certain criticality or involvement in decisions about schooling among parents, which some schools would hope to foster" (p. 201). One has for her sake to hope that Ms Steedman never needs to apply for a job with the Consumers' Association. What would such authentically impartial people make of a candidate pro-posing to rate whatever produce caused most dissatisfaction to its users as the Best Buy, and to commend its manufacturers for thereby encouraging "criticality or involvement" among their customers?

Real Concern got little attention in the specialist education press, where most commentators continued to speak of the NCB work as authoritative. Mrs Williams herself has continued to describe her offspring in this way, without attempting to meet any of the objections. Yet there was a curious but also significant sequel. The British Educational Research Association (BERA) took the very unusual step of publishing an Open Letter, announcing that its Executive Council was "deeply concerned" about *Real Concern*.

In particular they took exception to the accusation by Cox and Marks that the NCDS researchers had "doctored" their evidence, and were "excessively partisan" in their interpretation and presentation. What "equally concerned" the executive was that *Real Concern* was published under the aegis of the Centre for Policy Studies, "understood to be politically close to the Conservative Party", and yet "given the standing of objective educational research institutions" by the press. (That final contention must astound all who have ever published anything with the CPS, and have seen how our work is in consequence by the *Times Educational Supplement* (TES) dismissed as coming from a notoriously 'right-wing' think tank.)

Everyone, and not only Conservatives, is, of course, bound to approach any task and any question with many relevant preconceptions, and even with some relevant prejudices and biases. This is an inescapable limitation of the human condition. However, what is always within our power, and what we should and—providing that our desire to find and to tell the truth is sufficiently strong and overriding—we shall be forever scrupulous to do is to recognise all these personal prejudices and biases for what they are, and to refuse to allow them to distort or to corrupt our judgement. All this being so, the proper policy for sincere and honest inquirers is to start by either putting all the cards on the table or none, and never fallaciously to infer that because someone started with some prejudice or bias, therefore their conclusions must necessarily be correspondingly tainted.

BERA was at fault on both counts; a fact which has, surely, to be construed as some indication of their own unconfessed political commitments? In the first place, while BERA was eager to reproach Cox and Marks for their (to BERA) unacceptable Conservative associations, it took care to notice neither the internal evidence of partiality in *Progress in Secondary Schools* nor the external fact that Mrs Williams had appointed as Chairman of the Advisory Group for that whole project the aforementioned Professor A.H. Halsey. He had served as an official advisor to the Labour Secretary of State for Education (1965-8), and has never disguised his commitment either to socialist Procrusteanism in general or to "Labour's equality machine" in particular. BERA then proceeded to take it for granted, without further argument, both that committed Conservatives cannot be, whereas our opponents cannot but be, objective.

Here the behaviour of BERA, like that of the British Sociological Association (BSA) in an earlier affair, provides a very clear indication of the direction of the prevailing wind in the worlds of social science and policy research. Gould (1977) raised a question whether certain much-published workers in these fields were in fact sincerely pursuing truth, and whether their actual political objectives were indeed those to which they pretended to be devoted. The Executive of the BSA promptly summoned Gould to give an account of himself. He, very reasonably, refused to respond, save by forthwith resigning his membership. For it emerged that what this Executive wished was not to determine whether he could prove his charges but rather to reproach him for daring to criticise fellow professionals—who were, apparently, to be presumed or even assumed innocent whether or not they had been proved guilty (Flew, 1985, Ch. 8)!

(ii)   As soon as the 1980 Act became law the NCES began to prepare the Examination Results Research Project, which has itself so far resulted in three reports: *Standards in English Schools* (Marks *et al.*, 1983); *Standards in English Schools: Second Report* (Marks and Pomian-Srzednicki, 1985); and *Examination Performance of Secondary Schools in ILEA* (Marks *et al.*, 1986). Once again we have to emphasise that these studies of the results of individual schools, which first became available only when that Act took effect, were all privately financed, and were all executed by people who were not and never had been employed in any college, school or department of education. For, as has already been suggested, such facts have a wider significance.

Why few, if any, of the academics employed in those institutes, schools and departments leapt forward to exploit this rich new vein of research material is certainly not to be explained entirely by appealing to a truth recently uttered in a rather different context: "Education is a notoriously undemanding field of study" (Sowell, 1984, p. 160). Just as people seeking employment as teachers have often been asked for a declaration of faith in 'the comprehensive principle', so teachers of future teachers have been discouraged from saying or doing anything which might raise doubts about comprehension. The exceptional author of *Comprehensive Schooling: The Impossible Dream?*, who is a lecturer in a school of education, was warned by a friendly senior that the publication of such a book would likely prejudice his career prospects. However, he went ahead regardless, concluding: "First, that the comprehensive system has failed in practice, and second, that the theory underpinning comprehensive schooling is contradictory and incoherent" (Shaw, 1983, p. V).

The lack of official support for this particular NCES project fits into a general pattern. For the DES too is nowadays careful neither to present its statistics in ways which might provoke awkward questions nor to initiate any enquiries of its own which could reach similarly embarrassing conclusions. Earlier I described the DES as one element in the pro-comprehension lobby. That this is so is not a matter of party political dispute. For Mrs Williams herself has also said it:

> The Department of Education and Science, when I first was a minister in 1967, was still marked by the selective and meritocratic values of the 1944 Education Act... Gradually the Department moved towards supporting the reform of secondary schools on comprehensive lines. Comprehensive reorganisation replaced selective secondary education as the banner round which the Department rallied (Williams, 1981, p. 184).

Mrs Williams might have added, though here she would have been a less ideally qualified witness, that there have been similar transformations in specialist educational journalism and in the bureaucracies of the main teachers' unions. Anyone wanting to enter or to progress in either of these fields had better not have, or if they have would be ill advised to reveal, any doubts about the dissolution of the grammar schools or even perhaps about socialist Procrusteanism generally.

(a) When *Standards in English Schools* was first published both the authors and their work were subjected to an all-out campaign of vilification. By the time when they complained to the Press Council the TES had already printed 120 column issues of attack to a mere 20 of description or defence, the former including one quite extraordinarily scurrilous feature by a Professor of Education (Wragg, 1983). Much was made—especially by spokespersons for the LP, for the TUC Education Committee and for the NUT—of an internal and therefore supposedly confidential document in which DES statisticians were said to have 'rubbished' this "seriously flawed" and "grossly incompetent" work.

Although the harried and hounded authors were not to be permitted to see what was to them a professionally damaging document, nevertheless this internal and confidential DES paper was, in whole or part, widely leaked to persons believed to be trusty fellow members of the pro-comprehension lobby. Fortunately one of them, jibbing at such DES dirty tricks, and respecting that principle of natural justice which requires that those accused must always be informed of exactly what they are accused, eventually showed the critique to the criticised. They were then able to demonstrate, in a face-to-face discussion with the statisticians, arranged and chaired by the Minister at the House of Commons, that the supposed fundamental flaw was not in fact a fault in their own work but the result of a simple misreading on the part of their critics.

These DES critics at once apologised, withdrawing their original reservations but not their several commendations of a pathbreaking and exhaustive enterprise. These commendations had, of course, never been quoted by

any of those making so much of the leaked critique. The DES statisticians
also agreed to release more information about the social class composition
of school intakes, information which will make possible a still more adequate allowance for such differences. All this was clearly recorded in a
statement issued by the DES on the results of this confrontation between
the authors of *Standards in English Schools* and those who had supposedly
'rubbished' their work (28 November 1983). However, to that statement as
made available in the House of Commons a DES hidden hand had added an
earlier and completely superseded letter; presumably in the hope—a hope
which was in the event not disappointed—that journalists committed to
universal compulsory comprehension would eagerly misconstrue this as
invalidating the later confessions and apologies of the DES statisticians.

It is what happened next, and perhaps still more what did not happen,
which is so relevant to the argument of the present chapter. For most of
those who had made so much of the alleged 'rubbishing' by the DES statisticians never withdrew or apologised for their false assertions, but instead
continued to treat both the authors of *Standards in English Schools* and the
NCES as if they had indeed been not substantially vindicated but
utterly discredited.

Thus, true to form, the TES again repeated the phrase 'serious flaws'.
Similarly true to form, *The Teacher*, house organ of the NUT, first followed
the execrable example of the TES and then compounded this falsificatory
fault by flatly refusing to print any corrective protest from Cox and Marks.
That DES statement of apology was issued on 28 November 1983. In what
was clearly a later letter to *The Times* (3 December 1983) Giles Radice,
the then Labour Party Parliamentary spokesperson on Education, simply
ignored all withdrawals and continued to attack the NCES and defend the
DES. A very similar letter, signed by both the President of the National
Association of Head Teachers (NAHT) and the General Secretary of the
NUT, appeared three days later still (6 December 1983). Such, look you,
are the elected leaders of those who ask us to entrust all our children to their
care, unconditionally and with no rights of escape!

The fullest accounts of this extraordinary and extraordinarily instructive
affair so far available are first, an article in *The Times* (8 December 1983),
by Ronald Butt and not—significantly—by their Education Correspondent;
and, second, an imaginative reconstruction in *The Sunday Times* (11
December 1983), by the authors of *Yes, Minister* and not—still more
significantly—by that paper's Education Correspondent, Peter Wilby. On
this occasion Wilby excelled both himself and all others in stubborn persistence. For it was on the same day and in an adjacent column that, without so
much as mentioning the subsequent embarrassments and apologies of the
DES statisticians, he continued his own polemics both against Cox and
Marks and against the "right-wing" and hence unreliably "partial" NCES.

"Officials at the Department of Education and science," Wilby wrote, "have mounted a campaign to discredit their report. The officials argued—with good reason—that the report was flawed."

(b) We can, finally, derive salutary instruction from the misbehaviour of Giles Radice, Peter Wilby, Fred Jarvis, John Swallow and old uncle Tom Cobbleigh and all. For it is scarcely possible that they would have persisted in employing such discredited arguments had they themselves believed that there was anything better available. Here we have another and more compelling token of a powerful and improving type of argument which might lead us to speculate that, when earlier he published Wragg (1983), the Editor of the TES was himself already fearful of the correctness of the conclusions drawn by the authors of *Standards in English Schools*. For, again, it seems improbable that the Editor of a supposedly non-political, specialist journal—had he in his heart really been certain that their work indeed was, and could straightforwardly be shown to be, a farrago of falsehoods generated out of partisan incompetence—would have given a platform to such desperate demagoguery. Certainly—and fortunately—this particular column, all too aptly entitled 'Personal', and chiefly consisting in ad feminam suggestiones falsi about and against the Baroness Cox, was very different from what we are more used to finding printed in that journal.

Although we can but conjecture what the actual motivation of all these people was, and is, we are nevertheless able to feel pretty confident in determining what it was not, and is not. For, once we consider what the so-far unrefuted—and so-far, it seems, irrefutable—conclusions of *Standards in English Schools* were, it becomes quite obvious that what that motivation most certainly cannot be is a disinterested and overriding concern that all our children should reach the highest levels of educational attainment of which they are individually capable. (Originally, we should never forget, that was the sole stated aim of the whole Comprehensive Revolution.)

To enforce this last point it is not necessary to introduce long or numerous quotations. However, anyone who does in fact cherish such a commitment to across-the-board educational improvement will certainly want carefully to study the whole of both this first report and its two successors. Some of the findings do no more than provide more extensive confirmation of what was, although often wilfully ignored, already known. Earlier in this chapter we insisted that resource input is not regularly and positively correlated with education output. Here we have evidence that the contrary is nearer the truth, at least for education output as measured by national examinations: "Levels of expenditure provided another consistent correlation, but one which was persistently *negatively* related to examination attainment" (p. 14: emphasis mine). The authors add a comment which we shall need to remember when we reach Chapter 5:

Some of the LEAs with relatively high levels of spending are those which also cater for relatively high proportions of children from families of ethnic minority groups or who were born abroad. Thus, extra resources may be needed to provide for their special educational needs. However, the pattern is not uniform: several 'Big Spenders' which do NOT have large numbers of these children also have low levels of attainment. Conversely, a number of LEAs who spend less than the national average also have above average numbers of ethnic minority group children AND achieve above average examination results (p. 15).

What truly deserve the favourite headline description 'sensational' are all those findings which bear on questions about the actual educational effects of the Comprehensive Revolution. Since these findings are all based upon comparisons between the small surviving minority of secondary modern-cum-grammar school LEAs and the huge all-comprehensive majority, we can now readily recognise one compelling reason why not only Giles Radice and the Labour Party but also Fred Jarvis and the NUT leadership are so fanatically keen to overrun and clean up the last remaining pockets of resistance. It is that they urgently need, and must presumably want by destroying these control groups, to remove the possibility of making such revealing comparisons. How naively and generously mistaken was the young and innocent socialist sociologist Julienne Ford when, back in 1969, she described the Comprehensive Revolution as "an *experiment* with the life chances of millions of children" (quoted p. 8: emphasis supplied)! Most emphatically, 'experiment' never was the true name of the game.

Why, if the intended revolution was ever to be fully accomplished, this could not be so becomes cruelly clear the moment we consider some of the more sensational findings of *Standards in English Schools*; by far the most extensive survey ever made of examination results in the public sector: ". . . the secondary modern schools, so often depicted as the Cinderellas of the English education system, have attained very good examination results and have done very well for their pupils" (p. 17). To understand the following statements we need to know: that a bare pass at O-level is intended to be equivalent to a CSE Grade 1, with 'OC1 pass' being shorthand for either of these two equivalent performances; and that O-level/CSE points constitute a composite function intended to provide an index of performance in examinations of either kind:

> Perhaps most striking is the fact that pupils in secondary modern schools attained, on average, more O-level and CSE Grade 1 passes per pupil than pupils in all types of school in 4 LEAs, and more O-level/CSE points than the average for pupils in all types of schools in 6 LEAs. And, in English, they are outstanding in their levels of achievement: in no less than 17 LEAs in our sample, secondary modern school pupils attain more O-level/CSE points than the average for their counterparts in all other types of schools combined (p. 17).

Most sensational of all, however, is the overall conclusion of all the performance comparisons between "comprehensive and selective systems of schools". It is not surprising that the authors print this summary conclusion in block capitals:

THE RESULTS... STRONGLY INDICATE THAT SUBSTANTIALLY HIGHER O-LEVEL, CSE AND A-LEVEL EXAMINATION RESULTS ARE TO BE EXPECTED FOR PUPILS IN A FULLY SELECTIVE SYSTEM OF SCHOOLS COMPARED WITH PUPILS IN A FULLY COMPREHENSIVE SYSTEM OF SCHOOLS. THIS FINDING APPLIES TO ALL THE INDICES OF EXAMINATION SUCCESS WHICH WE STUDIED AND, ACCORDING TO OUR DATA, IS AS ROBUST AS THE GENERALLY ACCEPTED FINDING THAT EXAMINATION RESULTS ARE HIGHLY CORRELATED WITH SOCIAL CLASS (p. 61).

3

Clarifying Crucial Concepts

'The Prince of Wei,' said Tzu Lu, 'is awaiting you, Sir, to take control of his administration,—what will you undertake first, Sir?'—'The one thing needed,' replied the Master, 'is the correction of terms. . . . If terms be incorrect, then statements do not accord with facts; and when statements do not accord, then business is not properly executed;. . . Hence whatever a wise man denominates he can always definitely state, and what he so states he can always carry into practice, for the wise man will on no account have anything remiss in his definitions.' (Confucius, *The Analects*, XIII 3 (Soothill, 1910, pp. 607–11.))

'Whithersoever the wind, as it were, of the argument blows, there lies our course.' ((Plato's) Socrates, *The Republic* 394D.)

It sometimes seems that participants in debates about or within Edbiz are peculiarly liable to fall into conceptual confusion. They neglect to define what are for them key terms, often either collapsing or altogether failing to make crucial distinctions between different interpretations of those terms. Frequently, and in part presumably in consequence, they overlook the most obvious immediate inferences. Sometimes too they support cherished conclusions with arguments so excruciatingly bad that even their best friends must be embarrassed: thought must indeed be a painful process for such persons as these, and three minutes a very long time (p. 11, above).

Nor is the perhaps peculiarly poor quality of thinking in this area solely a matter of leaky logic or conceptual confusion, important though these are. Already in Chapters 1 and 2 we had to deploy distressingly many examples both of a refusal to follow lines of inquiry which it is feared might lead to uncongenial conclusions and of a determination either to ignore or even outright to deny unwelcome discovered facts, no matter what the evidence. All that is needed now, before proceeding to more purely conceptual issues, is to suggest that those intellectual and at the same time moral malpractices seem to be growing even more prevalent here— becoming progressively less venial and more flagrant as relevant evidence continues to accumulate.

For this purpose two or three quotations from the glossy 1986 Labour Party statement, from which earlier we drew two, at first sight, better things (p. 35, above), will be abundantly sufficient. Thus, after describing real increases in spending per pupil head as "This government's policies of squeezing the resources available to schools. . ." (p. 6), it proceeds to assert another demonstrated falsehood as a known truth: "It has now been established once and for all that a decline in provision means lower educational standards" (p. 7).

Again, after describing as "a complete myth" the incontestably true contention that maintained grammar schools "helped bright working class children to get a good education", it goes on to argue post hoc propter hoc. For—as if, even if it were a known truth that there had been an absolute improvement after comprehension, this would prove the comparative superiority of the new system—it proclaims: "Since the changeover to comprehensives, standards—even if judged by the narrow measure of examination results—have risen significantly" (p. 6). Here the nearest approach to any relevantly evidenced performance comparison between the two rival systems is still distant, and worse than worthless. It consists in falsely protesting that opponents "continually try to down grade comprehensives by comparing their examination results with those of selective schools" (p. 6).

Let it, however, be remembered that the NCES did indeed, as we have seen, make certain comparisons between some comprehensives and some selective schools. However, those selective schools, as we also saw, were the surviving, *negatively* selective ('creamed'), secondary moderns. Almost incredibly, these comparisons turned out to favour the so-long despised and rejected. What Bishop Berkeley would have called "the killing blow" is the finding in the *Third Report* that, using the index of O-level/CSE points (p. 66, above), ILEA's (all comprehensive) schools, with more spent per pupil head than under any other LEA, *on average*, and despite their including several excellent institutions:

> not only do less well than comprehensive schools elsewhere in the country, even in relatively socially deprived areas, but that they also do less well than secondary modern schools—schools which, by definition, are deprived of those pupils who would normally be expected to take GCE (p. 10).

The notion that debates within and about Edbiz embrace more wretched argument and more reckless assertion than others elsewhere may be a parochial illusion; like Wittgenstein's conviction that, in the particular Austrian village in which in the 1920s he happened to be working as a schoolteacher, human behaviour had descended to a low deeper than that reached anywhere else. What is certain, whether or not this is any sort of local peculiarity, is that many best-selling collections of essays in this particular area have been pervaded and corrupted by conceptual confusions. For instance, in the Penguin Education Special *Education for Democracy* none of the contributors spares a moment to explain what it is proposed to mean by the word 'democracy'; while their actual usage is certainly not consistent (Rubinstein and Stoneman, 1972).

A still more scandalous case is that of another collection published under that imprint, *Race, Culture and Intelligence* (Richardson and Spears, 1972). One might—had one been unfamiliar with similar productions issuing from the same source at that time—have expected that the editors of such a book would indeed "have attempted to step back from the debate itself and look at the concepts which underlie it". However, in fact *Race, Culture and Intelligence* is so far from containing the "close examination of the key ideas" thus promised in its Foreword that no one, from beginning to end, can spare a moment from execrating reactionaries and racists in order to spell out either what it is to be a racist or why racism is wrong.

So, once again, the same fundamental principle of natural justice is violated: the principle that no one should be accused of, much less condemned for, any offence unless the nature of the charge has first been explained. (Another such principle, that no one is to be judge in their own cause, is challenged every time anyone suggests—as the NUT so regularly does—that the last word about the performance of pupils should be given to those who have taught them. For this is to make teachers the ultimate judges of the effectiveness of their own teaching.) We can scarcely be surprised, though we may still be shocked, that *Race, Culture and Intelligence* also fails to define 'culture'. It therefore neglects to point the vital difference between, on the one hand, race, which most certainly is genetically determined, and, on the other, culture, which, equally certainly, is not.

3.1 Competition and co-operation

Already some of the crucial conceptual points have been made. Thus in Chapter 1 we noted the differences both between norm-related and criteria-related examinations and between an equal chance (an equal probability or likelihood) of achieving some objective and an equal chance (a fair and equal opportunity) of so doing. Later in this chapter we shall be seeing more of the importance of the second of these distinctions. That of the first is mainly that, in so far as GCE and CSE have been norm- rather than criteria-related, all direct comparisons between results in successive years, as opposed to comparisons within the same year, must be invalid. All the analyses performed under the NCES Examination Results Research Project were, therefore, of the latter sort (pp. 62ff., above). By contrast, the only

examination statistics cited in that 1986 Labour Party statement were not
(p. 6). As we read in Browning's 'Epistle of Karshish, the Arab Physician':
"It is strange." Or, rather, it would be were these particular policy makers
in truth exclusively or even primarily devoted to raising standards of
educational achievement.

Later, in an article in *The Times* (16 December 1986), Anne Sofer
repeated some of the same DES-supplied figures: 16 per cent of pupils left
school with one or more A-level passes in 1976 and 17 per cent in 1985;
while of those without A-levels, in 1976 8.5 per cent had five or more OC1
passes compared with 11 per cent in 1985. She construed this as a happy
and glorious vindication of the Comprehensive Revolution: "If the standards of our education system are behind those of some other countries, it is
because we started further behind, in that pre-comprehensive era often
evoked nowadays as a golden age."

In drawing this moral from her data base she committed two further
faults. She falsely assumed that West Germany, whose comparative
educational advantage she herself has most vividly in mind, had a pre-
dominantly comprehensive system. (She had, as we saw, earlier discussed
this Germany's advantage in the same newspaper.) She also overlooked
that the DES continues—for its own purposes—to confound the examination results of the independent with those of the maintained schools.
Because the performance figures of the former are so vastly superior the
very small average supposed advance over the last ten years may well have
been achieved only on that very narrow sector of the front. For while a mere
6 per cent of school leavers are from the independent schools, these get
about 16 per cent of all O-level passes, 25 per cent of A-level passes and 50
per cent of all grade As at A-level.

Chapter 2 developed the less sophisticated but none the less important
distinction between standards of resource input and standards of education
output: measures of the former being the quantities of cash, manpower and
materials put in while measures of the latter are measures of EVA—the
educational value added. One would think—to parody 'the implacable Professor' J.L. Austin—that collapsing this distinction was the occupational
disease afflicting all the supply-side interest groups, were it not so manifest
that it is both their ratio essendi and their prime occupation.

(i)   What was not done in either of the two previous chapters was to cite
any specimen of one excruciatingly bad form of argument which is
nevertheless widely and constantly employed. The reason for deferring that
task was that, had it been undertaken in the context of a critique of Anne
Sofer's 'A German Lesson for Our Schools' (p. 21, above), discussing it
there might have suggested that she too is one of its clients. Although I do
have my suspicions, the case certainly cannot be proved on the evidence of
that article alone.

The nerve of this lamentable form of argument is that a decisive reason for developing a single, uniform system of examining at 16+, or whenever else, is that abilities range over a continuum, across which the drawing of any sharp dividing line must be more or less arbitrary. Consider, for instance, the NUT pamphlet *Examining at 16+: the Case for a Common System*. Issued in November 1978, it confidently proclaims: "In maintaining two quite separate examinations, designed for pupils of different ability ranges, the present system is as divisive, and hence educationally indefensible, as the coexistence of grammar and secondary modern schools" (p. 2). For the same reason they go on to argue that in their own ideal, all-in, non-arbitrary world, "There would be no artificial division between 'pass' and 'fail' " (p. 6).

Yet, from the fact that the drawing of such a line at any particular point is always more or less arbitrary, we cannot validly infer that there can be no sufficient reason for drawing any sharp lines at all. In every sphere of human life it is for practical people imperative to draw decisive lines across such shading continua, and to insist that what falls below can and often must be treated very differently from what falls above, however hard or however indulgent this may appear to those coming almost indiscernibly close to the dividing lines (Flew, 1975, 7.13-7.24). Does anyone with three minutes to spare really need a professional philosopher to tell them that the dimensions of feet also range over continua but that this is an execrable reason for insisting that everyone be forced into boots or shoes of a single, uniform, standard size? (These would, no doubt have to be produced either by a central State Footwear Monopoly—British Boots?—or by a collection of LFMs on the familiar foolish ground that footwear is too important to the public good for its production to be left to altogether unsubsidised and centrally unplanned private enterprise.)

We must not, either by the extreme feebleness of the supporting argument or by the exasperated lightheartedness of the present response thereto, be misled to underestimate either the force of the drive to impose a single uniform examination system or the seriousness of the effects likely if this drive is allowed to succeed. Already the merger of GCE and CSE into a single GCSE has led, as predicted, to demands for simplification and for the removal of difficulties. The impact upon the standards achieved by the top 40 per cent, if the bottom 40 per cent were to be brought into a single all-comprehensive system, scarcely bears thinking about, yet must be, if the Gadarene rush is to be checked. Whatever happens at the bottoms of the scales, from the tops it is a matter of regression towards the mean. (Since precisely this is the object of 'progressive' taxation, if not by the same token of 'progressive' education, why is the former not called, more correctly, regressive taxation?)

(ii)   *Labour's Programme 1973* begins with a statement to be found also in many of its predecessors and successors: "We aim to bring about a society based on cooperation instead of competition, where production is for people's needs, not for private profit." Both these familiar antitheses are false. First, how do they think that it is possible in a pluralistic economy either to make a profit or even to stay in business at all save by supplying customers with goods or services which they want at prices which they are able and willing to pay? Of course, what people actually want may not be what (someone else would determine that) they need (Flew, 1981, Ch. V), but that is an excellent reason for suspecting authoritarian intentions in those who choose to refer to our needs rather than to our wants. Second, competition is not the opposite of co-operation. The true opposite of competition, at least in economic life, is not co-operation but monopoly. Firms or teams will not succeed either in commercial competition or in competitive team games without a deal of co-operation among their members. It is not for nothing that one of Britain's most dynamic contracting companies long ago adopted a hard-pulling tug-of-war team as its trademark.

(a) It is time and overtime to begin to analyse the concept of competition. The *first* thing to bring out is that competition essentially involves relationships between two or more competitors. In this essentially relational aspect it resembles both co-operation and equality: it takes at least two to compete, or to co-operate, or to be equal. You could say that this first conceptual fact makes competition, in the very weak sense just indicated, an essentially social notion: Robinson Crusoe cannot engage in any competitions on his desert island until and unless he meets Man Friday. Nor can he co-operate. Nor can he provide any purchase for the activities of the engineers of equalisation.

(b) The *second* proposition is different from, although it presupposes, the first. It is that competition essentially involves comparisons, and comparisons with another person or persons. Thus it is one thing to say that someone in some direction put up a better, or worse, performance than their own previous best, or worst; or that they in some way bettered or worsened their own former condition. However, we cannot begin to talk of competition until it is a question of making such comparisons betwen different persons. Any competitive bettering or worsening is always bettering or worsening relative to another competitor or to other competitors. This second conceptual fact makes any competitive performance a social action in the stronger, sociological understanding of that expression: "Action is social in so far as, by virtue of the subjective meaning attached to it by the acting individual (or individuals), it takes account of the behaviour of others" (Weber, 1904, p. 88).

Competition thus essentially involves comparisons. This is equally true of equality, but not of co-operation. The ideas of equality and of competition are similar in that neither has any necessary links with absolute position on any scale of achievement. Thus it is in principle possible to get and to stay ahead of all the competition, even though your position on some absolute scale is steadily declining; and equally possible in principle to fall and to remain behind all the competition, notwithstanding that your absolute situation is actually improving. Take an educational example. Suppose that we had been able to compare the performance of the independent and of the maintained schools in criteria-related examinations. Then we might have discovered either that the performance of the latter had been improving, although not enough to close the gap, or that, although the whole country had been in decline, the former still remained ahead.

It is this essential indifference to absolute position which those of us for whom equality of outcome is not a value find most alien and most repugnant in the Procrusteans, those for whom it is. If for you such equality is indeed a value then, it follows necessarily, that for you there must be at least some possible cases in which a more equal distribution of some sort of goods is to be preferred even where this greater equality is bought at the cost of a lower average, or even a lower minimum, absolute level (Flew, 1981). It is, surely, in terms of such Procrustean preferences that we have to understand much of the intellectual support for otherwise perplexing policies with regard both to the economy and to primary and secondary education. This moral will perhaps be more easily grasped if it is applied in the former context first.

The puzzle is why so many such people continue to call for the reimposition of something like the previous, confiscatory top tax rates of 83 per cent on employment and 98 per cent on investment income. They persist despite two fresh developments since the 1979 Conservative reductions: first, the undisputed revelation by the Treasury that a larger proportion of the total income tax revenue (26.7 per cent as against 24 per cent) is now coming from the 5 per cent who pay most income tax; and, second, a new American challenge, a challenge far more formidable than that of which M. Servan-Schreiber warned. With effect from New Year's Day 1988, the growth-minded USA will be welcoming tax-exiled high earners, job-makers and other wealth-creators with a new top federal income tax rate lower than the present UK standard rate!

We must not, of course, in contemplating such economically and fiscally destructive policies forget the (for any speech of his there) unprecedented ovation which greeted Denis Healey's promise to the 1973 Labour Party conference, that he would "make the rich howl in agony". Yet it would be not only uncharitable but also unrealistic to suggest that the support of such as Professors Halsey and Donnison also springs from sadistic envy rather than from their perverse Procrustean principles. This said, we have now always to be alert to applications of such principles in other contexts, and hence ready to recognise that and why it is that such people can be indifferent to, or even welcome, consequences which appal those cherishing either more purely educational concerns or more generously liberal principles.

(c) The *third* conceptual point about competition is that it essentially involves a striving by every competitor in some way to do better than all the rest of the competition. Thus, if someone takes part in some sort of race without trying to win, then we say—truly—that he is not, or is not really, competing in that race. It is a corollary of this third proposition that competition, like equality, is essentially concerned with relativities rather than absolutes. This corollary followed from the second proposition also. However, here it becomes easier to appreciate what is often an unlovely aspect of both ideas. At the end of an important and profoundly disturbing essay on 'The Economic Contradictions of Democracy' the author concludes: "It could yet be saved if contemporary egalitarianism were to lose its hold over the intelligentsia." Mentioning "concepts such as 'relative deprivation' in sociology, inequality (a loaded way of describing differences)" and " 'interdependent utilities' in economics", he deplores "the contribution of the so-called intelligentsia". This is "to focus all attention on relativities to the exclusion of absolutes" (Brittan, 1975, pp. 21, 27 and 28).

Whether or not we concur, we have to notice that competition too is essentially concerned with relativities, even as we go on to insist, as we surely must, on two things which are always neglected or even denied by protagonists of the "contemporary egalitarianism". First, competition, though conceptually concerned only with relativities, is often the practically necessary condition for promoting and securing the absolutely better. Second, it is perfectly possible for people engaging in competition to be aware of this first truth, and to be in fact themselves as much directed at absolute as at relative bettering.

These two true and ever topical points made, however, we do also have to allow that even conceptually there is a world of difference between trying to improve on one's own previous performance and trying to do or be better than someone else; between striving to improve the condition of oneself and one's family and trying to ensure that that condition is better than that of other people and their families. Aims of the latter of these two kinds can be unlovely, socially disruptive and insatiable, whereas those of the former are not. Most desires to do better *than others* are bound to end in frustration, whereas desires simply to do better are not similarly ill starred. The point here is very obvious, yet devastatingly decisive: if in any set of people everyone wants to do better than everyone else, then all except one, or even all, cannot but be disappointed!

Those whose own schooldays preceded the Comprehensive Revolution will doubtless be able to recall something of an unacceptable face of competition in primary and secondary education. However, let us conclude this Subsection with an instance from another time and another country.

While I was working on *The Politics of Procrustes* the wife of my publisher returned from Japan with the tale of a mother who made a practice of requiring her children to do their homework while she herself watched the most exciting television programmes—what expatriates in that country call 'Samurai Westerns'. Afterwards she gave her children vivid accounts of these violent and enthralling ongoings in hopes that such accounts— retailed at school with adornments—would tempt other children to neglect their own learning tasks!

(iii)   Turning from theoretical to more directly practical questions it ought to be, yet apparently is not, obvious that fair and open competition, though understandably uncongenial to reluctant and sluggish competitors, is one sure, if not the only or the surest, means of maintaining and/or raising standards in or of whatever it may be that the competition is a competition to achieve or to produce. There is abundant and compelling evidence for this conclusion both from experimental psychology and from everyday experience in all manner of fields. Without belabouring a contention which only the most incorrigibly indoctrinated would dare to challenge outright, it is perhaps just worth mentioning Richard Lynn's (1977) 'Competition and Cooperation' as a source of references to the findings of educational psychologists (pp. 107-13).

There is also some reason to believe that at least in some areas and with some people continuous as opposed to discontinuous feedback of information on success or failure tends, as a matter of contingent fact, to improve performance. *Trial and Error and the Idea of Progress* cites some experiments on efforts to acquire a simple skill, in which groups with discontinuous feedback "improved over a dozen trials from being on target forty per cent of the time to achieving fifty per cent on target performance"; while the groups with continuous feedback "started with nearly fifty per cent success and improved it, over the same period, to sixty-four per cent success" (Pirie, 1977, pp. 78-9 and 83).

(a) The question remaining is how it is possible for so many schools, schoolteachers and education pundits to continue preaching, in the face of evidence so overwhelming, against all competition and all competitive values, all the time contrasting these with co-operation and co-operative values, as if the two pairs must always be mutually exclusive. The absence of qualification in either case is remarkable. For not only competition but also co-operation ought to proceed always within the limits of law, and to stay subject to the prescriptions and proscriptions of morality. We always should ask: 'Competition in what areas of activity?' and 'Co-operation in the pursuit of what ends?'

The answer to our remaining question must be that the educational involvements of these people, and their 'policies for education', are not, in our previous and deliberately narrow understanding (p. 58, above), strictly educational. Additionally, or perhaps even alternatively, they often have what they themselves doubtless see as a conscientious concern to exploit the state monopoly system as a means for promoting and sustaining an ultra-egalitarian and—what might in fact turn out to be a very different thing—a socialist society.

Several contributors to *Education for Democracy* (Rubinstein and Stoneman, 1972) are frank in confessing such additional or alternative objectives. For instance, in an article under the menacing title 'The Comprehensive School: Labour's Equality Machine', Marsden reassures himself "that the narrowly meritocratic emphasis on streaming and academic results. . . will be a temporary phase" and soon "the internal dynamic of reorganisation should begin to assert itself" (p. 139). "These early disappointments for egalitarians emphasise that the community and the meritocratic schools represent quite different ideals. . . meritocrats and egalitarians will want to evaluate education, even the 'development of talent', by different criteria" (p. 140). We have too already heard Professor Edgley urging socialist teachers to insist on "raising the question 'Education for Industry, or—in its present form—against it'?" (quoted p. 26, above).

Such socialist teachers expose themselves here to challenge on two counts. First, how, in a country in which for a long time a majority even of Labour voters have been opposed to any further nationalisation, can a policy of making pupils unfit for any private employment consist with professions of either commitment to democracy or concern for the future welfare of those pupils? Second, even supposing that Clause IV of the Constitution of the Labour Party does within the foreseeable future become the law of the land, what are the prospects for a country which has to import most of its raw materials and a large part of its food if the resulting state monopolies cannot compete effectively with alternative foreign suppliers in selling exports to pay for those necessary imports? Perhaps those who have spoken of a "a cold Haiti" (Andreski) or "honorary membership of the Third World" (Boyson) have been exaggerating. Yet there certainly are some tendencies in that direction within British Edbiz.

(b) Notoriously someone once said that the Battle of Waterloo was won on the playing fields of Eton College. Much mocked though this saying has been, it does contain a modicum of unfashionable truth. For (disproportionately) many of Wellington's officers were indeed alumni of that ancient institution, and, since war is the most deadly serious, and deadly, of competitive team games, those military teams whose members best cooperate with one another, like similarly co-operative teams in all other spheres, greatly increase their chances (probabilities) of winning a victory.

Repeating this saying about Waterloo offers one more occasion for insisting upon the absurdity of assuming that co-operation and competition are always antithetically opposed. Certainly there are occasions, in business and elsewhere, when a choice has to be made between alternatives of co-operation or competition. Two firms, for instance, may have to decide whether to compete against each other for a big contract, each of the two submitting its own rival tender, or whether to form a consortium, submitting one joint tender in competition with the rest of the field. Then there are also cases—most strikingly and most familiarly in competitive games—where some co-operation is a condition of the possibility of the competition itself. I cannot play tennis at all, to say nothing of winning or losing, unless someone is willing so far to co-operate as to give me a game.

The article 'Competition and Cooperation', to which reference has already been made, notices that, traditionally, "Cooperative attitudes have mainly been fostered through team games" (Lynn, 1977, p. 111). It then goes on to agree with the traditionalists that "it is difficult to develop cooperative attitudes in academic work" on the grounds that "academic work is almost entirely an individual and not a team activity" (p. 112). Certainly the subject of all learning and failure to learn is the individual student. The Marxist Lecturer in the Sociology of Education who, after sneering at "The assumption that the individual is more important than the group or class. . . .," then went on to complain that "It is never made clear why most assessments are based on notions of individual competition rather than collective work", was far gone beyond redemption (Sarup, 1982, pp. 9 and 20).

However, no recognition of the fundamental truths which, he claims, pass Sarup's understanding suffices to rule out the possibility of introducing co-operative and at the same time competitive team contests into the academic side of education. There is, surely, room for an explosive growth of such co-operative competition in academic learning, with the rival schools and rival forms striving to reach higher average levels of scholastic achievement; their different performances being scored, of course, by independent, external, and, as far as can be, objective examinations. By giving those at the top of the class an incentive to help the laggards to improve, rather than complacently to preen themselves upon their own superior achievements, such an innovation could do a lot to beautify the previously unacceptable face of educational competition. A Parthian shot: could not the general refusal even to consider any such suggestion be yet another case of the private boarding school virus infecting the maintained sector, such an innovation being seen as an unsporting tactic in the great game in which the object of the teachers is to teach and that of the pupils not to learn?

3.2 Democracy and equality

In his wittily entitled *Sense and Sensibilia* the ever-formidable Austin (1962) picked and reproached 'democracy' as his example of "a notoriously useless word" (p. 144). However, he had, uncharacteristically, got it quite wrong: persistently and systematically abused, yes; useless, most emphatically not. For it is the only or the best available word for saying various very important things. We need to discover what these things are by distinguishing, if not three precise senses, at any rate three areas of meaning. We can find mnemonic labels for these in the concluding resolution of Abraham Lincoln's Gettysburg Address: "That governments of the people, by the people, for the people, shall not perish from the earth."

(i)(a)   *First* in that order is the understanding in which the word has no essential reference to anything political. The big *Oxford English Dictionary* glosses this, with little enthusiasm: "In modern use often more vaguely, denoting a social state in which all have equal rights, without hereditary, or arbitrary, differences of rank or privilege." It is with this sort of concern, usually, that people speak of democratising an educational institution or a department of state.

This, therefore, is the usage most generally favoured both by contributors to *Education for Democracy* and by sociologists of education. Thus in the former we read: "Without absorbing the independent, and particularly the public schools, into the state system, any talk of education for democracy remains a mockery" (Rubinstein and Stoneman, 1972, p. 88). An example of the latter is Pierre Bourdieu (1974), asking rhetorically, ". . . is not the best way of judging to what extent the reality of a democratic society conforms to its ideals, to measure chances of entering the institutional instruments of social elevation and cultural salvation open to individuals of different social classes?" (p. 43). So democracy here is, in a sense, 'of the people', but democracy in this understanding has no necessary connections with the government of anything.

(b) *Second* in the present ordering, although in every other way primary, there comes the application to methods of making state or, more generally, group decisions. If some group as a whole takes decisions by majority vote, then that is democratic. So, too, are institutions under which decisions are made by delegates, representatives or other officers who can in due course be voted out.

Two points require immediate further attention. First, notice the heavy non-paternalist emphasis upon what the voters themselves decide as opposed to what they might, by others, be supposed to need or what it may or may not be in their interests to have. Second, notice the emphasis upon voting out, not voting in. It is sometimes urged as a paradox of democracy that an electorate may give a majority to a party intending to make that the final free election. It is perhaps somewhat less often remarked that there must be parallel possibilities with every other form of government: an oligarchy might decide to hand over the sovereignty either to a dictator or to the populace; and so on. However, if, as I suggest, we adopt as part of our criterion of democratic legitimacy the possibility of—in a good old phrase— 'voting the scoundrels out' then we shall not be committing ourselves to accepting, as democrats, the verdict of that last election. In this more sophisticated understanding the guarantee of future free elections, and hence the permanent possibility of reversals, are elements of the essence of democracy. It is, therefore, an affront to democracy for any party to threaten irreversible changes, as in the 1970s and 1980s one of Britain's two majors has taken to doing. The democratic alternative is to promise measures which, once implemented, you hope and expect that almost no one will in fact want to undo. In an earlier and happier period it was a Labour Prime Minister who therefore insisted: "Democracy is not a one-way street."

(c) The importance of the first of the two emphases in the previous paragraph emerges more fully as we enter the *third* area of meaning: not 'by the people' but, rather, 'for the people'. Consider such increasingly common political labels as 'German Democratic Republic' or 'People's Democratic Republic of the Yemen'. Those devoted to democracy in our second understanding may too quickly put down these employments of the term as just so much flagrantly mendacious propaganda, but that is not the whole story, and for us here the other part is the more important.

Consider two revealing and authoritative statements. The first was made by Janos Kadar, addressing the Hungarian National Assembly on 11 May 1957, one year after the friendly neighbourhood tanks of imperial normalisation had installed him in office. The second comes from Abdul Kharume, First Vice President of Tanzania, and it was made on 7 July 1967 at the anniversary celebrations of the ruling and, of course, only legal party on the Tanzanian mainland. Mr Kharume, who has since been assassinated, was, as his Afro-Shirazi party in Zanzibar still is, strongly influenced by advisers from the German Democratic Republic. The Tanzanian government had recently rounded up everyone in Dar-es-Salaam without visible means of support and driven them out into the countryside. The two statements ran:

The task of the leaders is not to put into effect the wishes and will of the masses. . . The task of the leaders is to accomplish the interests of the masses. Why do I differentiate between the will and the interests of the masses? In the recent past we have encountered the phenomenon of certain categories of workers acting against their interests.

Our government is democratic because it makes its decisions in the interests of, and for the benefit of, the people. I wonder why men who are unemployed are surprised and resentful at the Government. . . sending them back to the land for their own advantage.

It is evident that Mr Kadar and Mr Kharume are not pretending to be democrats in any sense of our second sort. On the contrary: for them, as for Rousseau, the crux is not what anyone actually wants or decides but what satisfies the needs or serves the interests of the people; while for them, though not for him, what those needs and interests are, and who is to count as a person truly of the people, is for the party to decide.

(ii)   Confusions about equality are in the present context more damaging than confusions about democracy. This is in part because there are with equality more relevant and important differences to be confounded, and in part because most of the discussants here employ the word 'democracy' fairly consistently in an 'of the people' way, albeit without either explaining their own preferred usage or contrasting it with 'by the people' and 'for the people' alternatives.

(a) The *first* essential distinction is between the descriptive and the normative; between claims about what, it is alleged, either has been, already *is*, or in fact will be; and claims about what, it is suggested, ideally *ought* to have been, to be now or to become in the future. In the former kind the most vehement and often the most implausible claims about equalities as between human individuals and human sets are made by those who mistakenly believe that these are logically or in some other way presupposed by whatever contentions of the latter kind they are themselves especially concerned to maintain. There are even those, including some paid to know better, who appear to construe the claim "that all men are created equal" in the American Declaration of Independence as not merely presupposing but directly constituting the contention that "at birth human infants, regardless of heredity, are as equal as Fords"—a contention drawn from an edition of the *Encyclopaedia of the Social Sciences* issued in the days when, so long as black was your beautiful, you could buy your Ford in any colour you liked.

Nowadays such a descriptive equality in initial potentialities is not often outright asserted, or even quietly assumed, *as between individuals*. What both professing social scientists and those who put their reported findings to controversial use seem almost universally to assume, but more rarely assert, are similar equalities *as between sets*. Assumptions of this sort are made by all those—and today their name is legion—who insist upon concluding directly from set inequalities of outcome to set inequalities of opportunity (Murphy, 1978; 1981a, b). In defiance of both antecedent probabilities and subsequent experience these people insist on taking it absolutely for granted that, within the social sets which they are comparing, not only talents but also particular preferences and all other personal characteristics are distributed, if not perhaps exactly, then at least substantially, in the same way.

Professor Halsey is prepared to erect this stubborn persistence in fundamental false assumptions into a methodological principle. In a paper on 'Social Mobility and Education' he argues that egalitarians, among whom he is himself most prominently numbered, should assume, "unless there is proof to the contrary, [that] inequality of outcome in the social distribution of knowledge is a measure of *de facto* inequality of access" (Rubinstein, 1980, pp. 57-8).

In the respectable and rightly respected natural sciences it is as common as it can be proper to work on assumptions which are not known to be true. However, that is very different from resolving to insist upon maintaining assumptions known to be false. The fact that Halsey can proclaim his chosen, obscurantist methodological principle without, apparently, thereby discrediting either himself or his work in the eyes of his colleagues says something about the condition of the social sciences in Britain today; something which is as important as it is alarming (Flew, 1985, especially Ch. 8).

(b) The next task is to distinguish descriptive, would-be factual claims about equalities between individuals or sets from normative claims about the respects in which it is thought that those individuals or sets ought to be treated equally. Here it must suffice firmly to reiterate what has come to be known as Hume's Law (Flew, 1986, Ch. 9). For us now this implies that no proposition purely of the latter sort can either logically presuppose or strictly entail any proposition simply of the former. That granted, we have to distinguish three kinds of normative ideals of human equality.

The paradigm case of the first is provided by the Declaration of Independence. An initial careless glance might suggest that this affirms all to have been endowed at birth with equal potentialities. However, a more careful scrutiny will reveal that Mr Jefferson, not unaware of his own egregious talents, glossed this crucial clause as a claim not of fact but of right: "That they are endowed. . . with certain unalienable rights." In terms of the distinction explained earlier, the three specified are all of the option rather than the welfare sort (p. 15, above). This is the only one of these three ideals of equality which is, arguably, through the equal right to an equal vote, presupposed by 'by the people' democracy.

(c)The second ideal, and the first of the two urgently relevant to contemporary debates about education, has traditionally been defined by reference to a slogan of the great French Revolution of 1789: "The career open to the talents." The idea, the ideal, is that all the competitors arriving at the start line—wherever and whenever the race is to begin—ought at that point to be treated equally. If there has to be an inside track giving some advantage over the rest, then who gets it must be determined by a randomising mechanism, not by any kind of privilege or favouritism. Although it is usually referred to as equality of opportunity, it is less misleadingly thought of as an ideal of fair and open competition for scarce opportunities. Thus, in Article VI of the *Declaration of the Rights of Man and of the Citizen* we read: "The law... should be the same to all... and all being equal in its sight, are equally eligible to all honors, places and employments, *according to their different abilities, without any other distinction than that created by their virtue and talents*" (emphasis added).

It is most important to notice, and never to forget, that in all such competitions some of the competitors are bound to be advantaged, and others correspondingly disadvantaged, by what they are and what they have done or not done, suffered or not suffered, throughout the whole course of their previous lives. For instance, if it is a sporting contest, then some will have been well coached and/or will have trained hard, or, if it is an old-fashioned competitive written examination, for civil service entry or the like, some will have been well taught and/or will have studied hard. Some again will have had an ideal diet from birth, and before; some may have been at some stage damagingly undernourished; and some may have chosen, through overfeeding, to become overweight. And so on, and on and on.

These are several morals which might usefully be drawn here, but on this occasion the one to underline is that what gives or constitutes an advantage in a competition is not therefore and necessarily an unfair advantage. Yet it is only unfair advantages which have to be in some way removed or offset if the organisers are to escape the grave charge of treating competitors unequally. Indeed, anyone committed to equality of opportunity, and hence to competitions as their chosen allocative instrument, becomes thereby and necessarily committed to maintaining that not all actual advantages can be unfair. To illustrate: in my own student days it was in the one-mile track event a massive advantage to be Roger Bannister, but the Oxford University Athletic Club never thought that they needs must, in the fashionable name of fairness, either handicap or exclude him from competitions. (The object of handicapping, it perhaps needs to be remarked, is to secure not fair contests but close-fought and even ones. The handicapper is precisely not treating all contestants equally.)

If once we have understood the nature both of the ideal of equality of opportunity and of fair as opposed to unfair advantage in a competition, we have gained an even better position for understanding why the argument cannot go straight through from set inequalities of outcome to set inequalities of opportunity. Whether or not the conclusion happens in any particular case to be correct, if the argument is to constitute a valid demonstration, then it still has first to be shown that not only the relevant abilities but also the relevant desires and determinations are, in the sets being compared, substantially the same. Murphy makes it abundantly clear not only that in fact this showing is never even attempted but also that the committed egalitarian researchers more or less frankly concede that it cannot be shown, because it is not true (1978, 1981 a, b).

The nerve of the crucial fallacy here consists in a smart step *from* the contention that the chances or the probabilities that this competitor will win are not the same as the chances or the probabilities that that competitor will win *to* the conclusion that, therefore, these two competitors did not both have the same equal chance of success. This conclusion in its turn is then taken to carry the implication that the whole competition is unfair, if not deliberately rigged. However, any such argument, which appears in many more elaborate forms, depends always upon an equivocation. When the conclusion speaks of competitors having an equal chance to win, this is to be construed as saying only that the organisers are running things fairly and openly—treating all competitors equally. Yet the premise refers only to the probabilities or improbabilities of each particular contestant succeeding—and carries no implications that they are being treated either equally or unequally, in either a fairly or an unfairly run competition. If someone just is, for instance, the best sprinter, then the probability that he will win the 100 metres will be, must be, most unequally large. What is unfair about that? In any fair and unfreakish contest the best man has to win. By what other criterion would he be rated as, in this respect, the best?

(d) The third ideal, and the second of the two most relevant to current debates about education, has grown vastly more popular in recent years. The label 'equality of outcome' is apt and self-explanatory, either notwithstanding that or because it was introduced by the uncommitted. (Outright opponents prefer to make some partisan reference to Procrustes!) Few supporters do as yet actually demand either perfect equality of outcome or equality in respect of every sort of outcome. Most of those who start by demanding equality in, for instance, wealth or income are prepared to make some concessions, if usually reluctant and inadequate concessions, to permit a redeeming trade-off against economic efficiency. While they believe (that is, or profess to believe) that ideally everyone ought to have (and perhaps is entitled to have) exactly the same capital and income, nevertheless they are prepared to make grudging allowance for at least some differentials in order to provide some incentives to wealth creation.

Our egalitarians of outcome are also notably shy about applying their paraded principles in every field without restriction or even explaining to which fields they do not properly apply, and why. No one, or almost no one, seems to want to make all members of future generations so equal that they become identical twins, produced by the still to be developed techniques of big-batch human cloning. Yet, again, no one appears eager to offer to explain why, if equality without a prefix or suffix is to be accepted as good in itself, if not the supreme good, big-batch human cloning is not the radical and drastic Republican road to social perfection. Nevertheless, and all these reticences and inhibitions notwithstanding, there is no doubt but that this second most relevant ideal has been overtaking and replacing the first in its appeal to opinion formers (Flew, 1981, Ch. I-IV).

It therefore becomes important to realise that the two are indeed not merely different but incompatible. The crux is that the older ideal refers essentially to the establishment and conduct of competitions. Of their very nature—save in the rule-proving exceptional, unconsummated case where we have a draw or a dead heat—competitions must result in some inequality of outcome as between the several competitors. This is most obvious when the competition also serves as a means of allocating some kind of prizes among them. However, it is equally though less excitingly true where the scarce goods to be allocated are internal to the competition itself. For even where the inequalities of outcome are not compounded by the award of cash or kind prizes external to the competition itself, one or more of the competitors—dead heats and draws always excepted—must nothing more nor less than win, or, failing that, achieve a higher or lower position on some scale of merit. Such internal inequalities are almost bound to matter to the participants, if not much more widely: "Winning isn't everything," one leading American coach used to say, "but losing isn't anything".

An *Alice's Adventures in Wonderland* caucus race in which all participants know from the beginning not only that they will get prizes or placings but also that these prizes or placings will be the same for everyone is nothing but a nonsense, and not truly either a race or a competition. Furthermore, if in some putative contest the actual probabilities of success were ever known to be exactly the same for all participants, then the implication would be not that, for once, we had a truly fair competition—a competition in which at last everyone was being treated with perfect equality—but that the supposed competitors were really engaged in a kind of (possibly illegal) lottery rather than in an (always legitimate) trial of skill. So the older ideal of equality of opportunity necessarily must give rise to precisely that kind of inequality which it is the object of the newer ideal to suppress.

3.3 Excellence and elites, comprehension and selection

When Samuel Brittan expressed the hope that ('by the people') democracy "could yet be saved if contemporary egalitarianism were to lose its hold over the intelligentsia" (quoted p. 75, above), he was thinking primarily of the economy. However, the same unlikely development might also be the salvation of the state education system. Certainly it is necessary to take the measure of that "contemporary egalitarianism" if we are ever fully to understand either why not only 'competition' but 'excellence' and 'elitism' also have for so many in Edbiz become bad words or why the militants of the Comprehensive Revolution have always been, and still remain, resolved to press on regardless of any strictly educational results. (By the way, it is, perhaps deliberately, misleading to put opponents of that egalitarianism down as *in*egalitarians, just as it would be equally wrong to pretend that opponents of classical Utilitarianism must be committed to the promotion of the greatest *un*happiness of the greatest number! What in fact *anti*-egalitarians especially eschew is making any sort of relativity, rather than some absolute, a value.)

(i)   Shortly after Margaret Thatcher was first appointed Secretary of State at the DES she received what must have been an uncongenial lesson on the nature and purposes of our largest teachers' union. For the NUT weekly, *The Teacher*, without actually going so far as to make explicit its own preference for egalitarian mediocrity, nevertheless saw fit to warn her against "those who preach the importance of excellence". She was further instructed not to be tempted by "arguments defending an elite in education" (26 June 1970). Here we need to recall, what was always officially overlooked in the years of the NUT-dominated Schools Council, that this is an industrial rather than a craft union, and that the great majority of its members neither are teaching nor are qualified to teach any hard subjects up to the highest secondary level (Naylor and Marks, 1982).

(a) In the same year the Editorial Introduction to a collection frankly entitled *The Red Papers*, proclaimed a similar doctrine: "Elitist academic education fails because it fosters the values of competition rather than the values of cooperation" (Hemming, 1970, p. 2). Waiving the question whether this Editor was not really pointing to what was in his eyes an unacceptable cost rather than to any strictly educational failure, we have here to insist that to achieve excellence in any sphere must be to become a member of an elite. As such, you are no longer, in whatever is the relevant respect, equal to those who have not yet achieved this particular form of, or perhaps any, excellence. So, if we are going to have any excellence we are going to have sets of persons who, with respect to that sort of excellence, though not necessarily in any other respects, constitute elites.

It is, therefore, no wonder that the Edbiz apostles of "contemporary egalitarianism" condemn 'competition', 'excellence' and 'elites' as very bad words. What ought to amaze us is the effrontery of those who, while thus eschewing excellence, present policies requiring and promoting this rejection as policies for the improvement of state *education*. Any philosopher inclined to join the chorus against excellence should be invited to reconsider an obituary tribute to Wittgenstein: "There are many sorts of human excellence. Not least among them is the excellence of one who devotes his whole life, giving up all else, to the attempt to do one thing supremely well" (Gasking and Jackson, 1951).

(b) Perhaps nowadays there is rather less direct and explicit abuse of excellence. Thus, without actually employing that once-forbidden word, the latest Labour Party statement does contrive to claim that "For socialists, quality and equality go hand in hand"; though only after insisting that acceptably "high educational standards" must always be "not just for the few but for *all* pupils" (p. 3: emphasis original). The hubbub of disclaimers of elitism and denunciations of elitists still, however, continues. Even in universities and other institutions supposedly striving to become centres of excellence we too often hear vice-chancellors and other spokespersons shamefacedly explaining that, while not of course being elitist, they do nevertheless rather feel that some standards of academic quality ought to be maintained, and even perhaps—greatly daring—the better, the better.

Yet before even beginning to discuss any of these accusations and denials, denunciations and apologies we ought to insist upon receiving answers to two questions: 'What is meant by the word "elitism"?' and 'Why is its referent so often repudiated as self-evidently evil?' What is it which makes some forms of selection for quality—boo!—elitist and bad whereas others, like getting a winning sports team by picking the best available players, are perhaps innocuous or even—hooray!—positively admirable?

In default of any better alternative response I propose a meaning which, if my proposal were accepted, would make 'elitism' for me, if not for all who now employ it as an undefined verbal missile, a very bad word indeed. Let us then from this day forward use 'elitism' as a general term for any doctrine or practice which demands or supports government by supposed experts, experts neither responsible to nor ejectable by the governed, experts prescribing what those subjects are, altogether without reference to what they themselves may happen actually to want, to be taken to need. Plato's Guardians—the philosopher-kings of *The Republic*—are the original paradigm case of such an absolute and irresponsible ruling elite; while, as the advocate a system of this kind, Plato himself must be scored correspondingly as the philosophical founding father of all elitism (Flew, 1981, Ch. V; 1983).

In our own time, of course, by far the most important of such elites are the ruling Marxist–Leninist parties, and the most numerous and powerful elitists are members, fellow travellers or other sympathisers of such parties. Suppose, therefore, that we do give a sense of this sort to the words 'elitist' and 'elitism'. Then we have to recognise that a great many of those presently most loud in their denunciations—including some contributors to *Education for Democracy*, *Education and Equality*, *The Red Papers* and their like—will have in honesty either to stop their ranting or else to reconstrue these words as words of praise.

Alternatively, if we are to go on describing and abusing, as elitist, any kind of discrimination and selection for quality, then we all need to recognise what we are doing. We shall—in the name of the strange, new, false god of equality of outcome—be committed to repudiating all standards of excellence in every field of human achievement, and that repudiation is, surely, not so much an educational as an anti-educational idea?

(ii)   Early in Chapter 1 we noticed that the resolution passed by the House of Commons to justify DES Circular 10/65 was as strictly educational as the most purist could wish: it argued, or at any rate asserted, that the Comprehensive Revolution had become essential if more of our children were to reach higher levels of educational attainment (p. 27, above). However, we have also seen reason to believe that many of the most active and articulate promoters of that 'great experiment' have had, also or alternatively, quite different ends in mind, ends which may in practice turn out to be incompatible with that originally professed, strictly educational objective.

By far the most important of these quite different ends is equalisation, either of opportunity or, more radically, of outcome. Oddly, perhaps it is this, and not education, which is the overriding interest of almost everyone working in the sociology of education. Mrs Jean Floud, for instance, the then Principal of Newnham College in the University of Cambridge, entitled a paper 'Making Adults more Equal: the Scope and Limitations of Educational Policy'. It thus appears that for Mrs Floud educational policy or a policy for education had nothing to do with teaching and learning. It just was a policy for enforcing Procrustean ideals of equalisation. "To obtain the maximum equalizing effect," she said, ". . . distribution must be not only independent of, but negatively related to, the distribution of inherited inequalities of fortune, including genetic make-up" (Floud, 1975, p. 50). It is clear that Mrs Floud agreed with a conclusion which she attributed, correctly, to Jencks: ". . . we must see to it that. . . the link between vocational success and living standards is effectively broken" (p. 38).

In his own 'Foreword' to the British edition of *Inequality* Mr Tyrrell Burgess writes: "This book has infuriated a great many people in the U.S. and promises to infuriate people here. It does so by stating the liberal and Radical assumptions about education and then testing them against the evidence. The assumptions are found wanting" (Jencks, 1972, p. 1). Having drawn some of what he sees as the more particular morals for Britain, Burgess continues: "If reformers are not to be permanently frivolous they must be interested in whether their policies are failing. At least Jencks and his colleagues provide a convenient check list. To almost any proposal for education we can now ask 'did it survive the Jencks test. . .?' " (p. 2).

The prime purpose of quoting these two passages is to bring out that the "liberal and radical assumptions about education", and any consequent "proposal for education", have absolutely nothing to do with education, simplemindedly construed as a matter of boys and girls being taught and learning, but it would be mean to continue without commending Burgess for so forcefully grasping the main thesis developed in our Chapter 2. It is also useful to be reminded of that thesis. For, although much of the hostility towards or complacency about findings on the results of the Comprehensive Revolution arises because the parties in dispute are—in the most literal sense—at cross-purposes, there is also plenty resulting from what Burgess perhaps too kindly describes as frivolity.

(a) When that revolution began the actually existing British models were large schools recruiting from what were in fact atypical neighbourhoods; neighbourhoods atypical in as much as the social mix among the parents was either pretty close to the national average or, if skewed at all, skewed upwards. Presumably it was with such models in mind that it was concluded that 15 form-entry comprehensives could match three form-entry grammar schools in producing viable sixth forms. (In fact by 1980 the average size of a comprehensive in England was, at 950 pupils, roughly half this.)

Again, when the revolution began, by far the most popular argument in favour was that it meant the end of the old 11 + examinations, selecting for admission to the maintained grammar schools. Certainly the most vociferous opponents of 'the 11 +' were middle-class parents who feared that their children could not make it (Shaw, 1983, p. 45; and passim). Here the objection was not to all educational selection as such but either, generally, to allegedly irrecoverable rejections at too early an age or else to particular features of the selective mechanisms actually employed. Indeed the existing model comprehensives were commonly and correctly commended for developing complex but flexible structures of streaming and setting in order to ensure that all pupils progressed both as fast as they could and in the directions in which they were individually most inclined to go.

The ideal of reproducing such model comprehensives throughout the whole country could not, for two reasons, be realised. In the first place, it was impossible to finance the massive construction effort required if the entire secondary school population was to be re-accommodated in 15-form intake schools. Even had it been possible it is doubtful whether there would have been much enthusiasm for the task, in view of the mammoth problems of discipline and organisation arising in such far from human size institutions. In the second place, a great many, perhaps most, neighbourhoods in Britain do not contain a social mix which approximates to the national average: there are lots of Spurley Heys and quite a few Parrs Woods (p. 58, above). Combined with the fact that the average secondary school is now only about half the proposed ideal size, this extreme diversity of neighbourhoods has resulted in the current *Crisis in the Sixth Form* (Naylor, 1981).

This crisis, which everyone in Edbiz ought to have foreseen but which for a long time activated only those notorious double-plus ungood crimethinkers the *Black Paper* writers, has of course been brewing up from the very beginning of the Comprehensive Revolution. We have already cited two sets of figures to show how wastefully scarce teaching resources have in consequence been used (pp. 31–2 and 58 above). For much more of the similar see Naylor (1981). Here we need merely to repeat the moral drawn from the earlier citations. It was that, far from providing a grammar school education for all, the Comprehensive Revolution has in fact deprived large numbers of children, and those largely children from working-class homes, both of the peer-group stimulus and of the A-level teaching from which under the old regimen they could have benefited so greatly.

(b) One consideration which seems to weigh heavily with several of the most articulate and enthusiastic supporters of the Comprehensive Revolution is the alleged divisiveness both of the declining grammar/secondary modern system and of the still-flourishing independent schools. This seems to be what motivates Mrs Williams (1981) in her continuing determination to destroy all independents: "The maintained system of education and the economy itself are crippled by this socially segregated system" (p. 158). In a seminal essay on 'Comprehensive Education' in general Crosland (1974) argued on similar lines:

> . . . by selecting for a superior school children who are already well favoured by environment, we are not merely confirming, we are hardening and sharpening, an existing social division. . . I will not argue the point in terms of equality. But I will argue it in terms of a sense of community, of social cohesion, of a nation composed of people who understand each other because they can communicate (p. 204).

Whether this supposed sin of divisiveness will in fact be cured, and how far the possibilities of communication between people from different backgrounds will in fact be increased, by universal compulsory comprehension must remain hard to say for sure until and unless those who feel so strongly reveal what they themselves would be prepared to accept as appropriate measures of their proposed variables. In the meantime the most clarificatory move open to us is to suggest a relevant distinction between two conceptions of the comprehensive school. According to one a school is comprehensive in as much as it caters for all the children from the appropriate cohorts living within its catchment area: this would be better called, traditionally, a neighbourhood school. According to the other, a school is only truly comprehensive in so far as it recruits pupils constituting a fairly representative cross-section of the population as a whole.

Those favouring this second conception are apt to reject performance comparisons between, on the one hand, grammar school cum secondary modern systems and, on the other, others which according to more ordinary usage are all-comprehensive. This they do upon the practically irrelevant ground that some or all of the schools in these latter systems are not by their own preferred criteria truly comprehensive. This seems to be true even of the most sober critic of the Examination Results Research Project (Gray, 1983). By the way, the main finding of this research, indicating the strictly educational superiority of the old system, has since been confirmed by the internal researches of the DES. It was revealed, if only rather secretively in their Statistical Bulletin 13/84 (Naylor and Marks, 1985).

Once given this distinction between two conceptions of what a comprehensive school is, or would be, it becomes obvious both that it is only a system of the second sort which could pretend to offer a complete cure for the social divisiveness which seems so to upset socialist intellectuals and that to operate such a system throughout the whole country would require an unthinkable and perhaps sheerly impossible amount of compulsory bussing. Selective schools, recruiting their pupils from all classes over much wider catchment areas, were in fact much more socially mixed than many, perhaps most, neighbourhood comprehensives. In *Social Class and the Comprehensive School* Dr Julienne Ford (1969), a dissident socialist social scientist, reported what should not have been a very surprising finding:

> The evidence from this sample then suggests that if any type of schooling diminishes the likelihood of class bias in informal social relations within the classroom this is not the comprehensive but the grammar school. . . (p. 103).

She added a plea which she must have realised that her fellow socialists were resolved to ignore:

> Indeed if one firm policy recommendation can be made on the basis of this study it is that the first step towards improvement of secondary education is not a blind pursuance of comprehensive reorganisation but adequate research into the likely effects of such reorganisation. . . (p. 131).

(c) Earlier in the present chapter we saw how in 'The Comprehensive School: Labour's Equality Machine' Dennis Marsden (1971) exulted in threatening "that the narrowly meritocratic emphasis on streaming and academic results. . . will be a temporary phase". Soon "the internal dynamic of reorganisation should begin to assert itself' (p. 77, above). How right he was can be appreciated by noticing that Crosland himself, having at first disclaimed the appeal to any kind of egalitarian ideal, almost immediately discovers that the demolition of divisiveness demands an end to streaming as well as to "a strictly neighbourhood pattern of schools" (we should at least be grateful that Crosland, perhaps recalling his own brilliant academic record, did not also insist upon following the NUT to reject any merely "artificial division between 'pass' and 'fail' "):

> Of course the elimination of separation at 11 + is only a necessary, and not a sufficient, condition of reducing the divisive effect of our school system. We should not much improve matters if selection gave way merely to rigid streaming within a strictly neighbourhood pattern of schools. This would re-create many of the old evils within a comprehensive system (Crosland, 1974, p. 204).

The ideal of rejecting divisiveness thus appears to be transformed into that of imposing equality. So it seems that we now have three conceptions of comprehension: non-selective, neighbourhood; social cross-section; and unstreamed, mixed ability. It might happen, although it is scarcely likely, that one and the same school could satisfy all three of these specifications simultaneously.

About streaming and setting no one, surely, will wish to dispute that this is at least intended to ensure that all pupils develop their several talents to the full? However, such arrangements—in as much as those talents differ and in so far as these arrangements succeed in their intention—must tend to increase inequalities of educational outcome. Mixed ability teaching, on the other hand—in so far as it is not in practice teaching mainly very small groups of like abilities—is presumably intended to promote equalities of educational outcome, through regressions to the mean.

How far in fact it succeeds in attaining this educationally deplorable objective must be for the researchers to tell us. The findings of the HMIs in their 1980 report on *Educational Provision by the ILEA* must have given some satisfaction to the present Procrustean political masters of that high-spending, ultra-politicised organisation:

> Because of lack of challenge many children are allowed to proceed at an unduly slow pace. . . Potential is considerably undervalued and teachers demand too little. . . There are. . . many classes and schools where expectations are too low and where. . . teachers assume that mixed ability classes should be taught at a pace which is right for the pupil of slightly below average ability.

4

Education Vouchers

Parents have one real superiority over the Government or the administrators of [school] endowments. Their faults are mainly the corrigible faults of ignorance, not of apathy or prejudice. They have and feel the greatest interest in doing that which is for the real benefit of their children. They are the representatives of the present, the living and acting energy of a nation, which has ever owed its sure and onward progress more to individual efforts than to public control and direction. They have the wish to arrive at a true conclusion, the data are before them, they must be the judges in the last resort, why should we shrink from making them judges at once? (Sir Robert Lowe, Chancellor of the Exchequer in a Gladstone Cabinet, speaking in 1869.)

[The economic theory of bureaucracy predicts] that the bureau will be interested in some kind of alliance with factor suppliers since factors will enjoy increases in rewards resulting from the sale of their resources to the bureau. . . . Most interesting of all in our context, it is predicted that the bureau will engage in promotional activities favouring its own services. It will be increasingly jealous of rival bureaux or private competitors. It will also urge the need for 'mergers' for 'proper co-ordination' or 'centralization' and ultimately for one exclusive monolithic body. (E. G. West, *Education and the Industrial Revolution*, pp. 98–9.)

This chapter will be comparatively short, both because much which needs to be said already has been said, especially in Chapter 1, and because voucher schemes are merely one kind of possible means for realising the end ideal of an independent education for all. A comprehensive national voucher scheme—comprehensive in the sense of including the parents of all children in at least some of the relevant cohorts—can scarcely become practical politics in Britain until a far higher proportion of existing schools

93

become, in one way or another, like the existing independent schools, management centres. This does not require immediate and total emancipation from the state system. It would be sufficient if most of the tax funds allotted to the education of each pupil—perhaps just all the lion's share presently provided by central government—were somehow to follow pupils directly to the school, and, when a pupil ceased to attend that school, were to be withdrawn at once.

However, in the perspective advocated here even a fully comprehensive national voucher system, with every school completely private and independent, would still be a little less than ideal. No doubt there will always be some (hopefully very small) minority of the poor or otherwise peculiarly unfortunate for whom special tax-funded support will need to be provided, and ought to be. However, it must be ultimately ridiculous to go on raising the necessary funds through general taxation, necessarily establishing at least one bureaucratic apparatus to do this, and then doling these funds out piecemeal to the particular entitled parents (but doing this always in the form of vouchers, later to be converted into cash by the schools receiving them), while again and necessarily employing the same or another bureaucratic apparatus to perform these two further factitious and now-redundant operations.

The simpler, cheaper and in every other way superior alternative would be to leave the money in the pockets of the taxpayers, allowing us to pay our fee cheques direct into the accounts of the particular schools teaching our children. Toughly realistic economists in the USA have a lesson for us all when they insist that from every dollar raised by taxation some substantial commission is extracted, to remain within the Beltway, before the redistributionist state machine returns—say—90 cents to the citizens. (The Beltway is what was at first christened, not very crisply, "the circumferential highway" around the capital city.) Those unwilling to learn from the USA can find a parallel in a saying of Trotsky: "Whenever anyone has something to distribute, he will not forget himself."

4.1 "... like canned spuds in a supermarket"

Soon after Sir Keith Joseph was appointed Secretary of State at the DES, and announced his "philosophical sympathy" for some kind of voucher scheme, the NUT—'predictably', as they would themselves love to say of opponents—rushed into print with a hostile pamphlet. In this they quoted the former Prime Minister Edward Heath: "This is a crackpot scheme by those who think they can sell education with vouchers like canned spuds in a supermarket." The introduction of the word 'canned' here will perhaps arouse suspicions that Heath does not often shop for his own groceries.

A little more to the present point, his distaste for the usual procedures in their distribution presumably began when *Private Eye*, with offensive intent, nicknamed him "The Grocer". It must have been grievously intensified after his own positions, first as Leader of the Conservative Party and later as Prime Minister, were, to his own manifest and unappeasable resentment, usurped by a lady who was herself the daughter of an actual, small-scale, street-corner grocer.

(i) Others may join Heath in thinking the idea of the voucher crackpot. Yet it most certainly is not, as both he and the NUT probably believed, new-fangled. Its first proposer seems to have been the Radical Tom Paine, an active sympathiser with both the American and the great French Revolutions. To today's readers the relevant passage from *The Rights of Man* perhaps sounds quaint. Yet it makes the heart of the matter quite clear. For the state to ensure that some basic service such as schooling is available to all who need it, it is sufficient to ensure that everyone should have the means to buy that service. It is neither necessary nor, he believes, desirable that the service itself should be provided directly by the state, thus becoming (one more) cumbrous and unresponsive state monopoly. Arguing that "A nation under a well-regulated government should permit none to remain uninstructed", Paine (1791) urged the payment ". . . to every poor family . . . of four pounds a year for every child under fourteen years; enjoining the parents of such children to send them to school, to learn reading, writing and common arithmetic. . ." (pp. 267 and 263).

An example to all subsequent proposers of costly reforms, he straightway proceeded both to work out what taxes would be needed to finance this proposal and to indicate administrative means of ensuring that his education allowances would in fact be spent, as intended, on elementary schooling. Fundamentally the same idea—providing tax funds for the private purchase of services which are themselves independently supplied—was revived in John Stuart Mill's (1859) classic essay *On Liberty*. There, in the context of an attack on state monopoly in education as the greatest possible threat to the freedom of the individual (quoted, p. 23, above), Mill wrote:

> Were the duty of enforcing universal education once admitted . . . If the government would make up its mind to require for every child a good education, it might save itself the trouble of providing one. It might leave to parents to obtain the education where and how they pleased, and content itself with helping to pay the school fees of the poorer classes of children, and defraying the entire school expenses of those who have no one else to pay for them (p. 161).

Mill continues, both recognising and rejecting *The Road to Serfdom* (Hayek, 1944):

> If the roads, the railways, the banks, the insurance offices, the great joint stock companies, the universities and the public charities were all of them branches of

the government . . . not all the freedom of the press and popular constitution of the legislature would make this or any other country free otherwise than in name (p. 165).

(ii) It is worth emphasising these Radical and classical liberal antecedents as well as suggesting, incidentally, how mistaken it is to think of Mill himself as a proto-Fabian, or even a premature Benno-Bolshevik (Flew, 1975b). This is worthwhile because the recent revival of the voucher idea began with the publication of Milton Friedman's *Capitalism and Freedom* (1962, pp. 86–98), and in Britain such proposals were promoted first by writers for the Institute of Economic Affairs (IEA). It was Friedman's book which introduced the expression 'education vouchers'. His point was that the allowance should be given not in cash but in the form of a voucher; these, though all having a nominal cash value, would be actually cashable only by the schools to which the parents chose to pay them.

(a) This association with the IEA, often described by the media as a 'right-wing think tank', has—with all those who want to be, and to be recognised as, properly left-thinking, believing and practising readers of the *Guardian* newspaper—been the kiss of death. Worse still, such people, and the journalists who cater for them, often rate Hitler's National Socialist German Workers' Party as 'ultra right-wing'; whereas all Communists, whether Muscovite, Pekinese or other, are to them on the 'left wing'. From there it is easy to go on, foolishly or maliciously, to suggest some affinity between the anti-socialist Freedom Association and the neo-National Socialist National Front, while all the time overlooking every actual similarity between, on the one hand, 'Nazi' or Fascist totalitarianism and, on the other, Communist. (Once, in an especially private and unbuttoned wartime moment, Sir Winston Churchill, who had used every opportunity to learn about such things, exclaimed that Hitler's Germany and Stalin's Russia were "as different as Tweedledum and Tweedledee"!)

(b) As for rejecting the idea of the voucher because it is unacceptably 'right-wing', the situation in the USA is rather different. A relevant referendum initiative in California was put forward in the names of two prominent professing leftists. However, in Britain the only such person to break ranks, albeit temporarily, from the phalanx fighting for a still more total state monopoly has been Professor Halsey. Presumably he glimpsed the truths that, by permitting parental consumer choice, the quality of the services provided by different schools would tend to become both better and more equal. If separate suppliers were competing for custom, then the enormous performance differences which at present appear both to exist and to persist even within the same LEAs (pp. 43–4, above) could scarcely be expected to survive for long.

All that is certain, however, is that Halsey's conversion occurred on the road not to Damascus but Carlisle, and was duly reported in the national press on the following day (8 January 1981). This conversion seems, also, to have been neither thorough nor lasting. Again one can only speculate that his own Clause IV socialist commitment to total state monopoly of "all the means of production, distribution, and exchange", and his reluctance to be put down as 'right-wing', won out over any desires for actual equality either of opportunity or outcome.

Having, characteristically, sought advice only from Professors Halsey, Dennison and their like, and having therefore made much of the powerlessness of the poor, the Archbishop of Canterbury's Commission on the Problems of the Inner Cities went on not so much as to mention education vouchers or any other means of exit from often wretched, neighbourhood schools. (See the 1986 Report *Faith in the City*, and compare Flew, 1986b.) Obviously these Commissioners had never heard of Cardinal Bourne, who in the 1920s advocated vouchers as a means of ensuring that even the poorest Roman Catholic parents would be empowered to send their children to Roman Catholic Schools.

Had the Commissioners been willing to seek advice and information from a rather wider range of sources or to consider any but socialist policies, they might, for instance, have learnt from the USA of the reasons why many desperate, usually Protestant, black parents struggle to get their children out of blackboard jungles within the public system and into usually Roman Catholic private schools, and why the Congress of Racial Equality (CORE), listening to those poor parents rather than to the 'liberals' who pretend to speak for them, has adopted education vouchers as a main plank in its political platform. Commissioners more enquiring and less politically blinkered might even have noticed, almost in their own backyard, a new independent school established in 1981 by the Seventh Day Adventist Church. John Loughborough is three times oversubscribed, by mainly West Indian parents, notwithstanding that many find it hard to pay even the church-subsidised fees of £600 a year. How much how many powerless parents would love to have the power of the voucher in their purses! (As much, no doubt, as all those enjoying power and position in the bureaucratic–educational complex, and all the socialist spokespersons thereof, want their subjects to remain powerless.)

(iii) It is curious that Heath and the NUT should have hoped to dismiss all such proposals by comparing the workings of an established state monopoly education system with the ways in which groceries are now marketed (at least in peacetime, and within non-socialist economies). For it was through detailed comparisons between precisely these two alternatives that E. G. West (1970) developed the first book-length case for the voucher (pp. 13–14, 22–5, 62–4, 182–3, 216–17, and passim). Since the enormous advantages of the grocers' (but not The Grocer's) alternative become obvious the moment we begin to think such a comparison through, we have here yet another occasion for reflecting how few people have a moment to spare for thought. (Bertrand Russell once remarked, in mordant mischief: "Many people would sooner die than think. In fact they do.")

These obvious advantages are, of course, only advantages for the customers and for the efficient suppliers; an observation which can tell us a lot about the opposition of such pillars of the bureaucratic–educational establishment as the DES and the NUT. Nevertheless it is not easy to make even those enormous advantages obvious to those who have been trained, or who have trained themselves, into an incapacity to appreciate the nature, workings and possible merits of competitive markets, a category of persons which apparently embraces not only the interested personnel of all the public bureaucracies but also most of our professing social scientists (Marsland, 1987).

The supply of food is, surely, even more important than the supply of teaching services, for unless our children are adequately protected against starvation they will not survive long enough for anyone to need to worry about protecting them against ignorance. Yet, however fiercely it might be fretted with anxieties that all our children should be provided with a national core diet (and that too a diet which would enable them in future years to meet the requirements of future employers), it is hard to imagine that any government subject to the discipline of free elections would even entertain the possibility of introducing measures—enormously expensive measures, necessarily requiring massive increases in general taxation—in order to provide all such children's food 'free' at the point of supply, or at the point of consumption, either in shops, or (eventually no doubt) in messes, all established and managed by Local Food Monopolies (LFMs). Had Edward Heath ever been so imprudent as to let slip that he was contemplating such a truly crackpot proposal, then Thatcherite 'resistants of the first hour' would have been able to get shot of his leadership much sooner than we did.

Had an oppressive system of LFMs somehow been allowed to grow up, then it is at least as difficult to imagine that most people would accept it unquestioningly. It becomes still harder if we further suppose that the system has developed to the stage where all children are allocated to whichever of the LFM's shops or restaurants the LFM bureaucracy shall in its always greater than parental wisdom—'for administrative reasons' and 'to ensure the economical employment of grocery and messing resources'—decide to be most suitable.

Usually with education this in fact turns out to be the establishment happening to be nearest to the children's homes. Nevertheless we do have in our imaginings to accommodate some ideological calls for all grocery shops or messes to be truly comprehensive. This means that we have to allow for proposals that some, perhaps most, children should be compulsorily bussed off, at the socialist politicians' pleasure, to feed always somewhere else, and that a long way from home. These proposals would, of course, be designed either to secure a properly undivisive social mix in every LFM mess or to spare the catering workers in any such establishment from suffering a 'creaming off' of the heartiest and least fastidious eaters.

It would be possible to continue almost indefinitely having instructive fun with such imaginative comparisons. Yet is is sufficient to add only, as the last twist of the knife, that parents desiring to alter the distribution centre or mess allocation decided by the LFM bureaucracy are not to be allowed recourse to some tribunal altogether independent of that same LFM, although they may try their luck with elected representatives either on the Local Food Committee or in the House of Commons. When F. E. Smith, the future Lord Birkenhead, defended some peculiarly preposterous proposal *Punch* published verses concluding with the command: "Chuck it Smith!" Someone should now produce a parody concluding: "Chuck it, Heath!"

4.2 Bureaucratic power or market power?

In December 1986 the Hillgate Group issued *Whose Schools?* (Cox, 1986), urging that immediate steps be taken to realise the ideal advocated in Chapter 1, above: "An independent education for all." Regular readers of *New Society* will not have been surprised to find that journal editorialising against proposals to break an established state monopoly, especially when these came from what they could, and naturally would, put down as "a right-wing group".

What might to some be more surprising is the ineptitude of their development of a (small 'c') conservative case. Almost every preface to any work issued by the IEA urges us, in considering alternative political and economic policies, to insist upon making only the appropriate comparisons: we must not allow ourselves to be seduced into comparing the alleged failures of actual markets with the promised successes of ideal governments. However, the Editors of *New Society* are so audacious, or so incompetent, as to attempt to defend the existing state monopoloy system against market alternatives by blandly and blindly assuming that state control could not and would not produce or tolerate exactly what in fact it has produced and does tolerate. Their editorial, 'Revamping the School System', therefore concludes:

> The government has a duty, especially when a proper education for the young is being touted as essential for our national survival, to make sure that children's education does not depend on their parents' ability to make the right choice (2 January 1987).

(i) *Whose Schools?* had, of course, deployed evidence, of the kind
already provided in greater abundance above: evidence showing how very
far it is from being the case that all the children for whom the state system
provides are actually getting an equally good and "proper education" and
reminding us that, under that existing system, many children are now con-
scripted into, and helplessly trapped inside, what their Directors of Education, if not all their parents must know to be sump schools (p. 16,
above).

The almost incredible ineptitude of the Editorial response in *New Society*
is bound to suggest that judgement may be being distorted either by interest
or by ideology. Certainly a glance at the advertisements, on the backs of
which these journalists are writing, will reveal that all the appointments on
offer are in the public sector. However, such systematic failures either to
appreciate the merits or to understand the workings of markets are, more
probably, the results of a trained incapacity; a product of the notorious
Sociological Bias against Business and Freedom (Marsland, 1987).

Anyone who had ever seriously thought about competition and
markets—with a view, before either approving or disapproving, to first
understanding— would surely have realised long since that we do not before
enjoying their benefits have to wait upon the arrival of the Greek Kalends, a
future which will never come, when all participants are at last both fully
informed and acutely aware of every difference in either quality or price.
Instead the truth is that, just as soon as some customers are perceived even
to threaten to take their business elsewhere, the present supplier starts to
feel the pressure; while all alternative, competing suppliers, once they
become aware of these threats, begin to feel a pull.

All of us all the time profit from the price- and quality-conscious shopping of people we never meet, whose care to serve themselves has as one
unintended consequence benefits to others. Especially at weekends, every
North American local newspaper includes pages of nothing but boring lists
of the asking prices of groceries and other items available in various competing stores. Presumably some careful people, buying for their families,
and all the 'little old ladies in tennis shoes'—some strictly other people, that
is—study these advertisements. They then proceed by their own purchases
and not purchases to make it worthwhile for all stores to cut cents off their
prices whenever they can. All the customers, therefore, benefit from the
more careful shopping of what may well be only a small minority.

Suppose next that we now apply this insight to the case of some sump
school—the sort which the local Director of Education knows to be poor,
and into which he therefore takes care not to conscript the children of the
potentially troublemaking middle classes. Suppose, too, both that the
parents in this William Tyndale have the new legal right to withdraw their
children, taking them to some other institution perceived as superior, and

that every such withdrawal is immediately followed by a substantial transfer of funds to that preferred alternative. Then it must, surely, be obvious that it will not be necessary for a majority or even for a large minority, much less for all the parents to exercise that right of exit in order to ensure that the heat is on for both the teaching staff and for anyone else with any effective responsibility for that William Tyndale?

Suppose now, what must be in the last degree unlikely, that none of these teachers and administrators take any effective steps to mend their ways. Then there is still no reason to think that any of the children whose parents have not bothered to remove them will be any worse off than they were before.

To this the usual response from the most shameless and sanctimonious defenders of the established monopoly is to insist that no one (else) should be allowed to do better for their own children until and unless all the rest are able to benefit equally. One of my most vivid memories from recent years is of seeing Thomas Sowell in debate convert a huge, mainly student and—because viscerally leftist—previously hostile audience with one single outburst of controlled fury: "Let my people go!" His Pharaonic and Procrustean opponents, who themselves all lived in prosperous suburbs, could not, of course, be expected to sacrifice their own children to Procrustean parental principles: "No," Sowell commented, "only other people's!"

(ii) When my wife—who teaches in a centre-city, multi-racial, and very definitely neither middle-class nor rural primary school—saw *Power to the Parents* as one on my list of possible titles for the present book she shuddered. Even without her richness of confrontational experience, I too should have shuddered at the thought which had then leapt to her mind. For she was picturing a school run by a committee elected by and from the parents of all the pupils presently enrolled at Reading St Johns. However, this picture is as inappropriate as, to anyone knowing that school, it must be frightening. Neither schools nor food shops are or ought to be run by committees elected by and from their customers. Those who urge that educational services should be provided, if not exactly like, then at any rate much more "like canned spuds in a supermarket", are not suggesting a reorganisation upon such 'co-op' or (in the original small 's' sense) soviet lines.

There are enormous and vital differences between, on the one hand, the political power given by the right to vote in elections to membership in controlling committees and, on the other, the economic power of withdrawing your custom from one supplier and transferring it to another. (The differences of both from the power conferred by election or appointment to membership of such committees are, of course, still greater.)

(a) In the present context the first thing to notice is that you can have the 'political' without the 'economic'. Thus, at the national level, you may have the legal right, and even the practical possibility of emigration, without an effective right to vote, or the other way about. Then, with regard to schools, you might have the right to vote to membership of the Governing Body without having the right, much less any practical possibility, of taking your children elsewhere; or, again, the other way about.

Certainly it is impossible to exaggerate the importance, at the national level, of regular and contestable elections; of the permanent possibility of in due course 'voting the scoundrels out'. Yet the political power conferred by a right to vote constitutes in many cases an extremely unsatisfactory substitute for the economic power provided by a right of exit and transfer. There is no doubt but that the educational case is one of those many. For a start, without that right of exit and transfer, all those finding themselves in the minority on any issue which matters greatly to them are irretrievably trapped, whereas, with it, minorities can be catered for in one set of institutions and majorities in another. (Whyever not? Why has everyone got to have black, just because black is what either Henry Ford alone or even a majority of purchasers prefer?)

(b) There is in markets nothing strictly analogous to the phenomenon of being outvoted; or exercising your vote yet having absolutely nothing to show for it. Because in most cases people have different amounts to spend, whereas in paradigmatically democratic elections everyone has one and only one vote, it is often assumed that the democratic political process must be inherently more egalitarian than the operation of markets. This is, however, by no means completely or straightforwardly correct.

It is simply not true to say that in contested elections every vote cast carries equal weight. Even under the fairest and most truly representative of electoral systems there must always be those who are outvoted, and whose votes are therefore ineffective; while, with the grossly unfair and unrepresentative first-past-the-post system used in Britain, it is notorious that votes for candidates of minor parties are usually in terms of seats won worth only a small fraction of votes for their major party competition.

By contrast, every customer paying the same sum for any product is by that token of precisely equal importance to the supplier. In National Socialist Germany the racist—and, in particular, obscenely antisemitic— weekly *Der Sturmer* used in odious cartoons to make much of the rational indifference of both businesses and churches to the race of, respectively, their customers and their contributors. No doubt much the same is, with appropriate alterations, true in South Africa today: a point on which the protagonists of divestment ought to reflect, but in fact will not.

(c) In the present context, to say that one person is exercising power over another is to say that the first person is getting the second to do or to undergo something which the first wants the second to do or to undergo, but which the second would not himself or herself independently wish to do or to undergo; while to say that the first person possesses power, but is not exercising it, is to say that he or she could exercise it if he or she chose (Flew, 1985, pp. 78–9, 87–8 and 90–92). Any such definition is bound to carry the perhaps somewhat paradoxical consequence that both electors and consumers can be exercising power when they are not themselves aware of this, provided only that their representatives or their suppliers are then doing or refraining from doing something, which they would not do or refrain from doing, were it not for perceived threats emanating from those electors or consumers. However, this paradox is, surely, no more unacceptable than that of saying that he is the Dictator although he is at present not dictating but fast asleep?

There is in some circles much talk of firms possessing market power because they are believed to *control* such and such a percentage share of the total market. However, to the extent that any market is competitive and not cartelised, such talk is altogether misleading and inept. For when, as in any such uncartelised market, the elements composing all the various shares are re-won or re-lost every time any individual token of the particular product type is bought and sold, no one truly *controls* any particular percentage share.

Actual market power, the sort properly possessed by consumers over against those wanting to become or to remain their suppliers, is not, typically, of the direct, face-to-face and (to many) always grating and obnoxious kind exercised by office-holders. Typically, that is, dissatisfied consumers choosing to shift their business to alternative suppliers have no need either to justify themselves to anyone else in what might be personally disagreeable confrontations or to struggle to get their own way by time-consuming lobbying and politicking or even to risk giving personal offence to their previous unsatisfactory suppliers. All these things, for all but nature's bullies and busybodies, must rate among the merits of market over against political alternatives.

By far the greatest attraction, however, both of independent education in general and of voucher schemes in particular, is that the whole point of producing educational services now becomes service to the consumers who are now no longer, as always under socialist or any other sort of monopoly production, suppliants to their suppliers. Two never-too-often quoted passages from *The Wealth of Nations* are as relevant to the production and distribution of educational services as to the production and distribution of food or of anything else.

The first of these passages refers to "the mercantile system". To this perhaps the closest contemporary analogy is the phenomenon indicated by Dennis O'Keeffe: "Like so much else in the British economy, our education system is treated by its workforce as fundamentally a source not of *produc-*

tion but of *employment*" (quoted p. 41, above). It is perhaps significant that O'Keeffe himself has for some time been engaged in a study of truancy— a form of rebellion against the compulsory consumption of education services. Smith (1776) wrote:

> Consumption is the sole end and purpose of all production; and the interest of the producer ought to be attended to, only so far as it may be necessary for promoting that of the consumer. The maxim is so perfectly self-evident, that it would be absurd to attempt to prove it. But in the mercantile system, the interest of the consumer is almost constantly sacrificed to that of the producer; and it seems to consider production, and not consumption as the ultimate end and object of all industry and commerce (IV(viii)49, p. 660).

Fully to appreciate the second Smith passage we need first to have savoured a repellently representative anti-voucher statement from a state school headmaster. This head was, unsurprisingly, also an officer in the NUT:

> We see this as a barrier between us and the parent—this sticky little piece of paper in their hands— coming in and under duress—you will do this or else. We make our judgement because we believe it's in the best interests of every Willie and every little Johnny that we've got— and not because someone's going to say 'if you don't do it, we will do that'. It's this sort of philosophy of the marketplace that we reject (quoted M. and R. Freidman, 1980, pp. 173–4; and compare 'Wants or Needs: Choice or Command?', in Flew, 1981, Ch. V).

Smith shows us that such suppliers of educational services as this headmaster want parents to continue to be, relative to himself and his colleagues, in the helpless and degrading situation of beggars. Worse still, he wants us to be like beggars before their begging has conjured any currency into their hands. Whether sticky or not, coins, cheques and banknotes are the conventionally recognised instruments of purchasing power.

> It is not from the benevolence of the butcher, the brewer or the baker, that we expect our dinner, but from their regard to their own interest. We address ourselves, not to their humanity but to their self-love, and never talk to them of our own necessities but of their advantages. Nobody but a beggar chuses to depend chiefly upon the benevolence of his fellow-citizens. Even a beggar does not depend upon it entirely. The charity of well-disposed people, indeed, supplies him with the whole fund of his subsistence. But ... The greater part of his occasional wants are supplied in the same manner as those of other people, by treaty, by barter, and by purchase (Smith, 1776, I(ii)2, p. 27).

4.3 The objects and the objections of officials

There was in Chapter 1 occasion to describe the origins of a DES document entitled simply *Education Vouchers* (pp. 22–3, above), the document which unfriendly critics later nicknamed *No, Minister* (NM). It is remarkable, and a depressing indication of the quality of the advice given by civil servants to the political chiefs in that department, that the presumably plural authors seemed never to have heard of the idea before the arrival of Sir Keith Joseph. Even then they refused to refer to any non-official sources. Rather than go to the trouble of consulting any of the accessible and abundant unofficial literature, they preferred to speculate upon the reasons which supporters conceivably might offer. Providing no definition even of the title expression 'education voucher' they naturally saw no need to indicate the possibilities of such alternative means of approaching the same ends as education tax allowances or education tax credits.

For these DES officials the object of the exercise seems to have been to abort the idea, overwhelming any approach to those emancipatory ends with objections rather than to use their skills to help solve the no doubt formidable administrative problems. In Chapter 2 we quoted Mrs Williams reporting her observations of a developing commitment to the Comprehensive Revolution in the DES (p. 63, above). Some years earlier the Viscount Eccles had from the opposition benches of the House of Lords expressed his own similar observations as a warning: "You cannot trust that great department any longer. . . . It is a very sad thing for an ex-Minister to say. But you cannot trust that department not to be biased" (7 October 1976).

Already in the nineteenth century the predecessors of today's DES were, as West (1970, 1975) again and again shows, serving up the statistics in ways calculated to encourage the expansion of the state sector, and hence of their bureau. However, both the evident bias of NM and the fact that it consists of little more than a list of all the objections which its authors could think of are reasons why we need to devote some attention to it here. The further evidence of bias reinforces previous warnings. The objections are a challenge.

(i) The authors offer four conjectures as to what might "be in the proponents' minds". The first two objectives thus distinguished are really one that "vouchers might be a means of increasing parental choice"; while the third is that "vouchers might be a means of making schools more accountable to parents". Fourth comes the suggestion that advocates of the voucher might think that "the increase of choice and accountability should tend to raise educational standards" (NM 3).

(a) Certainly this first DES conjecture is, like the other two, correct. Equally certainly, if either God or Man gives any person a choice, then there can be no irrefragable guarantee that that choice will be made as someone else would have preferred to see it made. Nevertheless we do in fact have good reason to believe that, in the real world of Britain today and tomorrow, parental choice and parental power would make for a general and substantial rise in levels of educational achievement. The contemporary onslaught on such achievement, and especially upon the independent assessment of standards actually achieved, manifestly does not come from parents qua parents. Instead it comes, and it is coming all the time, from many and various individuals and collectivists within the bureaucratic-educational complex itself. It comes, as we have already had many occasions to notice, from professing educationists, with the ear and in the eye of the media; from institutes, colleges and departments of education; from the now very socialist and politicised leadership of the NUT; from Procrustean intellectuals, longing to enforce a universal quality of outcome; and from all their like, if any.

Sensible parents, and perhaps most particularly sensible working-class parents, want their children to be taught, above all, what will qualify them for good jobs. Hence they also want the learning achievements of those children to be independently certificated by organisations which potential employers trust—neither by CSE Mode III, that is, nor by pupil profiles, save in so far as the claims made about and in these can be and are verified by parallel performances in independently assessed public examinations. Without the possibility and the actuality of such cross-checks both Mode III examinations and pupil profiles become devices for giving teachers the last word on the thoroughness and effectiveness of their own work.

(b) Far more interesting than any of the four conjectures actually offered by the DES authors is the fifth; which is not. For it appears, and surely significantly, never to have crossed the authors' minds that anyone would or could believe that the introduction of consumer choice and competition between suppliers might yield better value for money.

Earlier chapters have given several examples of similar resource inputs apparently yielding very different amounts of EVA. Since a voucher scheme, like a scheme for tax allowances or tax credits, should and presumably would include the private sector, it is time for a few public/private comparisons. There is indeed some positive evidence to suggest that—in education as well as in rubbish disposal and other municipal matters—we pay dearer for direct labour, and that a drive for privatisation would better serve the public. Partly because the private sector in education is small, and partly because so many of the schools in that sector are boarding schools, more of this comparative evidence comes from the USA than from the UK. In California this evidence constitutes conspicuous confirmation of Friedman's Law: "Everything government does costs double." For there, annual costs per pupil head in the state's public schools are over $3,000, comparing with less than $1,500 in the private; while in these independent schools the otherwise most disadvantaged children achieve markedly better academic results than their opposite numbers in California's maintained schools (West, 1981, Ch. 3).

In seeking such comparative data for Britain we have first to discount all those oft-quoted fee figures which include boarding costs. On the state side we start with the recoupments which LEAs charge each other for servicing pupils from outside their own boundaries. These are national, based on national averages, annually updated, but all need to be increased by roughly 20 per cent to cover debt charges on capital expenditure, national and local administration of (but from outside) the schools, and so on. For 1982/3 the recoupments were: £778 per year in primary school; £1,026 for 11–16-year-olds; and £1,606 for sixth formers.

If we compare the figures resulting, after making the appropriate 20 per cent addition, with the fees charged in that year by the independent Fox-bush School in Kent, we see that voucher holders wishing to go independent will not need to top up by a lot, if anything. Foxbush is a day school for boys, owned and run by a consortium of teachers, accepting all comers without selection, and apparently enjoying a good reputation. I have Mrs Marjorie Seldon to thank for its 1982/3 fee schedule: £1,035 per year for juniors (8–11); £1,350 for the middle school (11–16); and £1,395 for the sixth form.

(ii) Already in Chapter 1 we had to note the complacent effrontery of the authors' professed concern lest a voucher system should fail either to pre-serve an adequate core curriculum or to meet the needs of employers (pp. 23ff., above). In order totally to discredit these professions it is here suf-ficient to reiterate two devastating charges against the status quo which the DES officials were thus labouring to defend. First, in general, there are still no independently assessed examinations for that 'bottom 40 per cent' for which neither GCE/CSE nor GCSE is intended to cater. Second, in par-ticular, there are still no tests designed to ensure both that everyone leaves school at least minimally literate and numerate and that we know how well the state system is succeeding in securing or failing to secure these objectives.

Lacking still any such comprehensive systems of actual testing, perhaps the best thing we have to go on is *Literacy and Numeracy: Evidence from the National Child Development Study* (London: Basic Skills Unit, 1983). In the present perspective the most remarkable features of this available evidence are that it comes from a sample survey and that the members of that sample were not actually given any tests. They were simply asked whether they were themselves aware of any handicaps and, if so, how severe and in what directions. There is nothing essentially wrong with such investigations: sample surveys are a thrifty means of forming a rough estimate of distributions within the whole population, while, if you do want to know how people feel, it certainly is at least a good start to ask them to tell you. However, none of this is any way to find out precisely who the actual adult illiterates and inumerates are, what schools they came from and how the system might be so improved as to ensure that far fewer members of later cohorts are allowed to go out into the adult world so handicapped.

Equally remarkable is the fact that these facts were not underlined, nor was this moral taken, in the reports by the education correspondents or in the leading articles of the general press. Those in *The Times* (22 July 1983) were on this occasion typical. Under the headline "At least 2*m*. illiterate adults in Britain, official report says," Lucy Hodges, the Education Correspondent, gave a very straight account: "This estimate of the state of adult illiteracy . . . confirms earlier figures which were based on guesswork"; and, "Referring to a recent Gallup study on adult numeracy, which found young adults to be the most able group, the report says that in the adult population a large numeracy problem must be even more common."

Neither in that report, nor in the leading article to which it concludes by referring, is there any suggestion that there should be standardised tests in the schools, tests which could simultaneously constitute both an annual census, showing what exactly the present situation is, and an annual challenge, an incentive to do better next year.

(iii) In detailing perceived difficulties in operating a voucher scheme the DES authors oddly insist upon treating legal obstacles as if these were on all-fours with physical. It appears that to the Mandarins all the rules and regulations currently governing the workings of the bureaucratic–educational complex are like the laws of the Medes and Persians. They cannot be changed. However, if all substantial alterations in whatever is at present established are to be ruled out as apriori unthinkable, then what, for Heaven's sake, is the point of having high-priced public employees wasting their time and our money writing memoranda about major policy proposals, proposals which precisely because they would involve a major change of course, it is thus predetermined never can and never shall be implemented?

(a) The same authors adopt a similarly inertial approach towards the perceived physical obstacles. They seem to think it both relevant and sufficient to point out that any voucher scheme which is to make any real difference must demand substantial and disturbing adaptation from most of those involved. Well, fancy that! Precisely what proponents have been saying again and again in all those works, none of which the DES officials deigned to consult, is that the education voucher is a very simple device, which both could and should be used to bring about extremely extensive yet correspondingly salutary changes. Furthermore, the adaptations required are all and only of the kind which greengrocers, publishers, appliance manufacturers, professional partnerships and other more humble suppliers of goods and services have to make, and usually succeed in making, in order to meet the sometimes unpredictably changing demands of a paying and freely choosing public.

Certainly there are several regulations and even some laws which will need to be either amended or repealed if a voucher system is to be launched, but if this is an objection to such a scheme then it must be an objection equally to any and every other major innovation. Certainly, too, as in any market situation, changes in demand not merely could but will "create difficult management and organisational problems". So what are heads and other managers for, if it is not to solve sometimes tricky management and organisational problems?

As an example of the inertial approach favoured by these DES authors, consider their treatment of "the obstacles now in the way of maintaining or creating . . . spare capacity in the right places and at the level demanded" (NM 8). "The ebb and flow of children at will," they go on to observe, "could create diffiuclt management and organisational problems for schools, at least in the short term" (NM 8 (iii)). For these Mandarins sometimes laughingly described as 'public servants', the final horror is, of course, that "a voucher system could lead to a situation in which parental choices and decisions determined the character of the maintained school system" (NM 10).

The difficulty of such problems for the schools is in any case being exaggerated. Although the DES writers do recognise the possibility of moving in mobile classrooms, it is only to dismiss this as cabined and constrained by present Regulations (NM 8 (ii)). It appears, however, that they have neither heard nor thought of the possibility of employing the same plant for two shifts, which has for years been successfully done by such perennially popular schools at Stuyvesant High in the Lower East Side of the Borough of Manhattan. (Perhaps I may be permitted parenthetically to cite my own experience of an independent school evacuated from Bath to Uppingham in 1939, sharing all the buildings and grounds of another such school until 1945. This experience, as far as it went, completely confirmed all the main findings of Michael Rutter (1979) and his team.)

(b) *Education vouchers* makes no distinction between the difficulties to be expected in first introducing a scheme and those of operating such a scheme once it had become accepted and established. The authors are, if anything, inclined to underestimate the former mainly because they are reluctant to recognise the present extent of parental dissatisfaction. They are also inclined to overestimate the latter, this time because of a refusal to appreciate the dynamics of a competitive, market situation.

The DES, as we have already had several occasions to notice, appears to be encased in a quite breathtakingly insolent complacency. Our authors obviously consider the present condition of the maintained system to be in general so sound and so satisfactory that any extensive or fundamental change could scarcely fail to be a change for the worse. This is, in truth, inconsistent with admissions which, however tacitly, they are, by the exigencies of their polemic, elsewhere constrained to make. They refer at one point to "experience in the present independent school market, with its very wide range of educational standards" (NM 6). However, later— without, it seems, noticing the implications—they speak both of some maintained schools "which already have as many as three applicants for each available place" (NM 8 (iii)) and of others which, if conscripts were no longer available to fill the rolls, would be "contracting . . . creating a spiral of falling standards and further enforced contractions" (NM 11).

Any voucher system is thus expected to show up more so-far unidentified William Tyndales. These are taken at one and the same time to be both so numerous that the difficulties of their reform or liquidation would wreck any such scheme and so exceptional as to constitute no serious blemish upon the system over which the DES presides. Partly because the education bureaucracy is so well aware of the near impossibility of reforming such institutions, in present conditions and from the outside, our authors persist in neglecting the promise that market pressures would, by concentrating the minds of those running such sump schools, encourage an irresistable internal drive to improve.

With their customary ineffable and incoherent complacency, these same authors ask: ". . . would the greater adaptability of the schools be compatible with efficient staffing, with present methods of supplying and training teachers and with government oversight over teacher supply and training?" (NM 12). Who would think from this that for years now supposedly trained teachers have been pouring into our schools without so much as a paltry GCE O-level pass in Mathematics, or its equivalent?

We have left till last that haunting fear of "a situation in which parental choices and decisions determined the character of the maintained school system". What can the voucher person say, save that precisely this is what we intend? Maybe, greatly daring, someone will later make so bold as to challenge these Guardians with the most fundamental political question: 'What is the maintained system being maintained for, if it is not to supply the educational wants of the piper-paying British people; and, first of all, of the parents?' Also, if the voters can decide, then why not the parents, who are, after all, often the same people (Flew, 1981, Ch. V; 1983)?

It is, of course, a reasonable fear that it would become 'politically impossible' to persuade parent voters to surrender voucher rights had they ever enjoyed such rights for even a 'trial' period, which accounts for much of the desperate ferocity of the opposition to all voucher proposals. Whereas the present small but excellent Assisted Places scheme will certainly be abolished within hours of the entry of any Labour or Alliance minister into Elizabeth House, any big move towards a voucher scheme must create vested interests which it would be electoral suicide to challenge. After all, whereas it is one thing to talk about irresponsible and ill-informed working-class parents when you are speaking as one socialist intellectual to another, or one Whitehall Mandarin to another, it is quite another matter to say anything of the such out on the doorstep, while canvassing for the votes of the people whom privately you despise!

(c) We must, finally, return to the disquieting significance of the fact that it was permanent senior officials in the DES who presented the Secretary of State with this disgraceful document. It is, as we have indicated, unresearched rather than ill-researched, stuffily complacent, and—worst of all—grossly biased towards those supply-side interest groups among which both the local and the national bureaucracies must themselves be numbered. In an article on 'The Missing Bottom Line' the educational economist Gareth Williams emphasises the difficulties of "separating the expert knowledge of any group of specialists from the special interests of that group" (Moodie, 1986, p. 35). If he ever writes a textbook he could do worse than reprint *Education Vouchers* as exercise material.

Along with all its other faults, both of omission and of commission, it confidently urges one argument which we might have hoped to see mentioned perhaps, but never used, in what pretends to be a non-partisan paper. "How could one justify a situation," these DES authors ask, "in which a voucher did less to satisfy some parents than others?" (NM 9).

Certainly parents living in areas so thinly populated as to be served by only one single school could gain no direct benefit from the introduction of a voucher scheme, but then they would suffer no disadvantage either. So the stringent but generous Italian conditions of Pareto optimality are satisfied. However, these DES authors go overboard for an entirely different principle: a mean, malign, dog-in-the-manger principle; a principle characteristic of, and one would hope peculiar to, British socialism at its worst. This is the principle that no one is to enjoy any good unless everyone can and does enjoy that same good and in that same way.

After that nasty Procrustean thrust I am quite surprised that no one at the DES thought to bring the fashionably mindless accusation of 'queue-crashing' against those who, by making private provision, remove their children from any queues for maintained schools. Instead, the best, or the worst, that they could do was maliciously to misdescribe vouchers as "little more than a straight subsidy for parents currently using the independent system" (NM 5). Yet by what twisted, socialist thought processes can we describe as a subsidy a measure which spares some from paying twice: once through taxation and then again independently? Could these supposedly neutral public servants not try just a little harder to make their private political commitments less grindingly obtrusive?

5

Three Concepts of Racism

I want to be a man on the same basis and level as any white citizen—I want to be as free as the whitest citizen. I want to exercise, and in full, the same rights as the white American. I want to be eligible for employment exclusively on the basis of my skills and employability, and for housing solely on my capacity to pay. I want to have the same privileges, the same treatment in public places as every other person. (Dr Ralph Bunche (the first black American to serve as, among many other things, US permanent representative at the UN).)

... all the time I was writing *Black Britain*, I found not solace, comfort or tolerance, but tension, a disturbing desire to break, smash, riot, to bellow; "Whitey! one day you'll have to pay!" (Chris Mullard: Preface to *Black Britain*.)

Starting in the early 1970s the National Union of Students (NUS) adopted the policy of 'No platform for fascists and racists': anyone whom the NUS ruled to fall under this ban was by all means to be prevented from getting a hearing inside any institution of tertiary education. Now it may well be argued that those who will refuse to reciprocate cannot claim toleration as a right, although we may still decide to grant it out of charity or prudence. (It was in fact fears, which were in his day well grounded, that Roman Catholics would refuse to reciprocate which led John Locke to support similar restrictions.) However, this justification is not available to the NUS, which has apparently never even considered extending the scope of its 'No platform' policies to include Leninists. Certainly since World War II these have always been far more numerous and far more influential in Britain than those who could with any plausibility be described as Fascists. The Leninists themselves, however, have been among the most energetic supporters of such 'No platform' policies, both in the NUS and elsewhere.

In the absence of any definition explaining what racism is, and why it is wrong, the cry of 'Racist!' has become a ready means of silencing any opponent perceived as too formidable to be overcome in fair and honest

112

intellectual combat. At first the main academic targets were psychologists such as Arthur Jensen in the USA and H. J. Eysenck in the UK. Their offence was to have published evidence that there may be genetically determined differences between different racial sets; differences, that is—though, curiously, this exception was scarcely ever mentioned—other than differences in respect of skin pigmentation and similar racial defining characteristics (Flew, 1976, Ch. 5). Now the offensive has become more general, and is directed particularly at those such as Ray Honeyford, the former Bradford headmaster. He dared to question in print some of the policies which Bradford and many other LEAs have been and still are imposing in the name of anti-racism.

5.1 Racism as plain injustice

What, then, is racism? Why is it morally wrong? These two questions ought to be, yet much too often are not, both asked and clearly answered before anyone is denounced and ostracised as a racist, and before the consideration of policies for anti-racist education begins. Once the two questions are put in tandem, as they are here, the answers become obvious. If racism is to be a moral offence, then it must be a kind of morally bad, and therefore controllable, behaviour, rather than of false, or otherwise improper, belief. That is, however, not to deny that that kind of bad behaviour has been and is in some way grounded in, and supposedly justified by, particular sorts of general belief about matters of non-normative fact.

(i) Let us therefore define 'racist behaviour' as advantaging or disadvantaging someone for no other or better reason than that he or she happens to be a member of one particular racial set rather than another.

In choosing the word 'set' we are, as always, accepting Cantor's Axiom for Sets, under which the sole essential feature of a set is that its members have at least one common characteristic. In the present context the currently most favoured alternative words ought to be unacceptable to everyone sincerely striving to achieve a society which, though in fact multiracial, is, at the same time and creditably, colourblind. To speak, for instance, of 'the Black Community' is bound to suggest that all people whose skins happen to have that pigmentation are, and are expected to remain, both self-consciously united with one another, and self-consciously separated from the rest of us, by their shared racial characteristics—a particular skin pigmentation, and so on. To speak of the members of any racial set as by that very membership comprising a social community, a community properly and hence possibly permanently aware of itself as such, surely is, in the sense just explained, racist talk? Certainly to speak in this way is to endorse and encourage racial apartness; which, being literally translated into Afrikaans, is *apartheid*.

(ii) Given as our answer to the first question the definition proposed in the previous Subsection, then the treatment of the second question can be equally direct and decisive. Racist behaviour, so defined, is morally wrong because it is unjust. The first eloquent epigraph to this chapter is, in the most traditional understanding of the word 'just', a cry for justice.

Dr Bunche was insisting that he, and, of course, all others, should as a matter of absolute right be accorded their own several and individual deserts and entitlements. In particular, he was demanding that he should be appointed, or not appointed, to any position for which he might choose to apply strictly and solely on the basis of his own individual merits, or lack of them, and to be neither disadvantaged in any such contests by hostile discrimination against members of the racial set to which he happened to belong, nor advantaged by any 'positive' discrimination in favour of that same racial set.

'Positive discrimination', it should be explained, is the slimy euphemism employed to commend the particular, privileged racist policies favoured by the commenders. In the USA such policies of 'positive discrimination' are promoted by many who think of themselves as 'Radical' or 'left liberal'. However, they are rejected by every subset in the population discernible by Dr Gallup—including, much to their credit, blacks. In the second epigraph, Professor Chris Mullard's confession of hatred for 'Whitey' contrasts unpleasingly with Dr Bunche's straightforward call for simple justice. Both should be remembered when we see how prominent Mullard and his writings have been and are in the promotion of 'racial awareness' and of what claim to be 'anti-racist' initiatives in education.

Certainly justice requires that all candidates for any position, irrespective of their racial set membership, be treated equally. However, we have to recognise from the beginning that the equality which is thus essential to justice is not a substantial equality of outcome, either for individuals or for sets, but rather a formal equality of treatment for all relevantly like cases. To say that this sort of equality is formal is not to say that it is empty, inessential or unimportant: quite the reverse. The point is that, to be rules at all, the rules of justice, like every other sort of rule, must be applied equally to all relevantly like cases. Yet it would be absurd to confuse this formal equality of treatment, which is indeed a first essential, with the imposition of an equality of outcome, which would in many cases be flatly incompatible with the most manifest mandates of justice. What, for instance, should we think of what called itself a system of criminal justice yet demanded that convicted criminals be treated in all respects just like everybody else?

'Relevant' now becomes the key word, and the very substantial rather than formal truth is that there is nothing of any importance, or almost nothing, to which differences in skin colour are properly relevant. The one possibly legitimate exception coming immediately to mind is the choice of black actors to play *Othello* or white actresses to play Desdemona. However, "this instance"—unlike the one to which the subsequent words were originally applied—really is "so singular, that it is scarcely worth our observing, and does not merit that for it alone we should alter our general maxim" (Hume, 1748, I, p. 21).

5.2 Racism as involving disfavoured beliefs

In Chapter 3 we noticed that, despite a prefatory editorial assurance that all concerned "have attempted to step back from the debate itself and look at the concepts which underlie it", the Penguin Education Special *Race, Culture and Intelligence* offered no definition of 'racism', and provided no account of the connections and lack of connections between race and culture (p. 70, above). Their failure on the first count may be put down in part to a disposition to maintain that it is impossible to attach a scientific meaning to the term 'race'. (This contention is, of course, not necessarily inconsistent with the project of giving a precise sense to the word 'racism', although to achieve this would demand some philosophical flexibility.)

(i) Two things, however, clearly are agreed: first, that racism is ineffably wicked; and, second, that it essentially involves certain sorts of belief about matters of non-normative fact. All such beliefs have to be rejected because, it is always assumed, if they were to be accepted as true, then their truth would justify behaviour which really is—in our and the only proper sense—racist. The sorts of belief which are thus embargoed are beliefs that there are, if only an average, practically relevant differences between different racial sets, differences which, being genetically determined, are not subject to alteration by any amount of environmental manipulation.

(a) Operating as they do with a concept of this kind, however ill defined, these contributors necessarily become committed to resisting any research which might discover that some beliefs of the sorts so ferociously repudiated are, after all, in fact true. I have elsewhere both pointed and protested some of the resulting inhibitions upon free inquiry (Flew, 1976, Ch. 5). It remains here to display the imprudence of such commitments.

By thus founding their rejection of racism upon assumptions of factual equalities between all racial sets they expose it always to overthrow by the latest communiqué from the science front. Suppose that these desired equalities do not in truth obtain. Then, successful though the militants of this form of 'anti-racism' have often been in suppressing what they fear as possibly falsifying research, still they can scarcely hope indefinitely to prevent news from leaking out. (For what looks like a very recent success in their campaign of suppression, see, however, Halstead, 1987.) These people would also do well to reflect that, to independent observers, their very zeal to ban research might seem to spring from some anxiety lest its true findings should turn out to be upsetting.

(b) To the extent that these people really do feel unshakeably certain that the facts are what they themselves would wish them to be, their confidence constitutes a remarkable and incongruously religious phenomenon. Yet few of them accept any traditionally religious revelation. How and by whom do they believe that these more worldly truths were vouchsafed to them? Again, most would, with a greater or lesser degree of contempt, reject the theses that the Universe is created by a God and that human affairs are all subject to His, or Its, Providence. Yet in many cases they hold to conclusions which would perhaps be true within such a Providential order while nevertheless strenuously denying the only premises from which these conclusions could rationally be inferred (Flew, 1987).

Certainly it is not as reckless to insist that there cannot be any genetically determined non-definitional differences between different racial sets as it is to make the parallel assumption about the males and females of the species. For whereas racial defining characteristics are all obviously superficial, their sexual analogues are sometimes deeply internal and structural. This is not, of course, enough to stop some people from suggesting the contrary; dismissing as "[bourgeois] ideology" any assertion "that women are intrinsically different from men" (Sarup, 1982, p. 78; and, for further similar examples, compare O'Keeffe, 1986, p. 162). Sarup, however—who gives compulsory, examined lectures on 'The Politics of Multi-racial Education' in the School of Education in Goldsmiths' College—is in his choice of beliefs almost totally emancipated from evidential inhibitions. Thus, without feeling any compulsion to offer a reason, he says he doubts, what easy enquiries would have shown him to be true, that "the American civil rights movement has altered the *economic* position of blacks. . ." (Sarup, 1986, p. 96: emphasis original).

To those refusing to admit any non-normative propositions into their definition of 'racism', the question whether there are or are not such genetically determined differences between different racial sets can be of no more interest than the question whether there are or are not parallel differences between the set consisting of the redheaded and the set consisting of the blond. Yet it is perhaps just worth indicating why, if our scientists were to discover that there are, *at least on average*, we ought not to be surprised. Suppose that in 4004 BC the Creator had—as Sarup and the contributors to *Race, Culture and Intelligence* would have wished—arranged for the gene pools of every racial set to contain all the same genes except for those determining racial defining characteristics, and these all distributed in exactly the same proportions. Then, allowing for some differences in achieved fertility between different social subsets within the same racial sets, and for similar differences in both achieved fertilities and social distribution between different racial sets, still we should by now, surely, expect to find some difference in the distributions of genes in the gene pools of different racial sets? Not that it matters.

(ii) The main reason why so many people want to make the denial of any substantial and significant, genetically determined, educationally or occupationally relevant differences between racial sets essential to any radical repudiation of racism is that they wrongly believe that to accept such differences would be to justify what is, in the sense previously explained, rightly to be condemned as racism. One of the cooler contributors to *Race, Culture and Intelligence*—that is, I fear, comparatively faint praise—commends "UNESCO and a distinguished line of social scientists who have worked to expose fallacies of racism. . ." (p. 196). The persons quoted were, however, concerned with the truth or falsity of propositions rather than with the validity or invalidity of arguments.

(a) When this contributor does consider something which could correctly be described as one of "the fallacies of racism" he is at one with the rest. The fallacy is not exposed as fallacious, and opposed, but rather proposed as sound, and endorsed. Thus he contends that to rate some people higher than others "on a scale of measured intelligence is to say . . . that one group of individuals rather than another should have privileges" (p. 169). This contention is plainly false. It is not to *say* anything of the sort. What is true is that, in some particular social context, someone, *by saying* that someone else has such and such an IQ, may ensure that that other person is appointed to some position, and thus enabled to enjoy the salary and perquisites attaching thereto.

By thus failing to distinguish speech acts of two very different sorts this contributor falls into the Naturalistic Fallacy, the fallacy of trying to derive conclusions about what *ought* to be from premises stating only what already *is* the case. He thus accepts that we could make a direct and valid inference from some statement of supposed fact about the average characteristics of some racial group to a conclusion about how we ought to treat all the individual members of that group.

In what for philosophers are recent years some have maintained two directly relevant, revisionist theses here: not only that the now-famous final *ought/is* paragraph of Section 1 of Book III of Hume's *Treatise* was not aimed at what G. E. Moore was eventually to christen the Naturalistic Fallacy but also that that is, in any case, no fallacy. Having long since done my best elsewhere to demonstrate the falsity of both claims (Flew, 1969) there is no need for me to do more here than indicate again that, if the second implies that we cannot properly distinguish between an equality of rights and an equality of talents, and that the obvious fallacies of deducing either directly from the other alone are not fallacies, then this consequence must by itself constitute a sufficient refutation of all such reactionary revisionism.

(b) There is a further fallacy in any argument which moves straight from some statement of the average characteristics of some set to a conclusion about any of the individual members of that set. This too in its application to racial sets may properly be accounted one of the "fallacies of racism". For that I belong to some set which is on average less this or more that than another set, to which you belong, carries no implication that I, as an individual, am less this or more that than you. However much we may sympathise with the correspondent who told Jensen that "If the group is to be labelled intellectually inferior, I, as a member of that group, am also inevitably and automatically so labelled", his argument is, as an argument from an average, manifestly fallacious (Jensen, 1972, p. 15).

5.3 Race and culture

In 1972 the contributors to *Race, Culture and Intelligence* failed to provide an account of the relations and lack of relations between race and culture. Since then it has becoome increasingly common to collapse the distinction, mistaking it that racial sets must by the same token be cultural sets, and identifying the multi-racial with the multi-cultural. For instance, when in the later 1970s a municipal bus company refused to accommodate Sikh employees by providing a turban variant of its uniform, this bit of bigoted bumbledom was widely mistaken to be business for the Commission for Racial Equality (CRE). No one, certainly, who has ever served alongside Sikhs in the armed forces of the Crown can have the slightest sympathy with such municipal woodenness. However, equally certainly, Sikhism is a religion and a matter, therefore, of culture rather than of race.

Nor is it necessary either that a multi-cultural society be multi-racial or that a multi-racial society be multi-cultural. Canada, for instance, has been from its beginning, by the very terms of Confederation, officially bi-lingual and hence, presumably, at least bi-cultural if not multi-cultural, but it is only rather recently that a few of its cities have become visibly multi-racial. If too the referent of the expression 'Black Culture' is indeed as racially exclusive as that label suggests, then it is something which the CRE ought to be discouraging, just as it ought not to be, as it has been, sponsoring, but instead working for the dissolution of, Conferences or Associations of Black (or Asian) Lawyers, and the like. (See the lists appended to *CRE Annual Reports*, recording grants awarded to various named organisations.)

Since culture, as opposed to race, is acquired, and may change or be lost it must be, in principle, possible for any culture which is not racially exclusive to be imparted to or adopted by people of any race. Not only is this, in principle, possible, it has also, in fact, frequently happened.

Certainly the Roman Empire at its apogee was multi-racial, while any remaining cultural divisions were along social or geographical rather than racial lines. (In face of some of the falsehoods nowadays so malevolently spread in the name of 'anti-racism', it becomes worth nothing, if only parenthetically, that in the Ancient World slaves were very often of the same race as masters, as were the blacks when first enslaved by other blacks—before being later sold to the whites running the Atlantic slave trade.)

(i) The truth is, of course, that 'race' and 'culture' are just about as far as could be from constituting convertible terms. On the contrary, the innumerable respects in which one culture may be distinguished from another include almost everything else but those inherited racial and other physiological characteristics which may or may not happen to be common to all the members of the social set sharing that particular culture. For, in the broad sense beloved of professing social scientists, the culture of a social set comprises not only its high culture, if any—its music, literature, arts, science and so on (its culture in a narrow sense)—but also its language, its mating and child-raising practices, its religious and other traditions, its official and actual values and so on, down through the whole long list of the professional interests of anthropologists and sociologists.

(a) Once this distinction between a broad, social scientific and a narrow, humanities sense of the word 'culture' has been made we have forthwith to go on to say that, whereas every social set must have a culture (social scientific), not every social set does have anything deserving the name of a culture (humanities). For, surely, the wretched Ik—*The Mountain People*—must be allowed to have lost all culture in that second sense (Turnbull, 1973)? Yet in the first sense they did have a culture; for precisely that was the immeasurably depressing subject of the anthropologist's study. For in that understanding a culture consists in absolutely every kind of preference, disposition, social practice and what have you, and not only those involved in activities which are cultural in the second, narrower and perhaps more elevated interpretation.

(b) The collapsing of the crucial distinction between race and culture, and the failure to distinguish a broader and narrower sense of 'culture', together constitute one of the main reasons why it has become common to insist that "we cannot accept quality distinctions between cultures" (Richardson and Spears, 1972, p. 156). This particular, confessional quotation comes from the conclusion of a contribution from the Professor of Education in the Open University. He appears not to have noticed that this refusal must disqualify him from maintaining either that it is better to be well educated than ill educated or not educated at all or that any culture which is racist or sexist is, at least in that respect and to that extent, worse than another which is neither.

The same or similar formulations are now to be found in the documentation of the 'anti-racist' policies of many LEAs. I have myself seen them in official papers from ILEA, Brent and Bradford. In Brent the Council statement of this principle of cultural equality, to which all employees are to be required to assent, runs: "The recognition that all people and cultures are inherently equal must be a constant from which all educational practice will be developed." It is reasonable to conjecture that similar formulations either have also come or will also be coming from all the other LEAs which have summoned the contentious Professor Mullard, and his London University Race Relations Policy and Practice Unit, to guide their policies for 'anti-racist' education. They are Avon, Birmingham, Derbyshire, Hampshire, Haringey, Leicestershire, Manchester and Sheffield (Marks, 1987).

It is necessary to give and to emphasise this long list of large LEAs since in *The Times Literary Supplement* (TLS) the reviewer of Palmer (1986)—desperate to ensure that no one should be influenced by anything said in that book—chose falsely to pretend that the policies to which its contributors took exception would affect little more than "rural Berkshire". (For an area including Basingstoke, Slough, Reading and much of the rest of Britain's Silicon Valley, a description contemptuously intended to suggest hicks and hayseeds is—shall we say?—perverse.)

(c) The same rot has also penetrated the Church of England. Thus *Faith in the City*, the by-now notorious 'Report of the Archbishop of Canterbury's Commission on Urban Priority Areas', likewise condemns, while never defining, the sin of racism; and it too makes no distinction between the multi-ethnic and the multi-cultural. So what it wants "the Church—clergy and laity" to do is "not to lag behind teachers in affirming and understanding other cultures" (p. 304).

Although this demand for *affirmation* is several times reiterated, nowhere are we offered any account of what, in the present context, it is supposed to mean. Presumably the employment of that word is, in Freudian terms, a compromise formation. The Archbishop's Commissioners—collapsing the distinction between race and culture—presumably felt bound to maintain as eager 'anti-racists' that all cultures are equally good and equally valid. But then—as, however weakly, professing Christians committed to maintaining that it must be a fault in any culture to deny their revealed truth—they were inhibited from clearly and outright asserting this equality of quality. It is unkind yet scarcely unfair to suggest that their actual concern must have been with appearances rather than with the substance of the Faith. For nowhere do they even pretend to be deriving their political and economic recommendations from any traditional source of Christian authority (Flew, 1986b).

In a secular age it is probable that most outsiders are unaware that this today is par for the course. When a collective of non-socialist but instead genuinely Christian sociologists and economists surveyed a representative sample of recent political and social statements from all the mainstream churches, they concluded that these were "sloppy, ill-thought out, ignorant one-sided, addicted to secular fashions, uncritical of conventional 'progressive' wisdom, hysterical, unmethodical in the use of sources and evidence, . . . and, most deplorable, uncharitable to those who disagree" (Anderson, 1984b, p. 3). Restrained no doubt by their own true charity, these critics left it to a Vice-President of the Rationalist Press Association to become the first publicly to challenge the sincerity of Christian commitment in some of those who draft such reports.

Certainly all the other charges brought by Anderson (1984b) against these other 'Christian' social and political statements can be sustained equally against the work of the Archbishop's Commissioners. For instance, they contrive never to quote any spokesperson for the 'doctrinaire monetarism' which they are so quick to condemn as uncaring, thus conveniently excusing themselves from the too-exacting task of explaining why the institutionalised fraud of inflation is, apparently, not merely consistent with but demanded by 'social justice'. And so on.

(ii) Once given a firm grasp on the distinctions between race and culture, and betwen the broad and narrow sense sof 'culture', we are ready to deal more fully first with the inability "to accept quality differences between cultures" and then with the assumption that multi-racial education has to be multi-cultural. The first source of that inability is, as we have seen, a failure to insist upon these two distinctions. However, since these claims about the inexpugnable equality of all cultures seem ultimately to have originated from people trained in, or otherwise affected or infected by, what is presented as social science, and since they themselves rarely disclose how this putative revelation was vouchsafed to them, it becomes worthwhile to indicate two further, equally unsound routes to the same false and educationally ruinous conclusion.

(a) A first clue is to be found in a throwaway reference to "the anthropological definition of 'culture' which refers to ways of life which all groups have and which are of equal vlaue" (Sarup, 1986, p. 14: mention quotes supplied). It is obvious that an author who had perhaps heard of Weber, but who was himself wholly lacking in logical acumen, might get the idea that Weberian *wertfreiheit* demanded not that—at least in their working hours—social scientists should refrain from attributing intrinsic values to any cultures but rather that they should assert that all are in truth equally valuable. This argument is so obviously unsound that to state it clearly and boldly should constitute a sufficient refutation.

The author of Sarup (1986) is, we are told, "a member of the editorial collective of *Radical Philosphy*". He is, nevertheless, capable both of defining 'dialectical materialism' as if it were, simply, materialism (p. 45) and of deducing that "the traditional nuclear family no longer exists in Britain" (p. 59) from the premise that "In 1981 one in seven, approximately 15 per cent of all families in Great Britain with dependent children ... were headed by a single parent" (p. 129). Since John Eggleston, Professor of Education in the University of Keele chose both Sarup (1982) and (1986) for the privilege of inclusion in the Routledge Education Books series, and since the School of Education at Goldsmiths' College not merely tolerates the lectures upon which Sarup (1986) is based but makes them compulsory and presumably examined, anyone involved in the hiring of teachers ought to view recent graduates from either institution with some suspicion.

That last is a point of a kind which does need to be pressed, every time. For the publications of those teaching in such schools, institutes and colleges provide the best if not the only index available to outsiders by which we can estimate what pupil teachers are being taught and how valuable or valueless the paper qualifications awarded to them actually are. *Caveat emptor*, which, being translated, is 'Buyer beware!'

(b) A second clue was given in our previous reference to "attributing intrinsic values". For another distinction essential here is that between intrinsic and instrumental value. To value something non-instrumentally is to value it as good in itself, irrespective of any possible further consequences of having it, whereas to value something instrumentally is to value it as a means to the achieving of some other as well as further end or ends.

To maintain that anything is non-instrumentally valuable is indeed to make a value judgement, which is, no doubt, an inherently contentious move. For it is to say that, regardless of consequences, whatever it is which is thus non-instrumentally valued *ought* to be preferred. However, to maintain that something is instrumentally valuable, adding the needed indication of the presumptively good end or ends to which it is alleged in fact to be a means, is to make a purely (would-be) factual and unequivocally true or false assertion. For it is to say, only and precisely, that what is thus instrumentally valuable in fact just *is* an effective means of achieving a presumptively good objective; and all this quite regardless of whether you or I or anyone else either wants or ought to want that particular objective.

The purpose of that brief and, hopefully, not too technical excursus into the philosophy of value is to bring out the full outrageousness of the contention that no culture (in either sense) may be said to be in any respect, or with regard to any possible objective, either superior or inferior to any other. A ban on the investigation of all such questions of instrumental efficiency, or on the publication of the findings, must constitute an intolerable restriction upon the freedom of inquiry, or of speech and writing. Yet exactly this is what is demanded when 'negative views' are embargoed, and everyone is required to allow that all cultures and all forms of linguistic expression are equally 'good' or equally *valid*.

(iii) Equipped with the various distinctions and other conceptual tools developed in the previous subsections we are at last in a position to dispose finally and decisively of the now manifestly false assumption that any properly multi-racial education must be, by the same token, multi-cultural. For, without either making or rejecting any always controversial claims about their intrinsic worth, we can discover and know that one feature of a culture (in either sense), or even one entire culture, is in fact a more effective means for securing certain ends, and this, if need be, quite regardless of whether these ends are in fact our own ends or anyone else's.

(a) Take the first case of languages. Whatever might be said about the attribution of such non-instrumental values as euphony or elegance, it would be—it is—simply silly to insist that every language is equally good for every possible practical purpose. Silliness is compounded into academic pretentiousness when this insistence is then supported by appeals to the alleged findings of uncited research (Honey, 1983).

Waiving all questions about complexity or redundancy, it is sufficient to indicate how ill advised it must be to attempt to employ a language lacking a vocabulary for discussing what you want to discuss. Of course, it is true that, had the history of these islands been very different, we might all be speaking and writing a language other than English, or some other dialect might have achieved the status of Standard English. Nevertheless, none of this speculative historical linguistics has the slightest tendency to show, as things in fact have been and now are, that it is not imperative for anyone proposing to make their home and their career in the United Kingdom to master English, and Standard English, rather than Urdu or Creole. If we were all proposing to live our lives in Japan and to be Japanese then the imperatives would be different, yet no less imperative: Japanese it would have to be, and Standard Japanese at that.

It is, therefore, sensible and indeed generous to provide special teaching of English for those immigrant children whose parents have yet to master our language. However, it is preposterous and grotesque for state schools to try—as some have done—to teach such children what are supposed to be their native languages. What are mother's knees *for* if they are not to learn our mother tongues *at*?

(b) The first case was that of language in particular. The second is that of culture in general. Here the advocates of multi-cultural education require us, at least in so far as non-white immigrants are concerned, to look back to the sources whence they came, rather than forwards into the traditions and culture of the nation into which they have chosen to join. Thus, at an early stage of the Schools Council's Education for a Multiracial Society Project,

Townsend and Brittan (1973) poured scorn on a situation in which, as they have it:

> Asian and West Indian pupils in junior schools, even in high immigrant areas, are more likely to learn about Alfred and the cakes than about Africa and India, while secondary pupils are more likely to know the causes of the Wars of the Roses than the causes of recent waves of immigration (p. 7).

Here, as so often, we should be willing to learn from the experience and the achievement of the nation which, in the century following the Civil War, assimilated by far the largest immigration in human history. At least in that period no one ever suggested that the US public schools ought to teach the children of immigrants in any language other than English, or that the history which those children were to learn there must be that of the countries which their parents had abandoned, rather than that of that "new nation, conceived in liberty" which they had now entered. To grow up as American every future citizen needed to know, as their successors today still do need to know, the meaning of Valley Forge and Yorktown, of Gettysburg and Appomattox Court House.

Those in the UK curious to discover why their parents or grandparents immigrated would best ask them for the true answer, rather than consult a teacher. For that teacher might well have been indoctrinated by the likes of Madan Sarup and be zealous, therefore, to speak of the mystic 'needs of Capital', or of the evils of 'colonialism', but never willing to attend to the individuals' hopes of bettering the conditions of themselves and of their families.

(iv) Of course, all this was, and is, and always ought to be without prejudice to the possibility and the desirability of preserving whatever cultural treasures the immigrant parents may have to contribute to the common store of their new country. However, this desirable possibility is, surely, best realised—as in the USA it has been—not by forcing some form of miscegenated multi-culturalism into the already overloaded curriculum of every single school but by leaving both the original immigrants and their descendants free to form their own several and various cultural organisations?

This they may and should do not only without let or hindrance but also without state subsidy. One excellent model is provided by the annual Steuben Day celebrations in New York City, in which German-Americans parade down Fifth Avenue, and the whole occasion is enjoyed as much by the spectators as by the participants.

(a) We do not, however, have to look so far in order to find models to imitate. New Britons of West Indian descent, to their own delight and to that of crowds of spectators, have for some years held annual carnivals in Notting Hill Gate. Again, since Cromwell lifted the ban on Jewish immigration, Jews have come to the British Isles from many foreign countries. Their descendants have been happy both to accept English as their mother tongue and to become themselves unequivocally and unreservedly British. State-maintained schools never provided nor were they ever asked to provide the children of these earlier immigrants with any teaching in or of Hebrew. Yet this was, of course, not intended to prevent, and has not in fact prevented, the parents from taking private steps to preserve both their religion and other elements of the culture with which their ancestors arrived.

(b) I have introduced the awkward expression 'New Briton' for a similar reason to that which the Australian Ministry of Immigration had for wanting everyone to speak and think of all landed immigrants as potentially 'New Australians'. It is to suggest that the aim of all public policy in this area ought to be so to assimilate all immigrants, and in particular all non-white immigrants, that they become English or Scots or Welsh who just happen to have skins of a minority pigmentation. Those to whom this development is unacceptable should, surely, never have immigrated to Britain in the first place? Anyone who wants "to remain—say—Bangladeshi ought to be planning later, if not sooner, to be returning to Bangladesh".

(c) The final phrase in the previous paragraph is a quotation from an essay published in *The Salisbury Review* (SR). It is worth repeating here since it appears to have appalled David Edgar, reviewing Palmer (1986) in *New Socialist* (January 1987). Having perversely devoted the whole of the first of his three pages to contributors to SR who did *not* contribute to that book, he concludes both his discussion of my contribution and his review by quoting the same phrase, which is not repeated in that contribution. He comments, finally: "Professor Flew may well have erased that last, chilling sentence from his memory. That doesn't mean we should delete it from ours" (p. 21).

Easy though it is to appreciate that after writing a piece so fevered, Edgar would have required some refrigeration, it remains difficult to be sure why this particular sentence met his need so satisfactorily. Perhaps the most plausible conjecture is that Edgar is one of the people—among whom some of those most influential in what Peter Simple calls the Race Relations Industry must be numbered—who want to conserve the entire non-white population as an alienated and anti-British minority, ready to be recruited as stormtroopers in the *New Socialist* cause.

Certainly there are those who consciously and categorically reject the ideal of assimilation. Thus Sarup (1986) maintains, most characteristically, that "to assimilate, for whites, means to stay the same; to assimilate, for blacks, is to discard their identity and all that culturally defines their existence" (p. 16; and compare Mullard, 1982, which Sarup is here commending).

Although such rejections are nowadays usually urged in the name of 'anti-racism', they should nevertheless be seen as themselves essentially racist and as such, therefore, altogether unacceptable. For, if the particular pigmentation of the skins of all members of some human set "culturally defines their existence" then the culture of that set becomes, necessarily, racially exclusive. Its exclusiveness is again, by immediate inference, racist. So to those who are sincere and consistent in their repudiation of all racism, and who are not beneath a false flag labouring to further some quite different aim, the proper ideal becomes that epitomised in the caption of one Conservative Party poster: "Labour says you're black, but we say you're British."

5.4 Racism as causing disfavoured outcomes

Section 5.1 explained both what ought to be meant by 'racism' and why racism so conceived is morally wrong. Section 5.2 proceeded to elucidate and explode one popular misconception. A second and far more damaging misconception is, unlike the first, often explicitly expounded by its promoters. Already in the 1970s this notion was providing a basis for policy in some other spheres. Then, with the coming of the 1980s, it began to have an ever-increasing impact upon the British educational system.

(i) We cannot hope, for instance, to understand the activities of that 'UNESCO in a clerical collar' the World Council of Churches (WCC), working through what it calls its Programme to Combat Racism (PCR), save in terms of this sort of neo-Marxist conception. (See, for intance, Smith, 1977 and Lefever, 1979.)

(a) This second misconception has a recognised but confusing name, 'institutionalised racism'. It is doubly confusing both because what is thus described as institutionalised is not necessarily racism and because the policies pressed by the promoters of this misconception necessarily must actually institutionalise racism. It is for this reason—and not because we want to deny the possibility of both giving sense to, and finding application for, a notion of institutionalised racism—that authentic anti-racists have to reject it. (True to form, the Archbishop's Commissioners employed this expression without either explaining or attempting to justify their usage.)

(b) I hesitate to repeat now, what I said in Palmer (1986), that I found the formulation with which I shall be working here in *Education for Equality* (EE). Early in 1983 this document was distributed to all teachers in Berkshire schools by the Advisory Committee for Multicultural Education, a sub-committee of the local Education Committee. I hesitate since the TLS reviewer made this his excuse for pretending that such ideas are largely confined to, and could do little damage in, "rural Berkshire".

Yet it is important to emphasise that both these ideas and the policies based upon them have in fact begun to spread far beyond the inner-city strongholds of what the media too complacently describe as 'the loony left'. For, although Berkshire had at that time a narrow Conservative majority, everything in EE—described by its author in my wife's presence as containing "a Marxist analysis"—was at once and without reservation accepted by the parent committee. Since I had in Palmer (1986) proceeded immediately to point out that several of the crucial paragraphs of EE reappeared, word for word the same, two or three months later in documents issued by ILEA, I have here to console myself as best I may by reflecting that there can be no defence either against reviewers so resolute to minimise and to misrepresent or against the editors who nevertheless continue to employ them.

(ii) In EE, under the italicised heading, *"The central and pervasive influence of racism"*, the key clauses of this latest redefinition were:

> There are certain routine practices, customs and procedures in our society whose consequence is that black people have poorer jobs, health, housing and life-chances than do the white majority. . . These practices and customs are maintained by relations and structures of power, and are justified by centuries-old beliefs and attitudes which hold that black people are essentially inferior to white people—biologically, or culturally, or both. 'Racism' is a shorthand term for this combination of discriminatory practices, unequal relations and structures of power, and negative beliefs and attitudes.

(a) Section 5.2 said what most needed to be said about the imprudence of defining 'racism' wholly or even in part in terms of beliefs about what are thought to be matters of non-normative fact. So the first point to notice here is one which must raise questions about the anti-racist good faith of those responsible for the above formulation. For this formulation appears to preclude the possibility of condemning as racist any but white people and white institutions. Yet some of our non-white immigrants—the Uganda Asians—had during the dictatorship of the monster Amin the bitterest experience of black racism. Nor are either the black or the brown varieties altogether unknown in the UK.

(b) A second feature of this redefinition is that it makes racism, at least in the first instance, a characteristic of social institutions rather than of individual behaviour. However the truth is that racism, as previously defined, is, like the violent causing of gross bodily harm, essentially intentional. It is for that very reason that it is peculiarly repellent. Yet the 'institutionalised racism' of the present redefinition—like what some professing social scientists call 'institutionalised violence' (Flew, 1985, pp.

51–2)—is to be so adjudged irrespective of anyone's actual intentions. By thus making irrelevant the most obvious answer to the question 'And why is racism morally wrong?' this second innovation presents its sponsors with the so-far unrecognised problem of providing an equally persuasive alternative.

(c) Either of these first two objections would constitute sufficient reason to send the redefiners back to their definitional drawing boards, but a third feature is by far the most objectionable. The key word 'racism' is being redefined in terms simply of consequences. The implications, above all for educational standards, are appalling. For the new definition embraces all, repeat all, "practices, customs and procedures whose consequence is that black people have poorer jobs, health, housing, education and life-chances than do the white majority". All such "practices, customs and procedures" are to be condemned, and condemned as racist, regardless of whether the 'black' disadvantage is or is not in fact due to hostile discrimination on the basis of racial set membership.

Again, and in particular, we are specifically forbidden to attend to, or even to admit, the vital relevance and importance of differences which are in the broad sense cultural. Everyone takes care never to mention, much less to consult, any of the works of the distinguished, Chicago-trained (and, incidentally, black) American economist Thomas Sowell (1975, 1983, 1986); works showing in case after case how sometimes spectacular differences between the records in the USA of sets of 'ethnic' immigrants from different cultural backgrounds simply cannot be attributed to the presence or absence of favourable or hostile discrimination.

Given this second alternative concept, and given too that, whatever the word is to be used to mean, racism has to be eschewed and abominated, then we are going to be asked to condemn and abandon any and every institution or practice the actual effects of which are that the racial distribution in any subset is substantially different from that in the population as a whole. If there are n per cent of blacks and m per cent of browns in the population as a whole, then there will have to be n per cent of blacks and m per cent of browns in every profession, class, team, area or what have you. Anything, but anything, which stands in the way of this presupposed ideal is to be denounced and execrated. It has to be, by redefinition, racist.

(iii) It is embarrassing yet it appears—in what Wittgenstein so loved to call "the darkness of these times"—necessary to insist that to point to implications of this redefinition is precisely not to say that these are explicitly asserted therein. Had EE said things so manifestly outrageous, outright and in as many words, then even the sleepiest and most complacent of Berkshire's Conservative County Councilors might have been alerted to what is going on. It is only because these consequences are *logically implied* rather than *explicitly asserted* that it becomes both possible to overlook them and necessary to point them out. However, once it has been pointed out, it ought to be obvious that and why they follow necessarily.

(a) From the review aforementioned it would seem that David Edgar has never mastered one most elementary and fundamental distinction between, on the one hand, asserting some particular proposition and on the other, asserting something else which, while not itself being that particular proposition, is nevertheless logically implied by it. For he began by quoting what I had maintained, and do still maintain, follows necessarily from this second redefinition of 'racism'. He then quoted that redefinition, and in triumph commented:

> To draw from that the message that Berkshire is demanding racial parity within assemblages of sportsplayers, musicians and Nobel laureates—or that the absence of such parity of itself implies racism in their selection procedures—is to go beyond caricature. *It just doesn't say it at all* (p. 20: emphasis added).

(b) Among the many furiously leftist reviewers of Palmer (1986), Edgar was not alone in failing to grasp an elementary point of logic. In the *New Statesman*, for instance, Jolyon Jenkins quoted a compelling demonstration of the scarcely contestable conclusion that—in the sense carefully explained in Section 5.1, above—'positive discrimination' must be just as racist as 'negative'. This demonstration, falsely and without argument, he then put down as one token of a particular type of fallacy nicknamed in Flew (1975); proceeding to exult in what he thus mistook to be an elegant refutation of Flew.

There is a twofold justification for attending here if only for a moment, to some of the delinquencies of these hostile reviewers of Palmer (1986), an earlier work describing and denouncing what is today being so widely promoted in the misappropriate name of anti-racism. In the first place such attention may generate the charitable thought that some at least of the scandalous misrepresentations in such journals as the *Guardian*, the *New Statesman*, and *The Freethinker* may have sprung from an unfamiliarity with, and a consequent incapacity for, critical thought—critical, that is, in the unprejudicially appraising sense, not the necessarily hostile (pp. 38–9, above).

Any self-satisfaction arising from so generous an exercise of charity is, however, quickly extinguished. For if these chosen champions of the left really are as unfamiliar with and as inept in critical thinking as, on the charitable view, they seem to be then this fact is bound to suggest something extremely alarming about what in many of our tertiary institutions is presently being provided as education—or, more particularly, as (capital E) Education. We have to ask, even if we cannot excogitate any means of discovering the true answer, how many lecturers—and, in particular, how many lecturers in institutes, colleges and departments of education—have been, in the comparative privacy of the classroom, presenting to their students such materials as we can now see publicly and shamelessly displayed in Sarup (1982, 1986). How many too, without ever forcefully drawing any argued dissent to their attention, have been expecting those students, on pain of failing, to represent that material uncritically in written examinations, or for other forms of assessment (Scruton *et al.*, 1985)?

(c) Although there is no doubt but that the Conservative County Councillors of Berkshire did fail to appreciate the logical implications of the supposedly neo-Marxist redefinition of 'racism', many others have drawn and are drawing, and have acted and are acting upon, practical conclusions warranted only by its acceptance. Individual teachers and entire educational institutions thus have been and are to be condemned without appeal simply because black pupils, and in particular black boys, are disproportionately represented in the 'sin bins'; and all this with no thought of the possibility that they may also be disproportionately represented in the sets of actual sinners. Methods of assessment thus have been or are to be rejected for no other or better reason than that some racial set performs disproportionately well or disproportionately ill, without any consideration of the possibility that that set may actually be disproportionately good or bad at whatever that method of assessment is intended to assess; just as it was sometimes, indeed often, thought a sufficient condemnation of the old 11+ examinations that children from the Registrar Generals' lower social classes were disproportionately unsuccessful:

> One of the best known cases of discrimination is the fact that most black children are put in the lowest streams and are overrepresented in special schools. For example, in 1971 immigrants formed 6.5 per cent of all pupils in educationally subnormal schools. The significance of this process has been described by Bernard Coard in his book, *How the West Indian Child is made Educationally Sub-Normal in the British School System* (Sarup, 1982, p. 105. For an account of the second crucial fallacy in Coard, 1971, see Palmer, 1986, p. 24).

(iv) Here, in discussions of race, we find all those fallacies already familiar from discussions of social class. There are the same forms of invalid argument moving straight from inequalities of outcome to inequalities of opportunity. There are the same failures, or refusals, to allow that human sets can differ in respect of the internal distribution of both abilities and inclinations. Also there are the same failures, or refusals, to recognise the ambiguities between 'opportunity' and 'probability' senses of such words as 'chance' or 'access' (p. 21, above).

To show that such arguments are not only invalid but also sustain conclusions which are in fact false, we need to cite some of Sowell's cases showing "how sometimes spectacular differences between the records of 'ethnic' immigrants from different cultural backgrounds simply cannot be attributed to the presence or absence of favourable or hostile discrimination". For instance, in the USA blacks are heavily overrepresented in professional basketball, while Jews have been about nine times overrepresented among America's Nobel Prizewinners (27 per cent to 3 per cent). So if we were to accept the proposed (and often imposed) redefinition, or anything like it, we should be required to put down any such overrepresentation, as well as all the necessarily consequent underrepresentations, to 'institutionalised racism'. This we will be required to do notwithstanding that we know perfectly well that these overrepresentations actually result from entirely honest and colourblind attempts to appoint the strongest candidates. (No one so far—with the possible exception of National Socialist propagandists in the 1930s—has even accused the totally Nordic Nobel Committee of unfair, pro-semitic discrimination!)

Again, suppose we were so unfashionable as to cite a Third World example of what truly is institutionalised racism—the various arrangements designed to ensure that the proportion of racially Chinese students in Malaysian universities does not exceed that in the population as a whole. Then should we be surprised to learn that "although there are approximately equal numbers of Chinese and Malays in Malaysian colleges and universities, the Chinese outnumber the Malays by more than eight-to-one in the sciences and fifteen-to-one in engineering" (Sowell, 1983, p. 139)? Certainly not if we had read a recent leader in the *Wall Street Journal* (17 February 1987) which, after mistaking the connections between 'positive discrimination' and 'negative' to be contingent rather than necessary, goes on to point out that Asians are vastly overrepresented in many elite institutions, especially in mathematics and the hard sciences:

> At Harvard, for instance, Asians make up 10% of the student body, some five times their share of the US population. It is widely believed that admissions officers at some schools are now using informal quotas, not to help this minority but to hinder it.

For the fraudulent and factitious 'institutionalised racism' defined by this new third concept—a racism which is not necessarily any sort of racism at all—the sovereign cure lies, surely, only in truly racist policies of 'positive discrimination'? These must, always and necessarily, involve complementary policies of 'negative discrimination'. For how else is it to be ensured that in every sphere and at every level all the prescribed quotas are filled and, correspondingly, none overfilled? The adoption of such a concept, therefore, a concept under which we are mandated to condemn what some—including, apparently, the Archbishop's Commissioners— would have us call 'institutionalised racism', most paradoxically yet altogether inescapably, demands that racism, in the primary sense, be everywhere and for ever institutionalised!

5.5 When black can be brown or white, and why

Even the most casual and uninquisitive of television viewers must occasionally have met, and perhaps been puzzled by, a new usage of the term 'black'. They may have seen, and been surprised to see, *Asians* urging the Labour Party to establish *Black* Sections. (Sarup, 1986, p. 99 asks "why doesn't the Labour Party create black sections?" However, he does not stay for the principled anti-racist answer given by the present majority on the National Executive Committee.)

Again, such viewers may have seen the newly elected Lord Mayor of Bradford claiming to be the first *black* to have attained such a position in England. Obviously this claim was, in the common understanding, false. For he is Asian not black. Furthermore, it is doubly false since it was in 1913 that John Archer, who truly was a black and who had already been a Borough Councillor for 20 years, became Mayor of Battersea, the constituency which, by the way, in 1922 elected Shapurji Saklatvala as the first Asian and first Communist MP (Palmer, 1986, p. 66).

(i) The practice of the Commission for Racial Equality (CRE) is confused and inconsistent. Sometimes they use the word to refer only to blacks, sometimes to all non-whites, and sometimes their intentions are obscure or indeterminate. All those promoting what we have distinguished as the third concept of racism follow, however, a consistent new usage. Thus EE proposes so to redefine the word 'black' as to include, unequivocally, "*both* Afro-Caribbean *and* Asian people", while simultaneously extending 'Afro-Caribbean' to embrace everyone previously accounted black (p. 3: emphasis original). It is at this point that the ILEA documents add their own supplementary paragraph:

> Other groups . . . usually referred to as 'ethnic minorities' also suffer varying degrees of prejudice and discrimination. These include Chinese, Greek Cypriots, Turkish Cypriots, Turks, Vietnamese, Moroccans . . . Irish . . . Jews. . . . *In using the term 'black' in this paper it is not the Authority's intention to exclude any minority group* (emphasis added).

(a) About the first of the two purposes of these verbal manoevres, all the documents which I have so far been able to consult are quite frank. It is to encourage all non-whites to see themselves as members of a more or less permanently alienated collective of victims, victims of an always and exclusively white racism and victims who cannot be expected themselves to do anything to better their individual conditions, other than support the right left-wing political campaigns. As EE explains, "The term 'black' emphasises the common experience which both Afro-Caribbean and Asian people have of being victims of racism, and their common determination to oppose racism" (p. 3).

Remembering the simultaneous redefinition of 'racism' in terms of all existing British institutions we have to construe this as confirming earlier suggestions of revolutionary intentions, intentions which are by Sarup and many others most frankly avowed (Sarup, 1982, 1986; and, for quotations from other spokespersons, compare Palmer, 1986, Chs 2, 5 and 6).

(b) The second and, of course, never so frankly avowed purpose is so to collapse distinctions between different sets of non-whites that it becomes possible to maintain that any relatively poor economic or educational performance by any such sets is (if not wholly then certainly in the main) attributable to (always and only) white racism. If and in so far as the object of the exercise is to unite all non-whites into a potentially revolutionary army of the aggrieved, then it becomes impeccably rational to strive in every way to deny, obscure or minimise all differences between subsets within the set of the non-white.

It is, however, equally obvious that this is not true if the objective is the officially stated aim of the whole Race Relations Industry. That officially stated aim is admirable and altogether unexceptionable: the CRE, as it likes to tell us in its advertisements, "was set up by the Race Relations Act 1976 with the duties of working towards the elimination of discrimination and promoting equality of opportunity and good relations between different racial groups generally".

Whenever that truly is the aim it becomes impossible to emphasise too strongly the importance of NOT thinking of all immigrants, or even of all non-white immigrants, as one homogeneous mass. For there is already a good deal of material to show that, especially in the second generation, Asians are reaching higher levels of achievement than blacks, and hence evidence to suggest that white racism cannot be the sole factor accounting for black failures, at least not unless we insist, in the teeth of the evidence, that what white racism there is is exclusively or mainly anti-black.

Consider, for instance, another finding of the NCDS. The NCDS has, it seems, discovered that whereas in the first generation all immigrants— West Indian, Asian, and Irish too—live, on average, in above-averagely overcrowded conditions, and whereas with *both* the West Indian *and* the Irish a considerable disparity persists into the second generation, with the Asians the disparity has, in the second generation, disappeared completely (Fogelman, 1983).

(ii) As a further indication both of the motivation behind, and of other vested interests in, this seemingly perverse and arbitrary redefinition of 'black' let us turn to the *1982 Annual Report* of the CRE. In the body of the text the Commission asserts that "ethnic minorities have taken more than their fair share" of youth unemployment, supporting this with the statement that "In June 1982, the Commission published a survey of inner city youth unemployment . . . which indicated that 59% of young people of West Indian origin were unemployed as compared with 41% of their white peers" (p. 9).

(a) It is clear that the CRE believes, or at any rate would like the rest of us to believe, that this certainly "potentially explosive" disparity is due to white racism, to discrimination against non-whites as such, and, therefore, that it falls within the CRE's statutory terms of reference. Yet on the very same page they present in diagram form fuller and slightly different figures. These show that their wholesale claim, extended to all "ethnic minorities", is simply false; that their suggested explanation of this 59 per cent to 41 per cent disparity, in terms of white discrimination against all non-whites, must be mistaken; and, hence, that the cherished corollary conclusion, that to destroy it is their own peculiar and appointed business, falls to the ground. For the diagram reveals other disparities in inner-city juvenile unemployment. Its figures are (not 41 but) 42 per cent for Whites, 59 per cent for Afro-Caribbeans and 40 per cent—a little less, that is, than for Whites—for Asians.

(b) There are two morals which we should draw from this sort of evidence, the first primary and the second consequential. The primary moral is that we should now look for *most of* the explanation of underachievement by any underachieving immigrant group, not in white, or even in non-white, racism but in cultural differences, in the broadest sense, between those groups and others.

Suppose, for instance, that it is universally the case in British schools, as one ILEA survey showed decisively that in their area it was, that 43 per cent of the children from West Indian families have only one parent at home, as against 5 per cent of those from Asian and 20 per cent of those from all families. Then that (in the broadest sense) cultural fact alone might be sufficient to explain most if not all the present scholastic underachievement of our British Afro-Caribbeans. For there is a great deal of evidence to show the educational relevance of having a father at home and caring; although, remarkably, this evidence, along with all other evidence emphasising the particular importance of the family, tends to be ignored by professing social scientists committed to some general doctrine of environmental omnipotence (Morgan, 1986, especially pp. 56–7).

(c) The second and consequential moral to be drawn from a study of that *1982 Annual Report* is that we badly need research focusing on cultural differences rather than racial similarities. For if only our researchers—in this encouraged and supported by formidable vested interests—were not so obsessed with race and racism, we might have evidence also of significant differences in performance between those coming from different parts of the Caribbean. It was, after all, non-racial differences between inhabitants of the different islands which killed the project of a West Indies Federation. Again, it was cultural rather than racial differences which led to the division of the Indian subcontinent into first two, then three, not always friendly nation states.

(iii) The vested interests are indeed formidable. We have had occasion before to remark that those self-described as public servants are too often assumed to be, ex officio, inhumanly disinterested, but, of course, they are in fact no less and no more human than the rest of us. We need, therefore, to remember that the CRE is a quango, and that those who man it cannot but acquire personal stakes both in its survival and in its growth. As the then Registrar of the University of Keele once nicely said of a then opposite number in a vast institution: "He is not a man to welcome suggestions for the diminution of the area of his responsibilities." So, if we discover in CRE's *Annual Reports* an inclination to exaggerate the extent of the evil of racism we shall do well to recall the traditional warning: "Never ask the barber if you need a haircut" (Palmer, 1986, p. 59).

(a) At the higher levels the pursuit of the interests of the bureau is in the main a decorous matter—delicately and discreetly massaging the evidence in order to give an impression more favourable to those interests, and so on. However, at lower, less official levels hellions may be unleashed to misrepresent and abuse, with no holds barred, any opponent perceived as constituting a serious threat. Thus David Rose, chosen by the *Guardian* to dispose of Palmer (1986) in Rose's usual way (6 February 1987), alleged that the conclusion which I drew from this CRE evidence was "to suggest that discrimination is therefore a myth". What I had actually said was exactly what is repeated above: "That we should now look for *most of* the explanation of underachievement in any underachieving immigrant group: not in white, or even in non-white, racism; but in cultural differences. . ." (emphasis added). I will construe this misrepresentation as an ingenuous incapacity to appreciate the difference between *all* and *most*.

Rose further misrepresented my contribution to Palmer (1986) as contending:

> that the disadvantages suffered by black people are essentially their own fault— either through inherent genetic shortcomings, or through their failure to ' adapt' culturally to British society.

The first of these two further misrepresentations is the cruder and less interesting. For in fact the only references to genetics in the chapter in question were in the two final pages (pp. 28–9), and they formed part of an argument to the conclusions first, that "any relevant genetic differences which may eventually be discovered are going to be differences solely on average" and, second, that it is in any case not necessary, "in order to legitimate a repudiation of racism", to deny that there in fact are such differences between different sets.

Waiving all questions about Rose's apparent failures to lay hold on the differences between race and culture, and between the hereditary determination of the one and the environmental determination of the other, it is in the present context still worthwhile to point out that, to say that "*most of* the explanation of underachievement" is to be found in "cultural differences" is not to say that those differences which do form part of this partial explanation are anyone's blameworthy fault, much less to say that they are the blameworthy faults of the particular underachievers under examination.

Sometimes no doubt in fact they will be, but, notoriously, we are not properly to be blamed for every lapse which we could have helped yet did not: there are innumerable possibilities of extenuation and excuse (Austin, 1961). Still more to the present point, there may be nothing much which the particular underachievers could do in order to remedy the cultural defects from which they are suffering: this is most obviously the case with any children of any colour whose education may be suffering from the lack of a present and caring father.

Perhaps less obviously, it is equally true of all those children of any colour trapped in schools which, for whatever reason, are not providing adequate teaching in career-crucial subjects. It so happens, however, that in Britain today these victims must in fact be disproportionately non-white. Early in 1987 the HMIs issued their most shattering report ever, overconfirming the worst fears of all those whose studies and arguments *The Teacher*, the TES and all other apologists for the bureaucratic–educational complex had for so long regularly tried to 'rubbish' as discreditably and intolerably 'right-wing'. No attempt was or could any longer be made to pretend that everything which might be amiss was due to those (really nonexistent) 'education cuts'. For the schools which the HMIs had inspected were all run by ILEA, and therefore among the most generously resourced of all those in the maintained system.

The HMIs sat in on 200 science lessons. Yet, *notwithstanding that all the teachers had had some warning of the inspection*, the conclusion was that *more than half* these lessons were substandard: 15 per cent good; 30 per cent satisfactory but not good; 40 per cent less than satisfactory; and 15 per cent "unrelievedly bad". This situation they described, mildly, as "a matter for concern". They went on to detail instances of the grossest idleness and incompetence.

At the risk, perhaps long since incurred, of boring readers to rigidity, it has to be said yet again that such enormous spreads between the best and worst outputs yielded by the same resource input is exactly what we ought to expect when suppliers are not subject to any market disciplines (or indeed, in this case, to much discipline of any other sort). Nor must we ever forget that, if *Labour's Charter for Parents* and the wishes of the NUT were ever implemented, then idle or incompetent teachers—who were under this particular inspection actually in the majority—would, through pupil profiles uncheckable against the results achieved in independently assessed public examinations, become the ultimate judges in their own causes. Having first ruined the wretched pupils, they could then commend their own work in producing what they chose falsely to say were superlative results!

(b) There are, in what for want of any other and better name we have to continue calling the Race Relations Industry, vested interests much more sinister and more powerful than the bureaucratic. So far their greatest triumph as been the diversion and redirection of the committee which eventually reported under the Chairmanship of Lord Swann. That report was issued by Her Majesty's Stationery Office (HMSO) in 1985 under a title embracing that committee's original terms of reference, *Education for All: The Report of the Committee of Inquiry into the Education of Children from Ethnic Minority Groups.*

Much has been said elsewhere about this deplorable document and, if it appears that it is having a substantial influence, much more will need to be said (see, for example, O'Keeffe, 1985). Here it will be sufficient to make one point only. This is that the majority allowed itself to be intimidated by an internal minority, backed by vociferous and militant external support, into the abject abandonment of any serious research designed to fulfil its original terms of reference. Those pressing for this disgraceful abdication had, as we have seen, good reason to fear that any honest and exhaustive investigation of the causes of educational underachievement, especially by Afro-Caribbeans, would reveal that this has in the main to be put down not to the racism of their white teachers and examiners but to what are, in the broadest sense, cultural facts both about the underachievers themselves and about their families. As *The Times* in its restrained way put the matter (15 March 1986): "Conflict within the Committee itself prevented it from pursuing its proposed factual survey into the social circumstances of successful and unsuccessful pupils in each major ethnic group."

6

Peace, 'Peace Studies', and the 'Peace Movement'

I don't believe in neutrality . . . People who think they can be devil's advocates and think they can present all sides of the argument and be objective are actually hiding behind their own political values. The starting point is that we live in an un-equal society and political education is about organising and thinking critically for change. (George Nicholson, the GLC member 'with special responsibility for Political Education' in ILEA, in the *Socialist Education Magazine* for Autumn 1982, p. 22.)

Our young people must be offered "a balanced view of modern society through political and trade union education." Central to this "balanced view" must be "Education for peace". (*Labour's Charter for Pupils and Parents*, 1985.)

The document containing the phrases quoted in the second epigraph, immediately above, seems to have found considerable favour with most of the teachers' unions. Also, notwithstanding that, among other things, it apparently proposed the abolition of all externally assessed public examinations, the destruction of all independent schools and the com-pulsory completion of the Comprehensive Revolution, the TES somehow contrived to describe the entire performance as "unexceptionable".

What today's new Labour Party counts as "a balanced view of modern society" is suggested by the first epigraph to this chapter. However, just in case that is wrongly dismissed as untypical, characteristic only of those too complacently picked out by most of the media as 'the loony left', we must also refer to ongoings in Cambridge, now a boom town about as far removed as could be from a decaying inner city. There, having won control of the Council, the Labour Party forthwith decided to introduce 'Peace Studies' into all the schools in the area. At the same time, making the object of that exercise perfectly plain, it also voted to provide funds for organisations active in the 'Peace Movement'; to support the 'Greenham Women' in a US lawsuit aimed at preventing the installation of cruise missiles in the UK;

to provide premises for a 'Peace Centre'; to hold the biggest possible public meeting in order "to publicise the nuclear free zone concept and the Council's attitude to civil defence"; to mount a major exhibition on the theme of peace; to invite East European artists to appear at the next Cambridge Festival; and to run 'peace seminars' for the education of the council staff. (See the *Cambridge Daily News* for 4 December 1984.)

6.1 A preliminary skirmish

It is, nevertheless, sometimes suggested that 'Peace Studies' and Education for Peace' are, or at least could be, something other and better than pro-Communist political indoctrination—propaganda for defencelessness against the Soviet power. Earlier in the year of the ongoings listed above the Master of a Cambridge college had actually asserted in a letter to *The Times* (6 January 1984) that even the present courses are "of unimpeachable intellectual integrity"! Two years later, in the more esoteric but equally respectable *Journal of the Philosophy of Education* we find Nigel Blake (1986) beginning an article: "Must we put a stop to Peace Education? The single purpose of this paper is to argue that we must not" (p. 27).

(i) The way in which Blake addresses this task is curiously indirect. It also reveals rather more than perhaps he intended to say both about the actual content of courses currently presented under the label 'Peace Studies' and about the true purposes of those now promoting and teaching such courses. For his second paragraph explains that the courses are "a political response" to "defence policies", policies which, he is so indiscreet as to confess, "Many of us believe . . . must be challenged by all available means" (p. 27). In the third paragraph he asserts: "There are perhaps three familiar arguments against Peace Education. None, however, are powerful or initially plausible. I find it more fruitful and illuminating here to rebut a different possible argument, one which I have not seen explicitly employed against Peace Education, but which is implicit in the kinds of political attack which have been mounted against the Peace Movement" (p. 27).

What is curious about all this, and in a way revealing, is that, rather than trying to meet the objections already made against what is actually being done under the 'Peace Studies' banner, Blake prefers, first himself to develop, and then to attack, what he calls "the Statist Case against Peace Education" (p. 27). This is a case which, on his own account, has been at most implicit, but never actually made. It would, however, also be a case even against a possible rather than any actual programme of 'Peace Studies'.

Of the opposition arguments which Blake lists as in fact urged, all three are dismissed in very short order; and all on the grounds that—whatever the merits or demerits of what in fact is being done, or for the foreseeable future is likely to be done, under the heading 'Peace Studies'—something other, and perhaps better, conceivably could be done. A certain academic aloofness, especially in a journal of philosophy, is often wholly appropriate. However, in this case it consists ill with the commitment, so frankly expressed in Blake's second paragraph, to a "political response to . . . defence policies", policies which, he frankly proclaims, "must be challenged by all available means".

In this perspective Blake's entire presentation and critique of what he calls "the Statist Case against Peace Education" must appear to be little more than a diversionary manoeuvre, presumably designed to distract attention away from the almost unprecedented and altogether scandalous exercises in partisan political indoctrination now being conducted under the auspices of so many of our LEAs.

(ii) The first objection noticed is that 'Peace Studies' is a non-subject. Academic conservatives have on occasion compared it not only with 'Women's Studies' and 'Black Studies' but also, more waggishly, with a project for 'Hole Studies'. (See Cox and Scruton, 1984, pp. 9ff.)

(a) This objection Blake meets by saying: "One could easily imagine a programme of studies which could appropriately be called Peace Education yet which had no truck with any supposed discipline of Peace Studies" (p. 27). True perhaps, although what we can easily imagine is scarcely relevant to questions about what is now actually being done.

What, however, is both relevant and important is Blake's short list of topics for inclusion in such an ideal programme of 'Peace Education', for it makes no specific reference to certain indispensable items. These are the essentials which are not, it would appear, in fact included in any of the syllabi previously published but which any possible programme amounting to more than the blinkered propaganda of what its spokespersons call 'The Peace Movement' would surely have to include. The reference is, of course, to the expansionary achievements and ambitions of the USSR and to the fundamental facts about a Leninist regime which, unlike those of the NATO countries, is subject to no internal democratic inhibitions.

The 'Peace Movements' both in NATO and the Warsaw Pact states do nevertheless have a lot in common, for both equally are dedicated to unilateral nuclear disarmament—by NATO. (Gwynne, 1985b, is of especial interest here. It gives an account of a conference in the School of Peace Studies at Bradford, ruefully attended by the authoress immediately after her return from visiting one of those countries in Eastern Europe already subject to the Soviet imperial power.)

(b) The second objection, like the first, is met by dismissing reference to the sordid actual in favour of a cult of the conceivable: ". . . it is alleged that Peace Education must be stopped because it is actually biased. I do not know whether this is true. But I see no reason why it must be true" (p. 27).

Blake's claim to nescience here consists a little awkwardly with his own earlier identification of 'Peace Education' with 'The Peace Movement'. However, if he does truly need and wish to learn, perhaps the best source of information about the strength and activities in Edbiz of the Campaign for Nuclear Disarmament (CND) and its allies is still Marks (1984).

The same and similar sources will also show the weakness of Blake's further observation: "There can be biased History or biased Religious Studies; yet no one suggests that these subjects should be banned, whatever other reservations they may have" (p. 27). In the first place it is not strictly correct to say that no one has ever suggested that either of these subjects should be banned. I myself, when young, argued, and in this at least was not altogether alone, that any Religious Studies should be studies of what religious people have believed and have done, but should never present any religious beliefs to children as if they were, what they are not, items of knowledge (Flew, 1968: this is something which my sometime pupil, given this reminder, may now recall).

In the second place, and much more to the present practical point, there are nowadays precious few teachers—and, it might sometimes seem, as few or fewer clergy—wholeheartedly and straightforwardly committed to traditional Christian doctrines. Even if there were many more, and even if they did feel tempted, or consider it their duty, to try to indoctrinate their charges, then they still could not hope to make much headway with members of a generation so totally secularised.

However, today, as elsewhere Blake would no doubt be eager to assure us, 'The Peace Movement' is a mass organisation. Furthermore, most of its members see it as a crusade. It also seems to have a peculiarly powerful appeal to teachers. For instance, the 1982 annual conference of the professedly non-political NUT rejected a proposal actually to affiliate to CND by only 114,000 card votes to 108,000. In opposing this resolution the union's President issued a significantly suggestive, carefully phrased disclaimer: "Teachers are not supposed to indoctrinate children, and we shall demonstrate our bias if we pass this." (See *The Times* for 14 April 1982.) It seems, therefore, to be neither disputed nor regretted that the indoctrination is being done, but it must not, or not too obviously, be seen to be done.

6.2 Conceptual truths, factual truisms and some favourite fallacies

Our present concern is with peace as opposed to war, rather than with—say—peace of mind. Certainly in this and perhaps in every sense peace, like both liberty and health, is something essentially negative, albeit a practically necessary condition of all manner of other more positive goods. Yet in all three cases there are those, uneasy with the idea that anything they rightly recognise as an important good should be thus negative, who insist on intruding their own positive values into these negative concepts.

(i) Immanuel Kant, for instance, at the beginning of the second paragraph of the Third Section of his *Groundwork of the Metaphysic of Morals*, objected to his own first and provisional account of liberty of the will: "The preceding definition of freedom is *negative* and therefore unfruitful for the discovery of its essence; but it leads to a *positive* conception which is so much the more full and fruitful." Notoriously, those who go on to develop a notion of 'positive freedom' proposes in its name to compel us to do things which (*they* maintain) are for *our* good (Flew, 1983).

Again, in its original constitution the World Health Organisation stated that "Health is a state of complete physical, mental and social-wellbeing, and not merely the absence of disease or infirmity. . ." The intentions of those who drafted this formulation were no doubt altogether admirable. Nevertheless it opened the way for psychiatrists, while pretending still to remain within the Hippocratic tradition, to strive to reshape their patients in directions which are not necessarily those chosen by those patients, but which certainly do accord with the ideals either of their psychiatrists, or of the states employing them or both (Flew, 1973).

To recognise the essential negativity of peace is relevant in as much as this conceptual truth provides the basis for an answer to a plausible challenge: 'If War Studies then why not—especially since peace is so much to be preferred—Peace Studies?' That argument does not, after all, go through. For the mere absence of war, gratifying though that must be in itself, cannot provide a positive uniting principle sufficient to define an academic area. So far at any rate, 'Peace Studies' remain more like 'Hole Studies' than they are like War Studies.

(ii) Peace, in our understanding, is, quite simply and very straightforwardly, the absence of war. Wars are started, waged and stopped either by collectivities or by individuals acting on behalf of collectivities. This point, too, like that of the essential negativity of peace, is both in a sense philosophical and, once made, undeniably obvious. Nevertheless, like so many similarly obvious and philosophical points, it does carry practical implications. Most immediately it suggests that the study of individual psychology is not going to be able to throw much light upon the causes of wars: something to remember if and when all the established academic groups start to demand a piece of the 'Peace Studies' action!

Another similarly obvious yet fundamental point is that—with some short-lived exceptions and others of no contemporary interest—wars are waged by and between states. In their turn states—again with certain exceptions which may for present purposes be ignored—are under the control of governments, and it is their governments which decide whether wars are to start, continue or stop. The short-lived and contemporary exceptions are civil wars, in which the party opposing what remains of the previous central government and state machine makes haste to establish its own alternatives, as was the case, for instance, in the Spanish Civil War of 1936–9.

(a) Different governments make their different decisions in different ways, and under various constraints. A few, a precious few—a tiny minority of the near two hundred represented in the United Nations—are ultimately accountable to a mass electorate. This kind of accountability constitutes a most powerful constraint. It makes it almost impossible for such a government to start or to conduct a war which is not perceived as either wholly defensive or likely to be short, cheap and distant, and very difficult to maintain a military establishment adequate to deter the hostile advances of powers the governments of which are not so constrained. We have here considerations which would, surely, be central to the long-term thinking of any peace campaign which—unlike, for instance, the World Peace Council—was not in effect and even in intention an instrument of Soviet foreign policy.

(b) The other present relevance of our third glimpse of the too-often neglected obvious is to remind enthusiasts for new programmes of 'Peace Studies' that an enormous amount of work bearing upon the stated aims of those programmes has been and is being done by people paid as historians or as political scientists. That reminder given it becomes incumbent upon those enthusiasts to provide generous hospitality both for that work and for the disciplines required to do it. They also need to think much harder than in Britain any have shown any sign of doing of what substantially different and equally or more relevant sort of work it would be appropriate to do as 'Peace Studies' research.

In fact here neither of these obligations is being met. Where, for instance, in any of the proliferating syllabi can we discover recommendations of works by mainstream historians, works such as *Studies in War and Peace* or *The Causes of Wars* by Michael Howard, sometime Chichele Professor of the History of War, and now Regius Professor of Modern History, in the University of Oxford? Such works are as consistently and systematically excluded from these syllabi as are those of Thomas Sowell from all the programmes for 'multi-cultural' and 'anti-racist education'. It takes no extraordinary powers of creative conjecture to recognise the similar and parallel reasons why.

Again, what we do find when we look down the list of current postgraduate research programmes published by the School of Peace Studies in the University of Bradford? These range from 'British Civil Defence Programmes' through 'Women in the Peace Movement' and 'Asian Education in Bradford' to 'Water Resources on the Palestinian Left Bank'. Then in the list of dissertations submitted in 1983 we have such remote and esoteric gems as 'The Failed Life and Achieved Poetry of

Sylvia Plath' and 'The Informal Education of the Post-school Adolescent' (Cox and Scruton, 1984, pp. 12ff.).

(iii) Continuing to review conceptual truths and factual truisms, the fourth such proposition to take on board is that it has been many years since any government, much less any people, has been even inclined to rate war any kind of good in itself. None now, surely, would contemplate war save in so far as the perceived alternative were by them regarded as even more intolerable. To say this, of course, is to say not that there is everywhere an overwhelming reluctance to wage war but that all governments would, if possible, prefer to achieve their objectives by other means.

(a) It is important to underline this fourth truth, for it is implicitly denied by those who accuse political opponents of warmongering. It is here wryly significant, and significant in many ways, that this charge has been and is loudly and widely urged against President Reagan, who is subject to every democratic constraint, and by people who never think to bring the same accusation against the government of the USSR, which is currently conducting a quite extraordinarily cruel colonial war in and against Afghanistan. However, even that imperial government presumably regards the waging of war as very much the lesser evil as compared with (to them) the intolerability of Afghan independence.

Those who implicitly or explicitly deny our fourth truistic truth often support that denial with an unsound argument, urging that it is governments which launch and maintain wars, whereas peoples are always anti-war. However, the first of these two claims is true only in an interpretation which makes it effectively tautological, while the second is false unless it is construed as meaning only that they do not regard war as good in itself. Certainly in the summer of 1940 the British people were at least as resolved as our government not to surrender; nor, after Pearl Harbor, were there many voices heard in the USA urging the President to arrange terms of capitulation!

(b) This fourth fundamental thus duly grasped, we are ready to appreciate two further points, at least one of which might be seen as a corollary. The first and more consequential is that, until and unless you have assessed the possible alternatives, it is silly to conclude that the initiation or continuation of war is the worst of all possible courses of action. This is again a point which once made, might seem too obvious to be worth putting. It is, nevertheless, commonly and, in some circles, universally overlooked. Where, for instance is the film or television critic who has not said of every latest realistic war movie that it demonstrates the futility of war? Yet how could the typical treatment, confined to the actual waging of a war, and without attending to the later consequences of that war, even begin to demonstrate anything of the such?

In the 1930s the conclusion that wars are always futile was standardly supported by a bold generalisation, itself usually sustained by no historical knowledge at all: 'No war ever settles anything.' Since World War I had been billed as the war to end wars some of these drastic generalisers were perhaps recklessly confounding two vastly different propositions: 'No war ever settles anything' and 'No war settles everything'.

There are, of course, innumerable instances to falsify that first recklessly ignorant generalisation. Consider, for instance, the splendid words of the inscription upon the Lincoln Memorial in Washington, DC: "In this temple, as in the hearts of the people for whom he saved the union, the memory of Abraham Lincoln is enshrined for ever." To this originally stated and eventually achieved aim Emancipation was added as a far from negligible bonus. (We must nevertheless be both saddened to contemplate the frightful costs of that second achievement, and perplexed that in the same period the freeing of the black slaves of Brazil and the white slaves of Russia should have been comparatively costless.)

(iv) There is another equally worthless argument, employed only since World War II, and then only with reference to nuclear weapons. It consists in urging that it is crazy for the superpowers to add or to update their arsenals of these armaments since both already have enough to kill all their enemies several times over. Such superpower moves may or may not be in some ways infatuated, but certainly, and by itself, the present argument does nothing to prove that they are.

In this case the begrudged moments of preliminary thought should have been about what it is now conventional to call conventional weapons: ordinary shells and bullets or, for that matter, arrows and spears. Powers going to war have almost always had enough of these to kill all their enemies several times over—if only those enemies were willing to position themselves suicidally, making no efforts either to resist or to reciprocate!

(a) The second and less consequential further point is that it is sometimes outright false, and almost always very misleading, to describe all military budgets as providing for expenditure on defence. This particular kind of confusion, along with many others, can be seen at perhaps its most confounded in the Report of the Brandt Commission. In a characteristically uncritical aphorism the Commission contends: "More arms do not make mankind safer, only poorer."

Suppose that the UN, perhaps inspired by a speech from the first Prime Minister of independent Grenada, had, against that prophet's predicted invasion of UFOs from outer space, launched a fabulously expensive, and indeed just fabulous, programme for the defence of Planet Earth. Then Brandt's aphorism would have been apt.

As a contribution to thought about problems of the real world, which is what the whole Report pretends to be, it is not. For the various separate military budgets thus fallaciously summed to yield a total expenditure on the defence of "mankind" are, of course, all budgets spent by separate, more or less sovereign governments on behalf not of mankind as a whole but of their own particular peoples. (Critical readers of J. S. Mill's *Utilitarianism* will be reminded of the way in which the psychological hedonists' insistence that everyone individually pursues their own greatest happiness leaves no one available for the collective pursuit of the greatest happiness of the greatest number.)

It now becomes obvious that at least some states and peoples have been and are made much safer by their military expenditure. Suppose that the state of Israel, for instance, had followed Brandt in eschewing all military spending as unacceptably impoverishing. Then, certainly, the state of Israel would have ceased to exist long since while, probably, much of its population would have survived, if at all, only in a condition substantially more wretched than anything suffered in consequence of its enormously burdensome actual defence spending.

When in this way we descend from fictitious global collectivities to concrete and individual fact it also becomes clear that it is not correct to describe all military as defence expenditure. If it really were, then how could there be actual or possible threats for all the defence provision to be defence against? Of course, it is not. There are actual threats, and real possibilities of future threats. To cite just one of the least disputable 'Third World' cases, Colonel Gadaffi has, ever since seizing power, spent hugely on armaments. Yet can anyone, keeping a straight face, assert that any of Libya's neighbours have been or are more threatening than threatened? Chad? Egypt? Tunisia?

(b) The way in which talk about defence can be misleading, as opposed to plain false, is by suggesting that the main object of the exercise must be to fight and to win any defensive war in which the state to be defended might find itself engaged. This does not have to be so, and in today's world usually is not so in fact. For the main objective, even the sole objective, may be — and of course in the case of NATO is— to deter possible attackers, and thus to forestall threats and to prevent rather than to win wars.

It is entirely consistent with the pursuit of this objective to hold that the outbreak of the war which you are labouring to prevent would be an unmitigated catastrophe, or even that it would not be in any real sense winnable by either party. Indeed the more firmly you hold to these opinions, the stronger your reasons for seeking and maintaining some effective deterrent. A deterrent is as such effective precisely and only to the extent that its possession forestalls the necessity of its employment. As the US Admiral Mahan said of British seapower in the Napoleonic wars: "Those far distant storm-beaten ships, upon which the Grand Army never looked, alone stood between it and the dominion of the world!"

(v) It is therefore, however emotionally effective, rationally absurd to present the unspeakably appalling consequences of bombardment by a salvo of multi-megaton nuclear missiles—as members of what call themselves 'anti-nuclear campaigns' or 'peace movements' so regularly do present them—as knockdown decisive reasons for abandoning your own deterrents, while still, of course, leaving such ultimate weapons in hands potentially or actually hostile. It cannot be too often reiterated that both Hiroshima and Nagasaki were, de facto, 'nuclear-free zones'. Though paradoxical, there was an invaluable nugget of truth in the old Roman maxim: "Si vis pacem para bellum" (If you want peace, prepare for war), a maxim later adapted and adopted by the USAAF Strategic Air Command: "Peace is our profession."

Here the important and crucial distinction is between, on the one hand, actually waging a defensive war and, on the other, deterring an actual or potential enemy from either attacking or securing compliance by threatening so to do. Once this distinction is grasped, as it seems that by the more militant 'peaceniks' it rarely if ever is, then it ceases to be any longer possible honestly to misrepresent the position of all those opposed to unilateral (and always non-Soviet) nuclear disarmament as epitomised in the nutshell slogan, 'Better dead than red'. It would be more although still not perfectly correct to sum it up as. 'Better some chance, and that not necessarily a very big chance, of being dead; rather than the near certainty of being red.' In any case those of us who are active friends of freedom and 'enemies of socialism' must expect under a Marxist–Leninist regime to be consigned to the slow death of the Gulag. For what even the least resisted of such takeovers could mean for 'enemies of socialism' see, for instance, Milosz (1981). By the Nobel Prizewinning poet, this is an account, first published in 1951, of the 1940 incorporation into the USSR of the three once independent Baltic republics, Latvia, Lithuania and Esthonia. For what a resisted Soviet occupation means today, consult the witness of martyred Afghanistan—a far-off country of which our new appeasers do not wish to hear.

So why should it be thought that defenders of deterrence do see our situation in the way in which such 'peaceniks' so stubbornly insist on saying that we see it? Here, as always when a case is persistently misrepresented by even moderately intelligent and well-informed persons, such misrepresentations ought to be construed as ungracious and backhanded admissions that the misrepresenters are at a loss to refute yet, for their own reasons, unwilling to accept, the case as truly presented.

There is a similarly revealing and damaging moral to be drawn from the well-sustained, indeed systematic, reluctance of the protagonists of 'Peace Studies' even to mention in their syllabi, much less actually to get their pupils to attend to, any powerfully argued deployments of the case against defencelessness (Marks, 1984; Cox and Scruton, 1984). The maximum concession commonly made to even a minimal fairmindedness is to mention in the syllabus, if perhaps nowhere else, one or two dull, stilted, punch-pulling, diplomatically inhibited pamphlets issued by the Ministry of Defence. For how could the indoctrinators be sure of making recruits to CND if they had encouraged their classes to attend to such vigorous, forthright and altogether uninhibited polemics as, for instance, Alun Chalfont 'The Great Unilateralist Illusion' in *Encounter* for April 1983 or Eric and Rael Jean Isaac 'The Counterfeit Peacemakers: Atomic Freeze' in *The American Spectator* for June 1982? (Both articles have also been separately reprinted as pamphlets in, respectively, London, England, and Bloomington, Indiana.)

6.3 'Peace Movements' where there is no war

Confronted by the many and various groups customarily calling themselves 'The Peace Movement', and usually accepted by the media at this their own valuation, some, but too few, non-movers have resented the implicit suggestion that a sincere concern for the maintenance of peace is narrowly proprietary, and confined to the militants of this movement. More particularly, everyone who refuses to surrender to the claims of CND—the Campaign for National Defencelessness—ought robustly to resent the insolent offensiveness of that organisation's employment as the title of its journal of the word *Sanity*.

  (i) In the perspectives opened by Section 6.2 we should also perceive it as strange, in countries which have in fact been at peace for many years, and in which no one is advocating war, that nevertheless there are nowadays often strong and vociferous movements describing themselves as 'Peace Movements'. In a free society, although only to the extent that it is indeed such, you might expect to find peace movements on two conditions: if a war was already in progress or if a proposal to start one was being seriously and actively debated. But why now, and why in several countries of Western Europe? (Several, but not all: the absence of such a movement in France is, presumably, to be explained by the presence of a strong and devoutly Muscovite Communist Party. It would there be just too obvious what such a movement was a movement towards!)

  Part of the answer to the general question about 'Peace Movements' must lie in failures to appreciate points made in Section 6.2, points which, though elementary and, once made, obvious, just as obviously do escape many persons not otherwise egregiously obtuse, but the clue to another part is a corollary of one of these same truistic points. For wherever it is the case that no government holds war to be somehow good in itself, there one could perhaps hope to find an absolute guarantee of permanent peace in ensuring that all demands made under threat of military force shall be accepted immediately.

This is indeed the openly proclaimed policy of the Anti-Tax Party in Denmark, which proposes the installation of a hotline with its pre-recorded answer (in Russian) to any ultimatum: 'We surrender.' It is, surely, significant that everyone identifies one and only one considerable source of ultimata to Denmark? (We simplify by here ignoring both the theoretical possibilities of incompatible ultimata and the more practical possibility that surrender would leave the captive nation still liable to be involved in the wars of its captors.)

(ii) It appears, furthermore, to be characteristic of all self-styled Peace Movements, not only in Western Europe but also—curiously and notably—in the Socialist bloc both to be demanding the one-sided nuclear disarmament of Western Europe and to be denouncing alleged American or allied (but very rarely if not quite never Soviet) 'imperialists', 'revanchists' and 'warmongers'.

This demand may be made for various and widely different reasons, differences of which anyone genuinely embarking on study of the issues needs to take account. Quakers and other pacifist supporters, for example, irrespective of whatever beliefs they may hold about the consequences of alternative courses, reject all employment of military force, whether nuclear or not, as absolutely and indefensibly wrong. Others, while not committed to this total rejection, are convinced that war, or at any rate nuclear war, is the worst of all possible evils. They recognise that it necessarily takes two sides to run a war, that there is no chance whatsoever of the USSR disarming unilaterally, and precious little of its agreeing to any really substantial progress towards verifiable multilateral disarmament. so, in hopes of removing all danger of the occurrence of so catastrophic a conflict, they call for the immediate one-sided disarmament of the side which just might be persuaded so to disarm.

A variant on the extreme pacifist position, one which can consistently be maintained by those who reject that extreme position and which has found some academically distinguished spokespersons, argues that it must be indefeasibly wrong to threaten to do something which, it might more plausibly be argued, it would indeed be inexcusable actually to do. If it would be morally wrong to respond to any actual Soviet first strike, whether counter-force or counter-value, by a counter-value or perhaps by any sort of second strike, then—it is argued—it must be wrong to threaten and to intend so to do.

It is very hard to have any patience with such factitious scruples, and well-nigh impossible to believe that they could be being sincerely urged by anyone at least reconciled if not positively and deliberately devoted to the achievement of a Marxist–Leninist world. As graduate students of philosophy some of us used sometimes to amuse ourselves by thinking up outrageous consequentialist counter-examples with which to challenge purist Kantian contentions that lying and other kinds of prima facie wrong doing must be in all circumstances and indefeasibly immoral. None of these farfetched examples could have been more outrageous or more challenging than the citation in the present context of soberly factual accounts of what an occupation by the Red Army, and the consequent installation of an irremovable Marxist–Leninist despotism, actually involves. So if anyone suggests to me, as I contemplate such a prospect, that I must not support the making of any threats which, arguably, it would be wicked to carry out, then I cannot but find myself, at least for once and momentarily, in partial agreement with Trotsky:

> As for us, we were never concerned with the Kantian-priestly and vegetarian-Quaker prattle about the 'sacredness of human life'!

(iii) Whatever their other merits or demerits, these pacifist and para-pacifist positions are thought through, and as such deserve a modicum of respect. However, the mass of the members and supporters of the 'Peace Movement' would seem to belong to one or other of two further sets, whom opponents may like mnemonically to distinguish as The Ninnies and The Nasties.

(a) The first of these two labels can be applied not unfairly to all who, not wishing to be troubled by hard facts or harder argument, respond to seeing *The Day After* or its like with the bleating, knee-jerk reaction: 'Ban the Bomb!' By this intellectual abdication they make themselves available for exploitation by anything calling itself an anti-nuclear or peace movement. The second and much less friendly label applies to all those who are consciously and deliberately working for that further and decisive shift in the world balance of power which must result from further successes for the policies of these movements.

It is correct to speak of "further successes". Perhaps the biggest was to delay or prevent the deployment of the so-called 'neutron bomb'. The central argument in that campaign was, significantly, first provided by Nikita Khrushchev, in his speech to a 'Soviet–Rumanian Friendship Meeting' on 11 August 1961. "The neutron bomb as conceived by American scientists," he said, "should kill everything living but leave material assets intact. They are acting as robbers who want to murder a man without staining his suit with blood, so as to be able to use this suit."

The great attraction of this new weapon, for all those who are concerned for the defence rather than the surrender of the West, was its promise of providing a decisive counter to the overwhelmingly superior tank armies of the

Warsaw Pact, a counter which, unlike any previously available nuclear weapon, would not in its use devastate large areas of Western Europe. Such use might also be thought less likely to provoke escalation to the strategic level than the use of more primitive tactical nuclear weapons. However, these attractions were, and surely significantly, no more attractive to the 'peace movements' than to Khrushchev. All concerned somehow managed to suppress grins at his characteristically comical suggestion that the uniform protective clothing of Soviet tank crews is some sort of natty, double-breasted, business suiting.

(b) The nickname 'The Nasties' fits all those whose support for 'Peace Movements' springs from a concern to promote Soviet power. At one time this set would have consisted almost entirely of members of fellow-travellers of Communist Parties in full communion with Moscow. Thanks to the growth of many if perhaps not quite fifty-six other varieties of Marxist–Leninists, some of which profess to disown whatever is taken to fall under the—one must suspect—deliberately indefinite description of 'Stalinism', that is true no longer.

It nevertheless remains the case, not very surprisingly, that Marxist–Leninists of all stripes, who seem in all 'Peace Movements' to exercise an organisational influence out of all proportion to their numbers, are rarely ready to admit publicly that, for them at least, the whole point and purpose of such movements is to promote Soviet power. Yet they can scarcely deny that—to employ what used to be favourite semi-technical terms among the cadres—'objectively' this must be the consequence of such policies, whatever the 'subjective' intents of any individuals. Those boldly claiming the Trotskyist name, of course, actually boast that, in all external conflicts, they stand 'unconditionally' at the side of the USSR, still characterised, a little oddly, as 'a workers' state' (Baker, 1981: one wonders what more the Nomenklatura needs to do in order finally to forfeit that intended commendation).

Extreme socialists of all stripes are usually predominant, if not always correspondingly prominent, in the leadership and control of these self-styled anti-nuclear and peace movements. They also play a similarly disproportionate part in the business of inducing labour unions and other organisations to commit themselves to support their political campaigns. Indeed, whereas it would be utterly wrong to assert that all their members and supporters have been and are either Marxist–Leninists or any other kind of ultra-socialist, it would by contrast be very nearly the exact truth to say that all socialist ultras do support the unilateral dismantling of all non-Soviet nuclear weapons. So much is it so that strength of support for this policy has become a chief criterion for the application of the expression 'ultra left-wing'. Yet it would not be quite the exact truth so long as there remain those for whom Beijing rather than Moscow is the Third Rome, and who therefore wish to see some countervailing force maintained against the 'hegemonism' of 'the New Tsars'.

(iv) Consider in this context the transformation of the British Labour Party which, having once provided and solidly supported one of the Foreign Secretaries most dedicated and most active in the foundation of NATO, is now totally committed to diametrically opposite policies: for the unilateral renunciation of the British nuclear deterrent; for the expulsion of all US nuclear forces; and for (what it is trying to sell as) "a non-nuclear *defence* policy".

This political phenomenon becomes intelligible surely, only to those prepared to open their eyes to the fact that those who brought about this transformation do positively and deliberately desire that decisive shift in the world balance of power to which these policies must inevitably contribute. It must, after all, be impossibly difficult for persons apprised, as we all are, of the enormous destructive potential of nuclear wepaons to persuade themselves that, in a conflict in which one side enjoyed a monopoly on such weapons and was not somehow effectively constrained from using them, the other side could be anything but totally at the mercy of those nucler monopolists. How many hours was it, after those first two demonstrations at Hiroshima and Nagasaki, before Japan surrendered unconditionally?

That the people whom we are talking about are not in fact themselves persuaded of this foolishness can be brought out by resolving another puzzle. The writers of opinion columns in the British press all expressed astonishment when three or four years ago Anthony Wedgwood-Benn and other able but 'very left-wing' members of the National Executive Committee of the Labour Party proclaimed that no threat is either coming or likely to come from the USSR. How, these editorialisers asked, could otherwise intelligent and well-informed politicians be so complacent and so blind?

Theirs was a perplexity which it takes only a small tincture of philosphy to ease. It is a matter of the logic of threats and promises. Which of your foretellings of your future behaviour towards me I shall perceive as threats and which as promises is in large part determined by what I myself happen to relish or to disrelish. If someone undertakes to kill me then—unless I am a candidate for voluntary euthanasia unable to kill myself—this undertaking has to be perceived as a threat. If someone undertakes to realise my own ideals, then their undertaking must, on the contrary, be seen by me as a promise.

Now, if we review both the whole aggressive external record of the Soviet regime from the conquest of Menshevik Georgia in 1920 to its still-continuing colonial wars in Afghanistan, and internal pronouncements from the leadership starting with Lenin himself, it becomes out of the question to deny that the rulers of the USSR have been and remain resolved to impose their social system wherever they are able to extend their control.

What, for instance, is Soviet sea power for? Listen to Admiral Gorshkov, the recently retired Commander in Chief of the Red Fleet:

> Soviet sea power, merely a minor defensive arm in 1953, has become the optimum means by which to defeat the imperialist enemy and the most important element in the Soviet arsenal to prepare the way for a Communist world.

For this, and for lots more of the similar, compare Greig (1981). This "compilation of Soviet statements on ideology, foreign policy and the use of military force" ought to be on every 'Peace Studies' reading list. In fact neither it nor any comparable substitute has so far been discovered in any such syllabus.

In the light of all this, do we really have to go on pretending that it is not precisely, or at any rate roughly, the same system of total and therefore totalitarian socialism—the social system for the universalisation of which Admiral Gorshkov built up the new all-oceans Soviet Navy—which those who have transformed the Labour Party are themselves labouring to impose? Whyever should those 'very left-wing' people, therefore, perceive overwhelming Soviet power as a threat? In fact they most manifestly, and altogether realistically, do not.

6.4 The contents of 'Peace Studies' programmes

In Section 6.1 we noticed the argument "that—whatever the merits or demerits of what in fact is being done, for the foreseeable future is likely to be done, under the heading 'Peace Studies'—something other, and perhaps better, conceivably could be done". Certainly, nothing could ever make 'Peace Studies' or 'Peace Education' an unitary discipline. At best it is bound to remain—like 'Black Studies', 'Women's Studies' and 'World Studies' (Scruton, 1985)—an artificial collection of scraps and pieces rather than a natural field of academic enquiry and instruction.

Equally certainly there is no possibility either at this time or for the foreseeable future of having in British schools any 'Peace Studies' which are not in practice, what at present they almost always are and are indeed intended to be, partisan and indoctrinative. Those many for whom every such course is in fact an opportunity to make propaganda—primarily for defencelessness and secondarily for all manner of other always leftist causes—are far too well entrenched in too many institutions, and far too strongly represented in the teachers' unions for any such possible ideal to be realised in practice (Marks, 1984; Cox and Scruton, 1984; Scruton *et al.*, 1985).

It is nevertheless worthwhile briefly to consider what would have to be included in a programme which really was to be "of unimpeachable intellectual integrity". This is worthwhile if only still more starkly to bring out how very far the present programmes are from meriting that magisterial commendation.

(i) Suppose, then, that we are concerned to construct such a worthy programme. Suppose, too, that the object is, as it certainly ought to be, to help students to think better and more fruitfully about the great issues of war and peace. Then one thing which we shall certainly want to include is some basic training in the critical (appraising) examination of the arguments most commonly deployed in controversies in this area. In the waspish words of one of the greatest of intellectual coaches: ". . . there is nothing so plain boring as the constant repetition of assertions that are not true, and sometimes not even faintly sensible; if we can reduce this a bit, it will be all to the good" (Austin, 1962, p. 5).

(a) Boring it may be, but it is much worse than boring when the constantly reiterated falsehoods and fallacies are being effectively employed to support catastrophic conclusions. Yet the syllabi, the promoters and presumably the teachers of the present courses make no room for any such training in the arts of appraisal. On the contrary, they seem to be themselves the eager clients rather than any kind of critics of most of the particular falsehoods and fallacies previously examined in this chapter.

That is, of course, one more reason why it is impossible to avoid the conclusion that the object of the exercise is not education but indoctrination. In so far as this is indeed the case, the teachers of 'Peace Studies' will not want their pupils either to learn relevant facts or to acquire critical capacities; not, that is, if those acquisitions are likely to undermine the convictions which these teachers are striving to implant.

(b) Nor is the indoctrination which is actually going on in the periods devoted to 'Peace Studies' restricted to the beliefs and attitudes of the propaganda for defencelessness. In Section 6.1 we noted how the adoption of a perversely positive redefinition of 'peace' licenses the subsumption of all manner of other perceived goods under that term.

For instance, it is in the world of 'Peace Education' also usual to redefine 'violence' in a way similarly perverse, distorting and enormously overextended. In the traditional sense, the sense in which violence has acquired and deserves its traditional ill repute, doing violence is the essentially intentional infliction of grievous bodily or sometimes other harm. In the new sense of 'violence', occasionally qualified as structural or institutional, although the suggestion of sinister intent is retained, almost anything of which the speaker disapproves can (however caused) be rated (an effect of) violence.

As one "practitioner" observes, "the extended definition of 'violence' . . . enables an extended definition of 'peace' " (Duzcek, 1983). It does indeed. For, as the same lady was to remark in a speech to a National Council of Women conference on *Peace Education in Schools* (3 March 1984), "this could include bad housing, poor educational and medical provision, systems of apartheid and discrimination, high unemployment, and poverty. At the international level one could name systems of imperialism, the arms race, or even the international monetary system." The expression 'structural violence', like the expression 'institutionalised racism', is thus a formula for finding violence, like racism, everywhere, including, perhaps especially including, places where, in the ordinary and ordinarily obnoxious understandings of these words, there is in truth neither violence nor racism to be found.

(ii) So far we have settled on one element which, to be genuinely educational, any programme of 'Peace Studies' ought to contain. However, once we are fully seized of the point that the concept of peace is essentially negative, we can scarcely fail to notice that this means that the innumerable situations to which it can correctly be applied may have little or nothing positively in common. In fact of course, they do not; but then, that being so, how can we be sure that there is a possible, practically important, intellectual discipline which this nominal expression can conveniently be recruited to designate?

(Parenthetically, this last is a question which may with profit be generalised to embrace also 'Women's Studies' and 'Black Studies'. There is no doubt but that peace and women and blacks are all very important. Nor is there any doubt but that there are similarly important questions to be asked and answered about each and all of them. However, none of this is by any means sufficient to warrant the desired conclusion. It is not, that is, sufficient to show that all the questions thus picked out should be investigated together in the same context. For neither the absence of war nor the presence of that particular sex nor any one particular pigmentation constitutes an adequate uniting bond. Indeed those who would deny this in the second two cases expose themselves to charges of, respectively, sexism and racism.)

Again, even if it be allowed that we do have in 'Peace Studies' the makings of an integrated and viable academic discipline, to allow this is very different from allowing that it is one which can properly and profitably be pursued at every level—from primary to graduate school. It is, no doubt, always rash to assert that there is anything which no one would be prepared to maintain. ("Some philosophers," C. D. Broad once wickedly observed, "would say anything—except their prayers.")

Yet, surely, there cannot be many who would want to make out that 'Sex Education' should have a place in the curriculum at every level from primary to graduate school? So, once it is admitted that not every subject which has a place at some has a place at every level, those who want 'Peace Studies' to be pursued either at all levels or at any particular level of the educational system will certainly have a further case to make out.

(iii) Continuing with the question of what, always allowing that we had to have programmes of 'Peace Studies', such programmes ought to contain, here are two suggestions to add to that first course on *Straight and Crooked Thinking*, with special reference to issues of war and peace (Thouless, 1930; and compare Flew, 1975).

(a) We should need a course in moral philosophy, with particular reference to the medieval doctrine of the just war and contemporary criticism thereof. Yet it would be a maimed and aborted course in either ethics or moral philosophy which confined itself to issues of war and peace. Nor has anyone any business silently to ignore Aristotle's warnings against attempts to teach material of this and similar kinds to the immature. Thus in the *Nicomachean Ethics* we read:

> Again, each person judges correctly those matters with which he is acquainted ... Hence the young are not fit to be students of Public Affairs. For they have no experience of life and conduct, and it is these that supply the premises and subject matter of this discipline. They are, moreover, followers of their feelings and will, therefore, get no profit from the study—since its end is not knowledge but practice (1094B28–1095A7).

(b) The indispensable practical background to all theoretical discussions can be provided only by history and, in particular the history of modern Europe and of North America, of World War II and of the USSR and its expansion. To be fully and effectively relevant this study would have especially to attend to the differences between governmental decision-making and the constraints upon it in NATO and in the Warsaw Pact; to the global objectives of the ruling elite in the USSR (Greig, 1981); to the opinions about armament and disarmament of dissidents who have themselves suffered under the absolute and irremovable power of such elites (Bukovsky, 1982); and to the experiences of those who have lived through *The Day After* a Soviet military occupation (Milosz, 1981).

(iv) Since the three essentials suggested above are substantial, and not previously admitted, it becomes doubly desirable to list a few things which present British courses in 'Peace Studies' do in fact insist upon including but could with advantage omit.

(a) Take, for a start, the list of lecture topics for the taught as opposed to thesis Master's degree in the University of Bradford. It is provided by an official brochure, *The School of Peace Studies*. This list includes "critical sociology and the idea of a just society" and "problems of Third World development" but no reference to the structure and aims of the USSR and of the other, subordinate states of the Socialist bloc. Both the two subjects actually mentioned are no doubt important topics, which deserve to be handled in a properly unprejudiced and sincerely enquiring way. What, however, other than the adoption of a factitious positive concept of peace, gives them a place in a programme of 'Peace Studies'?

It must be noted, by the way, both that 'critical sociology' is a code expression for a kind of Marxist sociology and that Bradford's study of Third World development shows no sign of attending either to Peter Bauer's criticism of 'development economics' and government-to-government economic aid or to the success stories of those previously poor countries which have heeded the advice of Adam Smith and Milton Friedman rather than that of Karl Marx and J. K. Galbraith.

Descending to the second and third years of the undergraduate course, we find a list including 'Social Alternatives', 'Race Relations', 'Politics of Developing Areas' and 'Social Psychology of Industrialism and Militarism'. Once again there seems to be going to be no direct treatment of any of the three matters which we have put forward as essential. Nor is it easy to discern either why the first three of the four topics quoted from the Bradford list are thought to be essential to an undergraduate study of peace, nor why Industrialism is thought to be signficiantly related to Militarism nor yet why, if it is, we are still supposed to welcome industrial development.

(b) At the school level again almost anything can be fitted in, or, rather, almost anything can be fitted in except what might possibly lead pupils to question crucial elements in the standard package of contemporary left-wing convictions and commitments. Document after document claims that "peace education" includes everything from teaching children courtesy and good manners to "equal opportunities" (always confused with equal outcomes), "human rights, justice, underdevelopment, ecology, militarism, arms spending, North/South, United Nations, co-operation"; even "a different history", together with the study of "conflict between nations" and of the "threat of mass destruction from nuclear weapons etc. and choices for action".

All the quotations in the previous paragraph come from what CND's teachers' affiliate Teachers for Peace (TP) offers as its definition of 'peace education', but they can all too easily be paralleled in many, many other documents issued by LEAs for the misguidance of teachers. The materials for 'Peace Studies' are usually selected very carefully, and always or almost always with specific and always left-wing indoctrinatory objectives.

Suppose, as this whole book has been advocating, that all our schools were independent management centres, and that all parents had the right to withdraw their children from their present schools and to take them to preferred alternatives. Then there is no reason to believe that this would bring an end to all political indoctrination in schools. For many parents, regrettable though this is, do positively want their children to be indoctrinated, rather than educated in critical, appraising thinking. However, the realisation of the ideal of an independent education for all could scarcely fail to reduce the total amount of indoctrination, if only because many of the periods now devoted to indoctrination would likely be squeezed out in favour of more career-relevant studies. Quite certainly, whatever continued simply could not be so overwhelmingly one-sided as it is now; in a pluralism of indoctrinators, none could be so lastingly successful as all those enjoying a monopoly.

Bibliography

This is intended to include all and only those works which are mentioned in the text but of which bibliographical particulars are not provided there.

ANDERSON, D. (Ed.) (1981). *The Pied Pipers of Education* (London: Social Affairs Unit).

ANDERSON, D. (Ed.) (1982). *Educated for Employment* (London: Social Affairs Unit).

ANDERSON, D. (Ed.) (1984a). *Trespassing? Businessmen's Views on the Education System* (London: Social Affairs Unit).

ANDERSON, D. (Ed.) (1984b). *The Kindness that Kills* (London: SPCK).

ANDRESKI, S. (1982). "Distortions of Education by the Vested Interests of the Bureaucracy', in Cox and Marks (1982).

ARISTOTLE (1941). *The Basic Works of Aristotle*, edited by R. McKeon (New York: Random House).

AUSTIN, J.L. (1961). 'A Plea for Excuses', in his *Philosophical Papers* (Oxford: Clarendon).

AUSTIN, J.L. (1962). *Sense and Sensibilia* (Oxford: Clarendon).

BAILEY, C. and BRIDGES, D. (1983). *Mixed Ability Grouping: A Philosophical Perspective* (London: Allen and Unwin).

BAKER, B. (1981). *The Far Left* (London: Weidenfield and Nicolson).

BALDWIN, R.W. (1981). *Secondary Schools: 1965–79* (London: National Council for Educational Standards).

BARROW, R. (1982). *Injustice, Inequality and Ethics: A Philosophical Introduction to Moral Problems* (Totowa, NJ, and Brighton: Barnes and Noble, and Wheatsheaf Books).

BAUER, P. (1976). *Dissent on Development* (Cambridge, MA: Harvard University Press).

BAUER, P. (1981). *Equality, the Third World and Economic Delusion* (London: Weidenfeld and Nicolson).

BLAKE, N. (1986). 'Peace Education and National Security', *Journal for the Philosophy of Education*, Vol. XIX, pp. 27–38.

BLUMENFELD, S. (1984). *NEA: Trojan Horse in American Education* (Boise, ID: Paradigm).

BLUMENFELD, S.L. (1985). *Is Public Education Necessary?* (Boise, ID: Paradigm, second edition).

BOYSON, R. (1974). *Oversubscribed!* (London: Ward Lock).

BOYSON, R. (1978). 'Verdict on Comprehensives', *The Free Nation* 29 September to 13 October.

BRITTAN, S. (1975). 'The Economic Contradictions of Democracy', in K.J.W. Alexander (Ed.) *The Political Economy of Change* (Oxford: Oxford University Press).

BROWN, M. and others (1986). *No Turning Back* (London: Conservative Political Centre).

BROWNING, R. [1833–64] (1970). *Poetical Works: 1833–64* (London: Oxford University Press).

BUKOVSKY, V. (1982). *The Peace Movement and the Soviet Union* (London: Coalition for Peace through Security).

BULLOCK, A. (1975). *A Language for Life* (London: HMSO).

COARD, B. (1971). *How the West Indian Child is made Educationally Sub-Normal in the British School System* (London: New Beacon).

COCKCROFT, W. (1982). *Mathematics Counts* (London: HMSO).

COLEMAN, J.S. and others (1966). *Equality of Educational Opportunity* (Washington, DC: US Government Printing Office).

COLEMAN, J.S. and others (1969). *Equal Educational Opportunity* (Cambridge, MA: Harvard UP). This volume is an expansion of the Winter 1968 Special Issue of the *Harvard Educational Review*.

COX, C. and others (1986). *Whose Schools? A Radical Manifesto* (London: Hillgate Group).

COX, C. and MARKS, J. (1980). *Sixth-Forms in ILEA Comprehensives: A Cruel Confidence Trick?* (London: National Council for Educational Standards).

COX, C. and MARKS, J. (1981). *Real Concern* (London: Centre for Policy Studies).

COX, C. and MARKS, J. (Eds) (1982a). *The Right to Learn* (London: Centre for Policy Studies).

COX, C. and MARKS, J. (1982b). 'Voluntary Schools Threatened', *The Free Nation* for September.

COX, C. and SCRUTON, R. (1984). *Peace Studies: a Critical Survey* (London: Institute for European Defence and Strategic Studies).

COX, C.B. and BOYSON, R. (1975). *Black Paper 1975* (London: Dent).

COX, C.B. and BOYSON, R. (1977). *Black Paper 1977* (London: Temple Smith).

COX, C.B. and DYSON, A.E. (Eds) (1969). *Fight for Education: A Black Paper* (London: *Critical Quarterly*).

COX, C.B. and DYSON, A.E. (Eds) (1970). *Black Paper Two* (London: *Critical Quarterly*).

COX, C.B. and DYSON, A.E. (Eds) (1971). *Black Paper Three* (London: *Critical Quarterly*).

CROSLAND, A. (1974). *Socialism Now, and Other Essays* (London: Cape).

CROSLAND, S. (1982). *Tony Crosland* (London: Cape).

DAVIE, R., BUTLER, N. and GOLDSTEIN, H. (1972). *From Birth to Seven* (London: Longman).

DAWSON, G. (1981). 'Unfitting Teachers to Teach: Sociology in the Training of Teachers', in Anderson (1981).

DEWEY, J. (1944). *Democracy and Education* (New York: The Free Press).

DONNISON, D.V. (1970). *Public Schools Commission: Second Report* (London: HMSO).

DUZCEK, S. (1983). 'Peace Education', in J. Thacker (Ed.) *Perspectives No. 11* (Exeter: School of Education).

EDGLEY, R. (1978). 'Education for Industry', *Radical Philosophy*, No. 19.

ELIOT, T.S. (1960). *The Complete Poems and Plays* (New York: Harcourt Brace).

ERICKSON, D.A. (1982). 'Disturbing Evidence about the "One Bet System" ', in Everhart (1982).

EVERHART, R.B. (Ed.) (1982). *The Public School Monopoly* (San Francisco, CA: Pacific Institute for Public Policy Research).

FLESCH, R. (1955). *Why Johnny Can't Read* (New York: Harper and Row).

FLEW, A.G.N. (1968). 'Against Indoctrination', in A.J. Ayer (Ed.), *The Humanist Outlook* (London: Pemberton).

FLEW, A.G.N. (1969). 'On the Interpretation of Hume' and 'On not Deriving Ought from Is', in W.D. Hudson (Ed.), *The Is/Ought Question* (London, and New York: Macmillan, and St Martin's Press), pp. 64–9 and 135–43.

FLEW, A.G.N. (1973). *Crime or Disease?* (London: Macmillan).

FLEW, A.G.N. (1975a). *Thinking about Thinking* (London: Collins/Fontana).

FLEW, A.G.N. (1975b). 'J.S. Mill: Socialist or Libertarian?', in M. Ivens (Ed.), *Prophets of Freedom and Enterprise* (London: Kogan Page).

FLEW, A.G.N. (1976). *Sociology, Equality and Education* (London: Macmillan).

FLEW, A.G.N. (1977). 'Democracy in Education', in Peters (1977, pp. 76–101).

FLEW, A.G.N. (1978a). 'The Philosophy of Freedom', in K. Watkins (Ed.), *In Defence of Freedom* (London: Cassell).

FLEW, A.G.N. (1978b). *A Rational Animal* (Oxford: Clarendon).

FLEW, A.G.N. (1981). *The Politics of Procrustes* (London, and Buffalo NY: Temple Smith, and Prometheus).

FLEW, A.G.N. (1982a). 'A Strong Programme for the Sociology of Belief', *Inquiry* (Oslo), 25, pp. 365–78.

FLEW, A.G.N. (1982b). 'Could there be Universal Natural Rights?' *Journal of Libertarian Studies*, Vol. VI, pp. 277–88.

FLEW, A.G.N. (1983). ' "Freedom is Slavery": a Slogan for our new Philosopher Kings', in A.P. Griffiths (Ed.), *Of Liberty* (Cambridge: Cambridge University Press).

FLEW, A.G.N. (1984). 'The Concept of Human Betterment', in K. Boulding (Ed.), *The Economics of Human Betterment* (London: Macmillan).

FLEW, A.G.N. (1985). *Thinking about Social Thinking* (Oxford: Blackwell).

FLEW, A.G.N. (1986a). *David Hume: Philosopher of Moral Science* (Oxford: Blackwell).

FLEW, A.G.N. (1986b). 'An Ungodly Muddle', in *Encounter* for September.

FLEW, A.G.N. (1987). 'Prophecy or Philosophy', Historicism or History', in C. Wilson (Ed.), *Marxism Refuted* (Bath: Ashgrove Press).

FLOUD, J. (1975). 'Making Adults more Equal: the Scope and Limitations of Educational Policy', in P.R. Cox, H.B. Miles and J. Peel (Eds), *Equalities and Inequalities in Education* (London and New York: Academic Press), pp. 37–51.

FLOUD, J.E., HALSEY, A.H. and MARTIN, E.M. (1956). *Social Class and Educational Opportunity* (London: Heinemann).

FOGELMAN, K. (Ed.) (1983). *Growing up in Great Britain* (London: Macmillan).

FORD, J. (1969). *Social Class and the Comprehensive School* (London: Routledge and Kegan Paul).

FRIEDMAN, J. (1962). *Capitalism and Freedom* (Chicago: Chicago University Press).

FRIEDMAN, M. and FRIEDMAN, R. (1980). *Free to Choose* (London: Secker and Warburg).

GASKING, D.A.T. and JACKSON, A.C. (1951). 'Ludwig Wittgenstein', *Australasian Journal of Philosophy*.

GLASS, G.V. and others (1982). *School Class Size: Research and Policy* (Beverly Hills, CA: Sage).

GOULD, J. and others (1977). *The Attack on Higher Education* (London: Institute for the Study of Conflict).

GRAY, J. (1983). 'Questions of Background', *The Times Educational Supplement* for 8 July.

GREIG, I. (Ed.) (1981). *They Mean What They Say* (London: Foreign Affairs Research Institute).

GWYNNE, J. (1985a). 'Peace Fighters', in *Encounter* for June.

GWYNNE, J. (1985b). 'A Peaceful Weekend', in *Encounter* for July/ August.

HALSALL, E. (1973). *The Comprehensive School: Guidelines for the Reorganisation of Secondary Education* (Oxford: Pergamon).

HALSEY, A.H. (1980). 'Social Mobility and Education', in Rubinstein (1980).

HALSTEAD, B. (1987). 'The New Left's Assault on Science', in *The Salisbury Review* for January.

HARGREAVES, D.H. (1982). *The Challenge of the Comprehensive School: Culture, Curriculum and Community* (London: Routledge and Kegan Paul).

HAYEK, F.A. (1944). *The Road to Serfdom* (London: Routledge and Kegan Paul).

HEMMING, J. (Ed.) (1970). *The Red Papers* (London: Islander).

HINTON, M. (1979). *Comprehensive Schools: A Christian's View* (London: SCM).

HOBBES, T. [1651]. *Leviathan*, in *The English Works of Thomas Hobbes*, edited by W. Molesworth (London: Bohn, 1839).

HONEY, J. (1983). *The Language Trap: race, class and the standard English issue in British schools* (London, National Council for Educational Standards).

HOPKINS, A. (1978). *The School Debate* (Harmondsworth: Penguin).

HOUSMAN, A.E. (1931). *Juvenalis Saturae* (Cambridge: Cambridge University Press, revised edition).

HOWARD, M. (1970). *Studies in War and Peace* (London: Temple Smith).

HOWARD, M. (1983). *The Causes of Wars* (London: Temple Smith).

HUME, D. [1739–40]. *A Treatise of Human Nature*, edited by L.A. Selby-Bigge and revised by P.H. Nidditch (Oxford: Clarendon, second edition 1978).

HUME, D. [1748]. *An Enquiry concerning Human Understanding*, in *Hume's Enquiries*, edited by L.A. Selby-Bigge and revised by P.H. Nidditch (Oxford: Clarendon, third edition, 1975).

JAY, A. and LYNN, J. (1983). 'Guess, Minister: a Ploy so Selective it Appears Beyond Comprehension', in *The Sunday Times* for 11 December.

JENCKS, C. and others (1972). *Inequality: A Reassessment of the Effect of Family and Schooling in America* (New York and London: Basic Books; republished in London by Allen Lane in 1973, with an introduction by Tyrrell Burgess).

JENSEN, A. (1972). *Genetics and Education* (London, Constable).

KANT, I. [1785] (1949). *Groundwork of the Metaphysics of Morals*, translated by H.J. Paton as *The Moral Law* (London: Hutchinson).

KUHN, T. (1962). *The Structure of Scientific Revolutions* (Chicago, IL: Chicago University Press).

LEFEVER, E. (1979). *Amsterdam to Nairobi: The World Council of Churches and the Third World* (Washington, DC: Georgetown University Press).

LEVITAS, M. (1974). *Marxist Perspectives in the Philosophy of Education* (London: Routledge and Kegan Paul).

LEWIS, J. (Ed.) (1986). *Educational Indoctrination: The House of Lords Debate* (London: Policy Research Associates).

LORD, R. (1983). 'Value for Money in the Education Service', in *Public Money* for September.

LYNN, R. (1977). 'Competition and Cooperation', in Cox and Boyson (1977).

MARGOLIS, J. (Ed.) (1969). *Public Economics* (New York, and London: St Martin's Press, and Macmillan).

MARKS, J. (1984). *"Peace Studies" in our Schools: Propaganda for Defencelessness* (London: Women and Families for Defence).

MARKS, J. (1985). *London's Schools: When even the Communist Party gives up!* (London: Aims of Industry).

MARKS, J. (1987). 'The New Model Labour Party in Action', *The Salisbury Review*, for January.

MARKS, J., COX, C. and POMIAN-SRZEDNICKI, M. (1983). *Standards in English Schools* (London: National Council for Eductional Standards).

MARKS, J. and POMIAN-SRZEDNICKI, M. (1985). *Standards in English Schools: Second Report* (London: National Council for Educational Standards).

MARKS, J., COX, C. and POMIAN-SRZEDNICKI, M. (1986). *Examination Performance of Secondary Schools in ILEA* (London: National Council for Educational Standards).

MARSDEN, D. (1971). *Politicians, Equality and Comprehensives* (London: Fabian Society).

MARSLAND, D. (1985). *Neglect and Betrayal: War and Violence in Modern Sociology* (London: Institute for European Defence and Strategic Studies).

MARSLAND, D. (1987). *Seeds of Bankruptcy: Sociological Bias against Business and Freedom* (London: Pickwick).

MARX, K. [1847] (1936). *The Poverty of Philosophy*, no translator named (London: Lawrence & Wishart).

MILL, J.S. [1859] (1962). *On Liberty* (London: Collins/Fontana).

MILOSZ, C. (1981). *The Captive Mind* (New York: Vintage).

MOODIE, G.C. (Ed.) (1986). *Standards and Criteria in Higher Education* (London: NFER-Nelson).

MORGAN, P. (1986). 'Feminist Attempts to Sack Father: A Case of Unfair Dismissal?', in D. Andersen and G. Dawson (Eds), *Family Portraits* (London: Social Affairs Unit).

MULLARD, C. (1973). *Black Britain* (London: Allen and Unwin).

MULLARD, C. (1982). 'Multiracial Education in Britain: from Assimilation to Cultural Pluralism', in J. Tierney (Ed.), *Race, Migration and Schooling* (London: Holt, Rinehart and Winston).

MURPHY, J. (1978). 'Education and Equality: the Professional Ideology of the Educational Pathologist', *Educational Studies*, IV1.

MURPHY, J. (1981a). 'Disparity and Inequality in Education: the Crippling Legacy of Coleman', *British Journal of Educational Psychology*, III, pp. 61–70.

MURPHY, J. (1981b). 'Class Inequality in Education: Two Justifications, One Evaluation but no Hard Evidence', *British Journal of Sociology*, XXXII2.

MUSGROVE, F. (1966). *The Family, Education and Society* (London: Routledge and Kegan Paul).

NAYLOR, F. (1981). *Crisis in the Sixth Form* (London: Centre for Policy Studies).

NAYLOR, F. and MARKS, J. (1982). 'The National Union of Teachers— Professional Association or Trade Union or. . .?', in Cox and Marks (1982).

NAYLOR, F. and MARKS, J. (1985). *Comprehensives: Counting the Cost* (London: Centre for Policy Studies).

NEAVE, G. (1979). 'Sense and Sensitivity: The Case of Comprehensive Education', *Quantitative Sociology Newsletter*, No. 21.

NEWCASTLE COMMISSION (1861). *Royal Commission on Popular Education* (London: HMSO).

NISKANEN, W.A. (1971). *Bureaucracy and Representative Government* (Chicago, IL: Aldine Atherton).

O'KEEFFE, D. (1985). 'Swann-song of Prejudice', in *Encounter* for December.

O'KEEFFE, D. (Ed.) (1986). *The Wayward Curriculum* (London: Social Affairs Unit).

OLLMAN, B. and VERNOFF, E. (1982). *The Left Academy* (New York: McGraw-Hill).

PAGE, L. (1984). *The Marxian Legacy: Race, Nationalities, Colonialism and War* (London: The Freedom Association, reprinted as Appendix I to Page, 1987).

PAGE, L. (1987). *Karl Marx and the Critical Examination of his Works* (London: The Freedom Association).

PAINE, T. [1791] (1984). *The Rights of Man* (Harmondsworth: Penguin).

PALMER, F. (1986). *Anti-Racism: An Assault on Education and Value* (London: Sherwood).

PARTINGTON, G. (1987). Review of R. Sharp (Ed.), *Capitalist Crisis and Schooling* (Sydney, NSW: Macmillan, 1986), in *The Salisbury Review*, for January.

PETERS, R.S. (Ed.) (1977). *John Dewey Reconsidered* (London: Routledge and Kegan Paul).

PIRIE, M. (1978). *Trial and Error and the Idea of Progress* (LaSalle, IL: Open Court).

PLATO. *The Republic*, trans. P. Shorey (Cambridge, MA, and London: Harvard University Press, and Heinemann).

POPPER, K.R. (1957). *The Poverty of Historicism* (London: Routledge and Kegan Paul).

POPPER, K.R. (1959). *The Logic of Scientific Discovery* (London: Hutchinson).

POPPER, K.R. (1966). *The Open Society and its Enemies* (London: Routledge and Kegan Paul, fifth edition).

PRAIS, S.J. and WAGNER, K. (1983). *Schooling Standards in Britain and Germany; Some Summary Comparisons Bearing on Economic Efficiency* (London: National Institute for Economic and Social Research).

RADNITZKY, G. and BERNHOLZ, P. (1987). *Economic Imperialism: The Economic Method Applied Outside the Field of Economics* (New York: Paragon).

REID, M.I. and others (1981). *Mixed Ability Teaching: Problems and Possibilities* (Windsor: NFER).

RICHARDSON, K. and SPEARS, D. (Eds) (1972). *Race, Culture and Intelligence* (Harmondsworth: Penguin).

ROBBINS, L. (1935). *On the Nature and Significance of Economic Science* (London: Macmillan, second edition).

ROWE, A. (1970). 'Human beings, Class and Education', in Rubinstein and Stoneman (1970), pp. 33–40.

RUBINSTEIN, D. (Ed.) (1980). *Education and Equality* (Harmondsworth: Penguin).

RUBINSTEIN, D. and STONEMAN, C. (Eds) (1972). *Education for Democracy* (Harmondsworth: Penguin, second edition).

RUTTER, M. and others (1979). *Fifteen Thousand Hours: Secondary Schools and their Effects on Children* (London: Open Books).

RYLE, G. [1931]. 'Systematically Misleading Expressions', conveniently reprinted in A.G.N. Flew (Ed.), *Logic and Language* (Oxford: Blackwell, First Series, 1951).

SARUP, M. (1982). *Education, State and Crisis: A Marxist Perspective* (London: Routledge and Kegan Paul).

SARUP, M. (1986). *The Politics of Multiracial Education* (London: Routledge and Kegan Paul).

SCHELLING, T. (1978). *Micromotives and Macrobehavior* (New York: Norton).

SCHUMPETER, J.A. (1963). *Capitalism, Socialism and Democracy* (London: Allen and Unwin).

SCRUTON, R. (1985). *World Studies: Education or Indoctrination?* (London: Institute for European Defence and Strategic Studies).

SCRUTON, R., ELLIS-JONES, A. and O'KEEFFE, D. (1985). *Education and Indoctrination* (London: Education Research Centre).

SELDON, A. (Ed.) (1985). *The Riddle of the Voucher* (London: Institute of Economic Affairs).

SHAW, B. (1983). *Comprehensive Schooling: The Impossible Dream?* (Oxford: Blackwell).

SMITH, A. [1776] (1981). *An Inquiry into the Nature and Causes of the Wealth of Nations*, edited by R.H. Campbell, A.S. Skinner and W.B.Todd (Indianapolis, IN: Liberty Press).

SMITH, B. (1977). *The Fraudulent Gospel: Politics and the World Council of Churches* (Richmond: Foreign Affairs).

SOOTHILL, W.E. (1910). *The Analects of Confucius*, edited and translated by W.E. Soothill (Taiyuanfu, Shansi: Soothill).

SOWELL, T. (1975). *Race and Economics* (New York and London: Longman).

SOWELL, T. (1981). *Markets and Minorities* (New York, and Oxford: Basic Books, and Blackwell).

SOWELL, T. (1983). *Ethnic America* (New York: Basic Books).

SOWELL, T. (1984). *The Economics and Politics of Race* (New York: William Morrow).

SOWELL, T. (1986). *Education: Assumptions versus History* (Stanford, CA: Hoover Institution).

STEEDMAN, J. (1980). *Progress in Secondary Schools: Findings from the National Child Development Study* (London: National Children's Bureau).

STEEDMAN, J. and FOGELMAN, K. (1980). 'Secondary Schooling: Findings from the National Child Development Study', *Concern* No. 36 (Summer).

STEVENS, A. (1980). *Clever Children in Comprehensive Schools* (Harmondsworth: Penguin).

STOVE, D. (1982). *Popper and After: Four Modern Irrationalists* (Oxford: Pergamon).

STRAUGHAN, R. (1982). *Can We Teach Children To Be Good?* (London: Routledge and Kegan Paul).

TAWNEY, R.H. (Ed.) (1922). *Secondary Education for All: A Policy for Labour* (London: Allen and Unwin).

TAWNEY, R.H. (1952). *Equality* (London: Allen and Unwin, revised edition).

THOULESS, R.H. (1930). *Straight and Crooked Thinking* (London: Hodder and Stoughton).

TINGLE, R. (1986). *Gay Lessons* (London: Pickwick).

TOWNSEND, H.E.H. and BRITTAN, E.M. (1973). *Multicultural Education: Need and Innovation* (London: Evans/Methuen Educational).

TURNBULL, C. (1973). *The Mountain People* (London: Cape).

WEBB, R.K. (1963). 'The Victorian Reading Public', in B. Ford (Ed.), *From Dickens to Hardy* (London: Cassell, reissued by Penguin in 1968).

WEBER, M. [1904] ' "Objectivity" in Social Science and Social Policy', in *The Methodology of the Social Sciences*, translated by E.A. Shils and H.A. Finch and edited by E.A. Shils (Glencoe, IL: The Free Press, 1969).

WEST, E.G. (1970). *Education and the State* (London: Institute of Economic Affairs, second edition).

WEST, E.G. (1975). *Education and the Industrial Revolution* (London: Batsford).

WEST, E.G. (1981). *The Economics of Education Tax Credits* (Washington, DC: The Heritage Foundation).

WEYL, N. (1979). *Karl Marx: Racist* (New York: Arlington House).

WHITE, J.P. (1977). 'Tyndale and the Left', *Forum*, XIX2.

WILKINSON, M. (1977). *Lessons from Europe: A Comparison of British and West European Schooling* (London: Centre for Policy Studies).

WRAGG, E. (1983). 'Personal', in *The Times Educational Supplement* for 15 July.

YOUNG, M.F.D. (Ed.) (1971). *Knowledge and Control* (London: Collier-Macmillan).

Index of Names

169